# THE STUDENT
# TEACHER'S HANDBOOK
## Second Edition

# THE STUDENT TEACHER'S HANDBOOK
## Second Edition

Andrew I. Schwebel
*The Ohio State University*
Bernice L. Schwebel
*Douglass College of Rutgers University, Retired*
Carol R. Schwebel
*Columbus, Ohio, Public School System*
Milton Schwebel
*Rutgers University*

  LAWRENCE ERLBAUM ASSOCIATES, PUBLISHERS
1992    Hillsdale, New Jersey                    Hove and London

Lawrence Erlbaum Associates, Inc., Publishers
365 Broadway
Hillsdale, New Jersey 07642

**Library of Congress Cataloging-in-Publication Data**

The student teacher's handbook / Andrew I. Schwebel . . . [et. al.]. —
2nd ed.
    p.    cm.
  Includes index.
  ISBN 0-8058-1039-0. — ISBN 0-8058-1040-4 (pbk.)
  1. Student teaching—Handbooks, manuals, etc.  I. Schwebel,
Andrew I.
LB2157.A3S9  1992
370 7. '33—dc20                   91-22394
                                 CIP

Printed in the United States of America
10  9  8  7  6  5  4

# Contents

# Acknowledgments

This book has been a cooperative venture in more than just its multiple authorship. We could not have undertaken it without benefit of what we learned from our many students over the years.

Of special importance to this book have been the logs that our student teachers so generously shared with us. We are deeply indebted to them.

We wish to thank Linda Kozusko of the English Department at Rutgers University for her perceptive observations and graphic descriptions of teachers at work, which we incorporated in the book.

We are also indebted to three educators, whose constructive advice enabled us to enrich the content of this second edition immeasurably: Dr. Frances Cagnassola, teacher in the Newark, New Jersey school system; Professor James Raths, University of Delaware; and Professor Richard Wisniewski, Dean of the College of Education, University of Tennessee.

Collectively, we have benefitted over the years from interactions with colleague teachers in many places. These range from the northeast, the south, the midwest, and the far west of the United States, as well as Canada, Mexico, Great Britain, India, and other locations.

We have profited enormously from the support of our publisher, Lawrence Erlbaum, the enthusiastic backing of our editor, Hollis Heimbouch, and the attention to the book shown by Robin Marks Weisberg in production and Sharon Levy in promotion.

Finally, our thanks go to family members: David Schwebel for typing the manuscript and setting up the system for indexing; Sara Schwebel for her patience and loving support; Ruth Lubinsky for freeing the authors to complete the first edition by lovingly tending two young children; and Dr. Robert Schwebel, another educator, for challenging questions that helped keep us close to the grindstone of reality.

# I
▼▼▼▼▼▼▼▼▼▼

# Beginnings

# 1
▼▼▼▼▼▼▼

# Introduction: The Realities of Student Teaching

Let us face facts. The student teacher's position is a demanding one: A novice, still a student, enters a new setting to use newly acquired skills, under the watchful eye of experienced professionals. This *is* a difficult position. Yet, most students meet the challenge successfully.

Teaching is a high-pressure occupation. At the elementary level, teachers share 6 hours a day, 5 days a week, 40 weeks a year with some 20 to 30 children. On school days, in fact, teachers often spend more waking hours with the children in their class than do the children's parents.

At the middle school, or junior high school level, teachers contend with major transitions in their students: rapidly maturing minds and bodies, greater social assertiveness (they talk up more), and the rainbow of emotions expressed by individuals in the throes of peer pressure. While adjusting to these internal changes, middle school students must also accustom themselves to having several different teachers.

At the high school level, teachers experience continual turnover of students during the course of the day. That means getting acquainted with 100 or more adolescents, some of whom at any given time are in the midst of the personally and socially disruptive changes of pre-adulthood. It also means managing a sizeable number of classes of young people who are at the peak of activity and energy. Some of these youngsters will be intellectually curious and excited by what teachers offer. Others may be unwilling students, simply waiting for their 16th birthday and the chance to legally end their formal schooling. Still others, although willing students, are drained by the pressure of after-school jobs they hold to

3

help their families financially, or to earn money for cars, "designer" clothes, and expensive entertainment.

To be able to cope with the demands of their job, teachers must first be well versed in the content they teach. They cannot with comfort or any expectation of success enter the classroom with only rote knowledge of a concept they plan to teach. Besides mastery of their field, their success depends on knowledge of human development, that is, the process of cognitive, personality, and social growth. Teachers must also be skilled in group leadership in order to maintain quality discussions and lead the class with continuity from one activity or topic to another.

As if all of that were not enough, during a typical school year, a teacher could be confronted with problems that ordinarily are in the province of psychologists, psychiatrists, counselors, social workers, hearing and speech specialists, and the juvenile division of the police department. Although teachers are not responsible for providing services to students with problems beyond their own professional competencies, teachers do play an important role in linking students with help-giving resources and do have to contend with students' problems as they are manifested in the classroom.

To many teachers the diversity of knowledge and skills required is a great attraction, as are the challenges and the bit of the unpredictable that add spice to their working life. These and other features make the profession a desirable one. You know that because you have chosen it.

We have deliberately highlighted the demands and pressures of the job because it is these that are uppermost in the mind of the student teacher. The fact that a disproportionate amount of space in this book is devoted to problems student teachers face rather than benefits they enjoy is quite deliberate. You know of the enjoyment and growth you will experience in practicing your profession. What you want is help in solving problems you are likely to face and in acquiring skills you do not yet possess. We have written the book with that in mind.

Many student teachers wonder whether they will be sufficiently prepared to deal with all the issues and questions that they will encounter in their subject fields. Also, they ask: Will I be able to manage the class? To plan and conduct high-quality lessons? You may have occasional frightening thoughts that the class might get completely out of hand. And then you may sometimes become preoccupied with those special problem cases, including the obviously disturbed child. Having these questions and thoughts is perfectly normal. You are moving forward into what for you is uncharted territory.

The student teacher, besides having all of the problems of the regular teacher (except final responsibility), will also encounter the unique ones associated with being an apprentice. In particular, the student teacher generally works in the proverbial goldfish bowl, under the observant eyes of the cooperating teacher and the college supervisor. Although you know you will learn much from their observations, nonetheless, their presence adds to the pressures of the student-teaching experience.

The problems student teachers encounter result from myriad causes. Some problems student teachers create for themselves, unintentionally of course. These may be a result of poor judgment or of the anxiety that the novel experience of student teaching arouses in them. Some are the problems inherent in the day-to-day life of teaching. Others are peculiar to the special circumstances of being a student teacher, such as feeling inadequate as a result of comparing one's own work to that of the experienced cooperating teacher.

We confront each of these types of problems, showing how they relate to the life of the student teacher and providing you with tools—the knowledge and problem-solving strategies that we think will help you contend with these difficulties if you encounter them.

## DEFINING THE DYNAMIC ROLE OF THE STUDENT TEACHER

In the centuries of training people for work through practical experience, specialty learning took place through the relationship between the master and the apprentice. The master was the expert in one of the arts, crafts, or trades of his time (a barrister or cobbler, a miller or stone mason), and the apprentice served as assistant and learner for various lengths of time. The apprentice learned his trade by observing the master; by engaging in the activities of the calling, first in small then in larger ways; and finally, under the close scrutiny of the master, by doing a complete product on his own.

In the process of learning to use the tools and materials of the craft or occupation, the apprentice also acquired the special language of the field, adopted the habits and specialized garments, and absorbed the general mode of thought of fellow craftsmen. In all, the apprentice became trained and socialized in preparation for a lifetime's work in the craft.

The 10, 15, or 20 weeks of your student teaching will have almost exact counterparts to the medieval apprenticeship system. One of its often unrecognized purposes is to contribute to your socialization into the teaching profession, to prepare you for your regular job by having you experience how real-life (i.e., not textbook) teachers behave in class, in school, and in relationships with students, other teachers, the principal, and parents.

Also, as the apprentice, you will be working with an experienced if not yet a master teacher. You will have opportunity under his or her scrutiny to use the tools and materials of your new trade, and to gain experience first in small ways with individual students and later in larger ways with groups of students and with the class as a whole. When this time comes, you will likely recognize that although the courses and the fieldwork that preceded it helped ready you for student teaching, it is the teaching experience itself that caps and gives fullest meaning to all your previous education and training.

The weeks of student teaching offer unusual learning opportunities, and you will want to get the maximum possible yield from them. It is for this reason that you should concentrate on yourself—on learning, developing skills, gaining confidence, and succeeding in crossing this major professional hurdle.

We recognize that this advice may make you cringe; it sounds selfish to think primarily of yourself, particularly in a help-giving profession such as teaching. But look at the facts. Yes, you want to help the children or adolescents in your cooperating class(es), and you will, but that is not your primary mission at this point in your development. The cooperating teacher will safeguard the students' interests. You are there to better your skills so that you can aid hundreds of students in future years. Think of this time as an investment in yourself, one that will pay dividends to students who will be in your future classes.

The long hours involved in your commitment during student teaching may interfere with your social life. If your work schedule becomes a personal bother, you will probably be able to handle matters by reminding yourself of the limited time frame, your dedication to your career, and the satisfaction you will have when the training period is over. However, if you have a spouse or a serious dating partner, he or she may express some concerns. In this case, frank discussion may help you avoid or remedy relationship problems. You can explain that your time schedule is not a function of your feelings toward him or her, but rather stems from the demanding characteristics of your student-teaching assignment (which is short in duration yet great in its long-term career significance).

It may be easier to keep in mind the need to give your professional growth top priority if you remind yourself (and your spouse or friend) of your reasons for choosing the teaching profession. Were you attracted by the way of life, by the opportunity to work with children or adolescents, by the time given to reading and study or by the doors it opens to serve other people? Or were your reasons seemingly more mundane but no less important? Recalling your goals will provide motivation to help you maximize what you learn during your student-teaching experience.

In writing this book we have had one objective: to develop material useful to you in making your student-teaching experience optimally rewarding. In doing this we have been guided by an orientation of realism. You will be doing your student teaching in the here and now. Your thoughts will be on effectively meeting the demands of that job and also on finding a teaching position for next year. To the best of our ability we have concentrated on those concerns.

If you have come to appreciate the benefit of theory in work, you can feel assured. We share with you the belief that *theory can be of great practical value* to the teacher, just as it can be in science, sports, cooking, and art. We have been straightforward about what you can do to prevent and avoid problems and how you can deal with those that cannot be circumvented. To accomplish this we drew upon theory and research and upon our experiences as teachers and supervisors.

## HOW THE CONTENTS OF THIS BOOK CAN HELP

Part I of this book is devoted to *beginnings,* by which we mean the beginnings of your student-teaching experience. We place great stress on this early stage (and even the weeks before it) in order to help you prepare for early successes.

Two themes that are repeated often are developed at great length in chapter 2: (a) The most effective way to deal with anxieties about new experiences is by preparing for them; and (b) the best way to avoid teaching problems is by thoughtful preparation for the work to be performed. One of the features of chapter 2 is the elaboration of a problem-solving method that you will find useful in your student-teaching period and later as a teacher.

Part II is devoted to the *crucial relationships* of the student teacher. Your success depends on your relationships with the students, the cooperating teacher, and the college supervisor. In the chapters devoted to each of them (chapters 3, 4, and 5), we indicate how to go about building constructive relationships and cope with the kinds of problems that student teachers have repeatedly reported. Chapter 6 is about building relationships with parents, the school principal, and others who are important in school life.

Part III focuses on *curriculum and classroom management.* Linkage of the two topics is deliberate because the content of your lessons and their presentation play a big part in forging your students' classroom behavior. In other words, what and how you teach can foster student involvement and discourage disruptive behavior just as easily as it can fail to hold your learners' attention and, in this and other ways, lead to classroom disruption. The problems of classroom control and management are discussed in great detail because we expect, from countless experiences of student teachers, that these issues loom large in your mind.

Part IV addresses some of the *student teacher's special concerns.* These include concerns of "today," by which we mean those prevalent during student-teaching days. Then there are concerns of "tomorrow," such as the stress associated with the approaching end of your college career and the beginning of your preparations to assume a regular teaching position.

Throughout the book we offer practical information and ideas. Some ideas were drawn directly from research studies and from our own observations in classrooms. Other ideas came from our own experiences as students teachers and teachers. Finally, many important ideas came from student teachers who shared their thoughts, feelings, and experiences with us in individual conferences, seminars, and daily logs (or diaries) of their student teaching experiences.

## LOGS ON THE REAL LIFE OF STUDENT TEACHERS

To help you cope with the real problems of student teaching, we have incorporated excerpts of many students teachers' logs. Some were written in the white heat of emotion, perhaps at the beginning of the student teachers' assignments when they were feeling frustrated, inept, or powerless; others, while they were burning with anger over a sense of having been treated unfairly, or close to panic about their difficulties in controlling the class; and still others, at moments of warm satisfaction over seeing progress in their students' work and of pride and confidence as they saw their skills developing.

The logs were written by student teachers to serve as aids to themselves. Although the logs were shared with supervisors, they were not graded. Instead, the supervisors used the material in log entries to help them gain a deeper understanding of the student teachers' experiences and needs. The student teachers derived other benefits from their logs as well. For example, in them they could ventilate feelings and reflect and record their growth as professionals.

Many dozens of logs were collected during several different academic years. Three states in the eastern and midwestern parts of the country are represented. The logs were written by men and women of diverse racial and ethnic groups who came from families of middle, upper middle, and working-class backgrounds. Although the log writers ranged in age from 20 to 35, most were in their early 20s. Their assignments were at the preschool, elementary, junior (middle school) and senior high school levels and their schools were located in urban, including inner-city schools, suburban, and rural neighborhoods.

The instructions given to the students writing the logs quoted in this book were essentially those proposed for your use in chapter 2. They were asked to reflect on their classroom experiences each day and to write about them freely, considering events that went well and those that did not and their best possible explanation for what happened. They were encouraged to express their feelings about the day and the people involved. They did—sometimes tearfully, sometimes joyfully, and sometimes with passionate anger. Their openness has made their documents valuable to themselves and to others.

The anonymity of the authors of the logs has been carefully safeguarded. Names of student teachers, cooperating teachers, college supervisors, and students are pseudonyms. The school names have also been changed, and no localities are identified.

Besides the logs, we have drawn material from personal interviews with student teachers in several regions of the country. As with the logs, pseudonyms are used and the interview excerpts are preceded by a date.


## PURPOSE: PRACTICAL AND USEFUL

We wrote this book to serve you in a very personal way. Our goal was to write it so the pages have the ring of real life about them. Now our hope is that you will find it so. We would not want you faulting this book as Shelly criticized another one in her log:

2/19: I've started to get into the book that my cooperating teacher recommended. There are some parts where I just have to laugh. I agree with the basic ideas, those of caring, warmth, understanding, etc. — but at the end of the book there are some suggested comments that you could make to a child in certain situations. These comments were unbelievable. I could never see myself saying these things to the children. You can't pigeonhole children. Just like we've said in curriculum, there are no hypothetical children. There are only the real children in your classroom. This book is all right for basics but. . . .

Although we expect that what we have written will be useful to you next year and perhaps beyond, our aim is to help you make your life as a student teacher easier and more successful today and tomorrow. As you read the pages ahead, we think it will be most useful if you regard each one as if it were written especially for you. More specifically, consider the ways each idea or thought that is presented bears on your life in the classroom at the present time.

A final point. One of the most important objectives of education — yours and each of your students' — is to reach the point of being an independent thinker. Those free to think and solve problems for themselves have power and control over their own lives and professional work. You can make much progress toward such independence during your apprenticeship. We hope this book helps you develop that kind of power.

# 2

▼▼▼▼▼▼▼

# Anticipation and Preparation: Contending With Anxieties, Fears, and Problems

"When I think about teaching my own classes, I'm excited, anxious, and a little scared. Especially I wonder if I can be a real teacher to them, someone who they will accept as the equal of their own teacher. I also wonder if the teachers at the school will respect me." That is what James felt a few days before beginning his student teaching.

His are normal feelings. It is normal to feel some anxiety in anticipation of a new experience, especially when you are going to be observed and evaluated and when your career hinges on success. Do you remember other first experiences, for example the first date, the first time you drove a car or, earlier yet, the first time you had to give an oral report to the class? Chances are you showed the normal human reaction of anxiety in one form or another: "butterflies" in the stomach, a bit of sleeplessness, a lowered appetite or its opposite, overeating and some digestive problems, or a combination of these. And chances are, moments after the new experience got under way, your anxiety level dropped considerably.

That is what you can expect about the "firsts" that are coming up: When you first report as a student teacher, when you first lunch in the teachers' room, when you first take over the class for a lesson, when you first teach a whole day.

Anticipating a new experience is usually worse than the reality itself. Worry about failing can grow out of proportion, especially considering that most times the cooperating teacher will go to great lengths to help you develop as an independent teacher ready to take over the class on your own. The same is true for the college supervisor, who desires to see you through a successful teaching assignment. And the school principal wants you to be successful too because,

10

if for no other reason, your success means a smoother running school.

The students? They are children or adolescents, with all the feelings and problems and stresses that children have. They expect and want you to behave like the adult you are. They do not want you to be one of them. Friendly, yes, but not their friend; understanding, yes, but not with the intimacy of a parent or peer; in other words, they want you to be the teacher, the adult who sees to it that they keep to the limits of behavior that are expected of them. They are not your opponents; on the contrary, most are friendly to and supportive of the student teacher.

## EXPECTATIONS ABOUT YOUR CLASSROOM

"I am happy when I think about taking over the class. But I guess I'm also apprehensive about taking over the class. I'm apprehensive because I don't know what to expect. It's like the unknown," a student teacher shared with her seminar group.

What are you apprehensive about? she was asked.

"That's just the point," she replied, "I've observed a lot and I know that my fears are groundless. My cooperating teacher is friendly and decent, and she likes being helpful. But sometimes the kind of help she wants to give is not what I want. But that doesn't take away from her wish to be helpful! I don't know. I just don't know what I'm worried about."

When a future anxiety-provoking experience has a lot of *unknowns* connected with it, we tend to fill in the unknowns with our own fantasies. And often we fill in the unknowns with uncomfortable scenarios that, frequently and thankfully, are far from what actually develops. Here are examples taken from the reports of student teachers, some elementary, some middle, and some high school.

> I expected the school to be modern, the climate to be cold and impersonal, and the staff to be distant. How different it all turned out! There is a very warm, close atmosphere among the teachers. They made me feel very comfortable. As to my cooperating teacher, she is warm, helpful, cooperative and very understanding. I really enjoy working with her.

This student teacher, a bright young adult, had a bleak outlook about the important experience ahead of her. Fortunately, circumstances corrected her false expectations. Here is another student teacher.

> I thought most of the children would be from middle-class families and that the teacher would be an older woman and probably very set in her ways. As it turned out the children are great; each is so special. Many of them stay full days because their mothers work. They are all friendly and most are not the *prima donnas* I expected. There are 23 children in the class, all from very different backgrounds.

The teacher turned out to be young, innovative, sensitive, very open to new ideas and she's going to be fantastic to work with and learn from.

On the one hand, not everyone is as pleased with the cooperating teacher and the children as these two student teachers were. On the other hand, hardly any of the worst fears student teachers have ever materialize.

The inaccurate expectations of the student teachers just quoted were corrected only after their student teaching got under way. One said, "I sure wasted a lot of energy and time with my worries. And I lost some sleep—not to mention peace of mind—needlessly. Oh well, now it's just water over the dam."

Of course, it does not have to be this way. A student teacher can test out some fantasies and fears. It is reassuring to visit the school to which you are assigned. It is better yet to see the classroom and best of all to meet your cooperating teacher and the students. "I visited my school back in October," wrote one student teacher, whose assignment started in February, "so I knew more or less what I could expect. The school I found was lovely and the room itself appeared to provide warmth and color and is conducive to learning. That's the way I found it when I started here a few weeks ago."

It is true, of course, that early visits to obtain information do not always reveal the kind of school or conditions that one would prefer. The school might turn out to be old and forbidding in appearance. Worse yet, the teacher might turn out to be, or at least appear to be, remote. Perhaps worst of all, the children might seem to be so different from yourself that you would be concerned about your capacity to understand and to cope with them.

Your early observations may be disappointing. Still, it is better to know the characteristics of your teaching assignment than to live with untested fantasies. All one can do with the unknown is toss and turn in bed over it, and have nightmares and impaired relationships with family and friends. You can deal with the "known." You can prepare for it. Here is an account of a student teacher's expectations and the real life of the classroom that unfolded:

1/15: I expected the school to be an old one in a poor neighborhood, and so it was. I had been told it would be like that, so I expected everything that I thought goes with that: poor equipment and very little at that. I also thought it would be poorly organized and hence that minimal amounts of teaching would occur. Then I expected the children would be wild whether in the classroom or on the playground. They would display minimal self-control, that is, a lot of battling, hitting, and teasing. The teacher, I figured, would always be screaming at the top of her lungs and reprimanding the children. You can imagine that I wasn't very happy about that and it surely didn't add to my confidence.

As it turned out, this old building in a depressed area was very well organized and had many advantages (e.g., a breakfast and hot lunch program, a reading program, a library, and a good gymnasium). The children displayed a lot more self-control than I had expected. They are very verbal and use minimal physical aggression in the classroom. They are also learning self-discipline about finishing their work. The teacher is very firm and consistent with the children. She fosters independence in the children.

Nonetheless, teaching here will be a difficult task, as the class is large and there are a lot of cultural gaps as well. I've noticed words used in ways I'm not accustomed to. Also there are a lot of other things which differ from my own background.

Your foundation courses probably stressed the need to understand the cultural diversity in a school. Chances are you learned the value of demographic information to aid in that understanding and the ways to get it. Here is the time to use that knowledge—to find out *in advance* the composition of your class and to be familiar with the cultures represented in it.

Let us sum up. Anxiety in anticipation of a new experience is normal. Some of it is even desirable, seeming to give us a bit of an "edge." More than a little of it, however, is a burden, and we should work hard to manage it so that it does not interfere with our sleep, our appetite, or our personal life.

Reality testing is the best antidote to anxiety about the unknown. One of the important realities of our pluralistic society is the diversity of our culture, including diversity in the use of language, in ways of communicating and relating, and in the values we hold. When you get acquainted with modes of communications and values that are strange and, therefore, anxiety provoking, they become no more alien than chow mein, curry, or wiener schnitzel. To borrow from the classic song, "getting to know you" is what we need to do, and the best time to start doing that with your cooperating teacher and students is as soon as possible.

## SELF-EXPECTATIONS

Have you ever paused and asked yourself, "What do I expect to gain from my student teaching assignment?" What you expect depends partly, of course, on the standards you set for yourself and on your own concept of yourself as a person. Your expectations will also be shaped by other factors, such as: (a) the similarity of philosophy of teaching between you and your cooperating teacher, (b) the class composition, and (c) the atmosphere in the school and especially in the classroom.

Let us look at the first one, *teaching approach.* Let us assume your upbringing and your own experience in school have given you a preference for a highly structured mode of teaching. Now you are assigned a cooperating teacher who is generally permissive and loosely structured in class organization. Under these circumstances, you have a right to expect more stress than if your approaches were compatible.

You may reasonably assume that you will have difficulty in adapting to the unaccustomed behaviors. Yet the experience could turn out to be an enriching one. You may find that incorporating some permissiveness makes your teaching more effective. The same expectation is appropriate in the opposite situation; that is, if you are permissive and the cooperating teacher is highly structured.

Let us look at the second of the three factors that should have a bearing on the expectations you set, the *class composition.* It is unfair to expect a low-achieving class to reach the same level of performance as a high-achieving class. That does not mean that you will not accomplish as much; it does not mean you will not be contributing as much; it does mean that your expectations should be in terms of progress and not in terms of level of performance achieved (e.g., grade levels).

One should, of course, set high standards in all professional work but not expect the impossible. In 10 weeks one cannot expect to remedy years of poor school performance and lack of readiness for the grade or subject you are teaching.

The last of the three factors, *school and class atmosphere,* cannot be ignored when you set your expectations. If there is tension in the school, a sense of distrust and perhaps quiet hostility among teachers or between teachers and administrators, the children will be affected. If tension is clearly present in the classroom, even if not in the school, it will affect the behavior and learning of the children. Under no circumstances could you do as well as you would have if a healthier atmosphere prevailed.

Under these circumstances your self-expectations about what you can help the children accomplish should be lower. Consequently, our advice to you is that you are on your way to being a professional. Be a "pro" and adjust as well as you can. Do your best. But bear in mind that you alone cannot control all the forces that determine what happens when you student teach.

## PREPARING FOR YOUR ASSIGNMENT

To do a good job of preparation, student teachers should have advance notice about their school assignment. Obviously you cannot survey the school and its neighborhood without knowing the name of the school to which you will be assigned. Colleges and universities that make last-minute assignments do a disservice to their students.

Because part of being an effective leader is knowing the context in which one works and in which the children and their families live, work, and play, you should use the period before the assignment to investigate the neighborhood. Your college supervisor can give you a start in obtaining useful information. Your cooperating teacher can help fill in the gaps.

One of us had the good fortune of taking a course in which an excellent plan for studying the community was used. (This sociology of education course was taught by Patrick J. Kelley, then at New York University.) The following modified outline indicates the kinds of useful information that you can obtain to assist you in understanding your school's neighborhood.

## EXPLORATION AND INVESTIGATION OF A COMMUNITY

   I. Get a map covering a radius of 10 blocks around the school in which you will be doing your student teaching.

  II. Find out as much as you can about the community, especially the following:

     A. Community agencies, such as

       1. Library
       2. Settlement houses
       3. Health facilities
       4. Fire house, police station, post office, etc.
       5. Institutions, public or private, that affect the community such as a university
       6. Welfare agencies
       7. Community organization and local YMCA and YWCA

     B. Community leaders

       1. Political leaders
       2. Religious leaders
       3. Educational leaders
       4. Other persons (formal and informal) who influence the community

     C. Curriculum resources, such as

       1. Factories and commercial enterprises
       2. Museums
       3. Parks
       4. Docks
       5. Transportation facilities
       6. Churches, synagogues, and other houses of worship

     D. Representation of ethnic and socioeconomic groups based on

       1. Available statistics (from agencies or census or from local college or university library)
       2. Observation
       3. Signs in neighborhood
       4. Available foods
       5. Other evidences

     E. Unique characteristics of the neighborhood

       1. Family life
       2. Community life
       3. Evidence of problems
       4. Evidence of strengths

 III. Suggested ways of gathering data and information

     A. Careful observation during neighborhood walks

B. Interviews with community leaders, storekeepers, and other appropriate persons

C. Visits to community agencies and to curriculum resources

D. Visits to government offices for statistical information

For you in your first teaching experience, Section II, D and E, of the chart are especially important. Nothing, absolutely nothing, is of greater importance to a teacher than being able to understand the experiences of his or her students. The very meaning of education itself varies from social class to social class and from ethnic group to ethnic group.

In many instances, "a college education," which was obviously of some measure of importance to you and to us, does not mean the same thing to the children. It has less value, in part, because in the past it was generally unrealizable; in part, because a child from a family dependent for three generations on welfare support has had no opportunity to know its meaning.

To use another example, children of extremely high-income families are likely to hold a different perception of the importance of education from yours and ours. They do not fear not having a job and an income after graduation. They do not need to have career plans in the same way that somebody from a middle- or working-class family does. Their outlook on life and their experience of life are bound to be different from that of children of lesser means. No one socioeconomic or ethnic group is "better" than another, but members of each group may experience school and the lessons and homework you assign differently.

## BECOMING PART OF THE SCHOOL COMMUNITY

Over the decades the teaching profession has undergone considerable change in the direction of freedom to live one's private life as one prefers. When your grandparents were in school the practices were very different. In some school systems if a woman married she lost her job. But that was not all. If a teacher was seen serving beer at home on a Saturday night, his or her contract was not renewed.

Those days are past. However, that does not mean that all of the public's social restrictions on teachers have been lifted. The proprieties in a school regarding such practices as speech or mode of dress are generally more conservative than on a college campus. Let us take dress as an example. Although there has been much change in teachers' attire since the early 1970s when, for instance, slacks were taboo for women in most districts, certain styles of dress are still considered inappropriate in a school building.

We would like to be helpful to you by being able to spell out what the "well-dressed" student teacher wears today, but that is not possible. Although the loosening of dress requirements for teachers has its advantages, it poses for you, much more than it did to your counterparts in years past, the question of "What should I wear?"

Our recommendation is to note the dress of the faculty in the school to which you are assigned and, within the boundaries of your own taste, to dress as formally or informally as they as a group do. Their model is useful because it is likely to reflect community expectations as well as the preferences of the board of education, the superintendent, and the principal. For your first visit, assuming that you know nothing about the informal dress codes of the school, you would be well advised to be conservative in your choice of attire.

We recognize that some people will find the need to dress to others' specifications distasteful, and we understand these feelings. Nonetheless, our bias takes this form: Student teaching is a time in your career when you will have trained personal observers to serve you in the on-the-job development of your skills in reaching and teaching children. Your goal should be to use these weeks to learn all you can about your profession and to seek to become the best teacher possible. Anything that might interfere with the reaching of these goals, such as antagonizing the observers by inappropriate dress or speech, should be avoided.

## COMMON CONCERNS OF STUDENT TEACHERS

One of the best prescriptions for mental health is to remind ourselves that we are not alone in our concerns. For that reason we dwell here on common concerns reported by student teachers.

Over a several year period, candidates for student teaching in one department at the University of Georgia were surveyed about their concerns (Murwin & Matt, 1990). At the beginning of their course in methods and curriculum and one quarter before their student teaching, they were asked to identify their 10 major concerns about student teaching (Matt, personal communication, February 21, 1991). The responses of 36 students showed that some or all of the following were very much on their minds:

- Discipline. Uncertain about what to expect . . . and how to handle it . . . and whether their ways of handling problems would meet with approval.
- Student Relations. Anxious that they might not get along with their students . . . might not be liked and respected . . . and that this outcome would develop for reasons over which they themselves might not have any control, such as their need (as student teachers) to maintain control over the students.
- Faculty Relations. Apprehensive about relations with teachers and winning their respect . . . troubled about what their relationship with the cooperating teacher would be like.
- Lesson Plans. Insecure about preparing adequate and acceptable lesson plans (Note: one survey was taken at outset of course that gave them preparation

and practice in this activity) . . . not confident that their plans would be found to be satisfactory.

- Methods and Motivation. Troubled about their ability to motivate and hold their students' interest.
- Self-image. Unsure about their ability to match the expectations of the people who would make judgments about them.

Another concern, whether supplies and materials would be adequate, was especially relevant to teachers in special fields like technology, art, and music education.

The students in this still-ongoing study seemed to be saying, "I don't know what to expect and how I'll handle it. Also, I'm not sure whether students and teachers will like what I do, and will like me. I hope I can live up to expectations." An earlier study, which took a different tack, shows some similar findings. The subjects in this case were already in student teaching.

The following list identifies the major concerns of 139 student teachers who participated in a research project (Cohen, Mirels, & Schwebel, 1972). The length of this list of concerns may make it appear that we are accentuating the negative. We are not. Regardless of what we write and of whatever reassurances you may receive elsewhere, we know you will have your share of concerns. Our purpose in presenting them and showing percentages of student teachers affected by them is to reiterate that it is common for student teachers to experience them. Student teachers who have no concerns had better get their pulse checked!

The participating student teachers were given a questionnaire built to assess the worries of student teachers during their school assignment. The 122 items on the questionnaire were chosen to cover the broadest possible range—from concerns about getting cooperation from the school's janitor to those about getting too personally involved with the students' problems. The student-teacher subjects were asked to rate each item indicating whether it caused: (a) "no concern," (b) "slight concern," (c) "moderate concern," (d) "great concern," (e) "such very great concern that it has led me to consider leaving the teaching profession."

From the 122 concerns, we first chose those that 50% or more student teachers rated as moderate, great, or very great concerns. From those we then selected the concerns that 25% or more rated as great or very great concerns. The concerns so identified are organized into the categories proposed by Fuller (1969), concerns about the self and concerns about pupils, and are presented here:

### Concerns About the Self

1. Relationships with cooperating teacher, college supervisor, other professionals and parents

- Receiving sufficient encouragement from my college supervisor and cooperating teacher
- Evaluation of my teaching by my college supervisor
- Adjusting to the expectations of my college supervisor
- Getting parents interested in their child's education
- Dealing with parents whose attitudes adversely affect their children's school performance
- Obtaining adequate assistance

2. Personal adjustment problems
   - Obtaining a good job placement after graduation
   - Worrying whether I am doing an effective job of teaching
   - Achieving a good understanding of my personal strengths and weaknesses with respect to teaching
   - Falling into routine methods of presenting material

3. Knowledge of subject matter
   - Teaching students to think through problems on their own
   - Finding ways of keeping up with new ideas in education

4. Control and management
   - Finding ways to control the students effectively
   - Finding sufficient time to cover the required material effectively
   - Providing all the pupils with opportunities for class participation
   - Leaving students back
   - Getting students to follow instructions
   - Finding adequate time for planning classroom work
   - Finding time to present current material not included in the regular curriculum
   - Finding enough time to give adequate individual attention to each student
   - Dealing with the classroom troublemakers
   - Dealing with students who interfere with others' work
   - Finding time to plan and rehearse special projects

5. Gaining emotional support from the students
   - Gaining pupils' respect

## Concerns About Students

1. Adapting the subject matter to the students
   - Presenting the work in ways which engage the students' interest
   - Presenting material in ways which foster understanding
   - Making up tests from which students can learn

2. Motivating students to learn
   - Getting all the students to participate in classroom discussions
   - Working with students who don't seem to care if they learn or not
   - Working with pupils who are not performing at grade level
   - Getting students to apply what they have learned to new problems
3. Learning progress of individual students and how this could be improved
   - Keeping the better students interested and busy while working with the slower students
   - Dealing with pupils who have emotional problems
   - Developing satisfactory ways to evaluate a student's progress
   - Discovering and developing the potential of each student
   - Adapting the assignments to the needs of the student
   - Diagnosing the individual needs of each student
   - Developing the full potential of the bright student in a class where most are average
   - Trying to assign grades fairly

If the list appears rather forbidding, you can at least be comforted by the fact that not all the concerns develop at once. Fuller (1969) discovered that student teachers typically experience concerns about themselves first. Until they deal with these, it is difficult for them to focus on the pupil-related concerns.

This seems reasonable. Student teachers need to feel somewhat comfortable and secure themselves before they can mobilize their energy and concentrate their attention on the children's problems.

However, student teachers, in the midst of the near chaos of the first weeks of adapting, become upset that they are worrying about themselves rather than about the children. This, they believe, is not the behavior of a responsible student teacher. Such a view is a mistaken one, as Fuller's work has shown. (Incidentally, the same pattern emerges in nursing students during their clinical assignments; Packard, Schwebel, & Ganey, 1979. Specifically, they are first concerned about their abilities and then, recognizing this, feel badly that they are worrying about themselves rather than their patients.)

It is also comforting to know that only 3 of the 122 items on the Common Concerns list aroused great concern or very great concern in 50% or more of the student teachers sampled (Cohen et al., 1972). These three were:

Obtaining a good job placement after graduation (81%)
Working with students who don't seem to care if they learn or not (52%)
Finding enough time to give adequate attention to each student (50%)

Not surprisingly, first and foremost among the items causing great or very great concern was that of addressing the issue of obtaining a good job after graduation. Every student teacher is conscious of the fact that his or her performance and the ratings he or she gets from the cooperating teacher and the college supervisor will have considerable bearing on his or her success in obtaining a job.

Next came concern about being able to motivate the "unmotivated" students. Implicit in this concern are fears about control of the class if the unmotivated become disruptive. The third greatest concern was worry about the time available to the teachers in today's classrooms. The student teachers wondered, given the press of time, if they will be able to be the good teachers they want to be?

When you are feeling overwhelmed early in your teaching, there is a tendency to blame yourself, to say somebody else would be working wonders. Do not blame yourself and do not put yourself down. Self-criticism is useful because it helps you do better, but self-condemnation is crippling. It drains your confidence while offering you nothing positive. When you are knee deep in concern, remember that the situation is temporary, that things will eventually get better, and that everybody has problems of one kind or another during student teaching.

Knowing that you are not the first or only student teacher with a reservoir of worries may not solve anything, but it will surely make you feel better. Helen put it this way in her log:

> 3/5: My lesson on plants was timed perfectly today. But I'm still having problems getting the children to listen or respond to me. The student-teaching seminar helped me here. It's comforting to know the rest of my classmates are having similar experiences and problems.

For generations, and still today as we have found in our most recent interviews, concerns like those discussed here have troubled student teachers. Remember, most of these individuals conquered their fears, coped with their stress, and went on to become effective educators.

## THE CONTROL-C METHOD OF PROBLEM SOLVING

In embarking on new ventures like student teaching, and then independent teaching, individuals who feel confident are at a great advantage. They know the realities of student teaching and have some of the concerns discussed earlier, but they are not thrown by them. They are able to keep their fears under control because they are confident that they will manage to cope successfully with whatever comes their way.

They get that kind of confidence by having the wherewithal to deal with problems. You don't have to be superman or superwoman to feel that way. You just have to develop skill as a problem solver. For that purpose, we have drawn on the literature on problem solving and on our own experience to develop a problem-solving system that you might want to master. We call it the CONTROL-C method.

The first point we want to make is that the eight-step CONTROL-C process may look complex but actually is simple and straightforward. As you see here, it is just a logical way of coping with problems. First let us examine some assumptions about CONTROL-C.

## Assumptions

The CONTROL-C method was developed on the basis of three important assumptions:

1. Usually there are several or more ways to cope with a problem in teaching.
2. To cope effectively with a problem you need to be able to recognize and appreciate the perspective of everybody involved.
3. Not every problem a student teacher faces is solvable.

These are discussed here, and then the CONTROL-C method is presented.

*Assumption 1: Usually There are Several or More Ways to Cope With Problems.*    Ours is the scientific age. When we have a problem, we go to the expert who is supposed to solve it. Our thinking is so dominated by a belief in the invincibility of research that we have become accustomed to think there is a right answer to everything. Such simplicity of solution rarely exists in problems that student teachers face. Usually there are many reasonable approaches to the problems encountered, with no one alternative seeming more obviously right than the others. Each possible approach has its own likelihood of success, its own payoffs, and its own costs. CONTROL-C was designed to help you select your best alternative to cope with a given problem.

For example, consider a class member named Johnny, a bright youngster who is always finishing seatwork quickly and interrupting the work of his slower paced neighbors by conversing with them. There are many ways to deal with him—for example, moving his seat, assigning him more work, scolding him when he talks, using him as a messenger, or developing his talent as a peer teacher. There is no one obviously correct solution to the problem.

Once a student teacher has a clear goal in mind, he or she is ready to select from the available alternatives. His or her decision is based on his or her values as an educator, his or her understanding of the child's interests, and his or her assessment of the relative merits of each choice. If one plan fails, the student teacher can experiment with another.

The same line of reasoning holds for interpersonal relationships and for any problems that develop between the student teacher and the two supervisors in his or her life. A diversity of alternatives can be established, and there is no one correct one.

*Assumption 2: To Cope Effectively With a Problem You Need to be Able to Recognize and Appreciate the Perspective of Everybody Involved.* For example, Johnny's disruptiveness could involve a number of people, including Johnny, his mother and father, the student teacher, the cooperating teacher, the principal, the school psychologist, and the student teacher's university supervisor. Each party in a situation has his or her own needs, goals, and so forth, and these affect how each sees a situation and what each wants to do about it. Some of the needs individuals have may not be immediately obvious, but if one surmises that they are there, one might be much more effective in problem solving. Although everybody's goal in Johnny's case might be to enable him to be a more effective learner and less disruptive to the class, the following chart shows what some covert (that is, not immediately obvious) needs of people in Johnny's case might be.

Psychologists sometimes call these covert needs *hidden agendas.* All people have them in situations that relate to their work and personal lives, which means in virtually all their relationships. There is nothing wrong with hidden agendas. Having them does not mean these people do not want to help Johnny. Quite the contrary, they all want to help him function better in school. However, if each person was aware of the hidden agendas of the others, the group might be better able to do what they all want—to help Johnny.

| *People Involved with Johnny's Problem* | *Possible Covert Needs* |
| --- | --- |
| 1. Johnny | To get attention from teacher and classmates. |
| 2. Johnny's mother | To be judged by school people as a concerned and good mother. |
| 3. Johnny's father | To be judged by school people as a concerned and good father. |
| 4. The student teacher | To not appear impatient when dealing with Johnny in front of the cooperating teacher and university supervisor. |
| 5. The cooperating teacher | To appear to the principal as a skilled teacher who is having difficult with Johnny because of Johnny's personality (and not the teacher's handling of the situation). |
| 6. The principal | To portray him or herself as a concerned administrator who cares about each student. |
| 7. The school counselor | To show progress in diagnosing and helping Johnny or to refer him elsewhere so that the responsibility is not in his or her office. |

| *People Involved with Johnny's Problem* | *Possible Covert Needs* |
|---|---|
| 8. The university supervisor | To be effective and to act to prevent having the problem involve his or her superior at the university. |
| 9. The university supervisor's superior | To avoid the growth of the problem to the point where the school no longer wants to use student teachers from the university. |

*Assumption 3: Not Every Problem a Student Teacher Faces is Solvable.* Regrettably there is not a Hollywood happy ending to every single classroom problem. Although not every problem has a perfect solution, in most instances the conflict situation can be improved to the point where those involved are comfortable. For instance, Mary may never be your most obedient pupil but, if she is treated in a certain way, her behavior can be modified so that she is only minimally disruptive to her classmates and to herself.

Another example of an unsolvable problem may apply to the cooperating teacher who is hypercritical and whose behavior is not truly cooperative. It may be too much to hope to form a perfect team with such a person. Yet, with the advice of the university supervisor, a working relationship can be established that is educational and at least tolerable, if not comfortable, to the student teacher.

## Using CONTROL-C

Your mind is the most important tool you have at your disposal as a problem-solving student teacher. When you inevitably stumble against an obstacle, apply yourself fully to addressing it, and you will feel more confident. The raw material for CONTROL-C is the information you yourself have collected. You process this information in steps that allow you to gain a deeper understanding of the problem and solve it in the way that makes the most sense to you, all things considered. The method personalizes problem solving to your particular situation and ensures that your needs and values are taken into account.

The eight steps of *CONTROL-C* are:

C Collect a bank of information.
O Ongoing identification of problems.
N New information collected.
T Take others' perspectives.
R Review coping procedures.
O Overview of problem and of alternative coping procedures shared with others.
L Link all information.
/
C Closure on one procedure.

These are now explained and illustrated by use of an example.

### C: Collect a Bank of Information

Use it to cope with current and future problems. For this purpose we suggest you keep a daily log of your experiences as a student teacher. In the log you should enter key events of the school day and your thoughts, feelings, and reactions to these. Write down what was good, what was bad, what you could have done differently to make things better, what you can do to avoid problems in the future. Also enter important events and reactions to your student-teaching seminar. Remember, effective log keeping involves more than just writing. It involves a personal, private thinking process. Note your deepest reflections and the range of emotions emanating from your classroom experiences, all for the purpose of gaining increasing mastery as a teacher.

Across the many miles and the time that separate us from you, we can sense your groaning reaction to the thought of having one more chore a day. We can sympathize with such a reaction and even add that a log is not essential; however, CONTROL-C is considerably more effective if you have a log to draw upon when you are confronted with a problem.

Obviously, to keep a log or not is your decision. We can only point out the advantages. The log (a) helps make CONTROL-C work more effectively, (b) systematically gives you a few moments to think through the events of the day, (c) offers you a regular opportunity to relieve stress and vent your feelings, and (d) allows you to develop a document that will later enable you to see your growth and get a sense of progress.

Perhaps the best argument for keeping logs is in Carmen's log, which she was required to keep during her student teaching.

> I just reread some of my earlier thoughts from the beginning of the month. Sometimes it's easier for me to explore things on paper. When I look back on my thoughts after a time interval, I see that not all of my ideas are logical. That makes this sort of thing valuable to me. I've been doing this journal-type thing since spring quarter. I wish I had kept a log of my thought-notes during my three weeks in the classroom winter quarter. It would be interesting to see my changes on paper. Easier, too. I've gone through a lot of changes since then. I'll bet this is much more interesting to me than to you!

*Example of C.*   Logs represent one kind of bank of information. Excerpts of logs are found throughout the remaining pages of the book.

### O: Ongoing Identification of Problems

Something is troubling you, and the situation needs remediation. The major task at this point is to make an accurate statement of the problem or the troubling situation. Describe it briefly, preferably in a sentence or two. Be sure that you are describing the problem rather than presenting a presumed cause or a proposed solution.

*Example of* **O.**   My cooperating teacher will not let me teach enough to satisfy me.

## N: New Information Collected

New and banked information is organized. Using your log (or memory), create a list of factors that could be playing a role in the situation. Get all possibilities down on paper so you can review them and reflect on them. Then decide which ones are your most promising "suspects."

*Example of* **N.**   Log entries on different dates included: "I didn't control the children today during my first lesson." "Mrs. P. didn't want to go to lunch with me today. I don't think she likes me." "Mrs. P. complained about the kids she gets from State [University]."

## T: Take Others' Perspectives

Remember the issue of "hidden agendas" discussed earlier. Try your best to get into the shoes of everybody else involved in any way in the classroom, and to understand and appreciate each of their perspectives on a given problem. Use whatever information you can to posit what is in their minds.

*Example of* **T.**   Mrs. P. doesn't think I'm ready and is afraid I'll ruin her class. She may assume if I observe her for a few more days I'll be better able to control the class. Mrs. P. is so much older: Maybe she treats all her student teachers this way—and protects them like her own children. Mrs. P. feels that the directives from the university only require I take over the full class for 4 weeks and that that's all I want.

## R: Review Coping Procedures

Generate a list of alternate ways of dealing with the situations. In doing this, think of what you have learned in the previous steps and also about the resources you have at your disposal.

*Example of* **R.**   I could talk to Mrs. P. about my early performance, or ask her to let me teach. Or I could ask her why she hasn't let me teach. I could ask my supervisor to talk to her and explain that it's OK if I take over the full class earlier than the last 4 weeks of the term. Or after the next lesson I teach, I could ask her directly for criticism. Etc., Etc.

## O: Overview of Problem and of Alternative Coping Procedures

Share the problem and your alternative coping procedures with resource persons, such as your university supervisor or cooperating teacher (if the problem is not directly related to them) or with friends or relatives. Have the resource persons help you review your thoughts about the issue you are facing. Once they have the relevant information, they can often provide a fresh view.

*Example of O.* You might choose to speak with one of the preceding persons or perhaps with several or all of them in planned sequence.

## L: Link all Information

With all of the preceding information at hand, review the alternative approaches, and assess the advantages and disadvantages of each. Consider the likelihood of each improving the situation. Consider all the people involved and the effect each alternative would have on you and them.

*Example of L.* Make a chart like the one in Table 2.1, and fill in all the boxes.

## C: Closure on One Procedure

Choose an approach, plan its use, and determine how you will evaluate the success of the selected approach.

*Example of C.* On the basis of the chart, you might decide to ask Mrs. P. directly why she has not allowed you to teach more frequently. While asking your supervisor would have been easier, you might conclude that it would be wiser and more mature to try to solve things yourself.

Your reasoning might be that this approach would win respect from both Mrs. P. and the university supervisor and, at the same time, build your own confidence. The plan might be to stay after school the next day to raise the issue with Mrs. P. Success could be measured by the number of lessons taught the next week. If there were no increase, then you could revert to the chart and select another approach.

Using the CONTROL-C procedure is not very different from the application of sound reasoning to problems in life in general. We give it such prominence here because you have probably not been trained in college to cope with problems in interpersonal relations. Also, some problems you will encounter in student teaching are almost certainly going to be of that kind. Although we have written this book solely to help you through some of the no-man's land of student teaching, we know that mastery of CONTROL-C will enable you to cope more effectively with interpersonal problems in your personal as well as your professional life.

TABLE 2.1
Problem Analysis Chart

| Alternatives | Likelihood of improving situation | Advantages | Disadvantages | Effect On | | | |
| --- | --- | --- | --- | --- | --- | --- | --- |
| | | | | Me | Mrs. P. | The children | My supervisor |
| 1. Talk to Mrs. P. about my early performance | | | | | | | |
| 2. Ask her to let me teach | | | | | | | |
| 3. Ask her why she hasn't let me teach | | | | | | | |
| 4. After next lesson ask directly for feedback | | | | | | | |
| 5. Ask my supervisor to talk to Mrs. P. | | | | | | | |

## FOUR STAGES TO STUDENT-TEACHING SUCCESS

We conclude this chapter with a description of the four stages of development that you are likely to experience during student teaching. These stages, derived from an analysis of the logs, are probably typical of the life of the student teacher. This is not to say that your experience will follow each stage exactly, or that each will be equally prominent. However, you can expect to find at least elements of each stage, perhaps more of some than others, during your teaching assignment.

### Stage 1: The Early Days

The first days are no honeymoon. They can be overwhelming, especially because the student teacher tries to absorb so much information very quickly. He or she drives him or herself: got to become acquainted with each child, got to learn the class routine and procedures, got to master the materials the teacher uses, got to learn his or her teaching techniques. Besides trying to master all that, he or she has to make sure that the cooperating teacher likes him or her or at least is on his or her side. Feeling overwhelmed and seeing the cooperating teacher functioning so well, and handling everything in stride, he or she feels awed. "Can I do it?", the student teacher asks him or herself.

### Stage 2: Becoming a Member of the Teaching Team

Through observation and immersion in class activities, the student teacher begins to get a more accurate picture of the class and its teacher. He or she begins to see the students as individuals and, at the same time, to gain a sense of the wholeness of the class, a group that operates as a unit. The cooperating teacher is not a name on an assignment sheet anymore, but rather a real live person. Effective as he or she may be as a teacher, he or she is not imbued as superman or superwoman, but simply as an able teacher who, being human and working with humans, has to cope with problems. The student teacher starts to generate ideas about what he or she would do differently if this were his or her class. He or she now begins to feel part of the class. The class recognizes him or her as a member of the teaching team. And the student teacher, perceiving the cooperating teacher as a person, has feelings that stem from their interaction, feelings like warmth, respect, and anger.

### Stage 3: Soloing as a Teacher

"The chalkboard shuffle and flounder" is also an appropriate title for this stage. The observation period is over and the student teacher tries his or her wings. He or she solos! All of the topics and problems discussed so often in the college classes, and fantasized and dreamed about (including an occasional nightmare?) are now real life, here and now, today. Preparation, presentation, timing, movement of pupils from one activity to another, assisting one group while monitoring the class, discipline, and discipline again—all these confront the student teacher at one time.

In Stage 2 the student teacher's morale had risen rapidly over the first stage. In Stage 3, unless he or she is careful, his or her morale can nose dive. If the student teacher wants to feel bad about something, there is always something to feel bad about. For instance, if he or she compares his or her performance with the cooperating teacher he or she will surely find him or herself inferior—and yet he or she may fail to attribute his or her inferiority to the differences in their experience. But he or she need not do that. He or she can find instead positive things to take note of, the progress he or she has made, and his or her success each day in coping with something he or she was unable to cope with before.

There are no yardsticks for student teachers at this point, only feedback from the cooperating teacher and the children, which they can reflect upon and learn from. There are three patterns to choose from in this stage: Some feel defeated by the situation, label themselves failures, and give up; others feel defeated, but place the blame elsewhere, usually on the cooperating teacher and sometimes on the college for having prepared them poorly; but most student teachers feel okay about Stage 3, viewing it as just a passing phase, difficult indeed, but one that they will weather successfully, in part by using a problem solving system like CONTROL-C.

## Stage 4: Feeling Like a Teacher

After passing through the storms of Stage 3, the student teacher settles down to the job of working with his or her pupils and, in the process, transforms him or herself into a teacher. His or her time with the cooperating teacher will be drawing to an end. From here on, whole days are his or hers to plan and execute.

From the weeks of classroom experience he or she has begun to develop his or her own style, and further, he or she has come to feel "at home" in front of the class. He or she knows there is much more to learn. But he or she accepts the reality that one does not become a master teacher in 10 weeks or 10 months. Above all, now he or she has much more confidence: When the new school year rolls around and he or she takes over his or her own class as a full-time teacher, he or she will be able to handle the job.

# Relationships

# 3
▼▼▼▼▼▼▼

# Relationship With the Cooperating Teacher: The Foundation of Effective Student Teaching

This chapter focuses on the cooperating teacher relationship, the foundation on which a successful student-teaching experience is built. If you form a supportive bond with your cooperating teacher, you will be able to overcome almost any professional problem you encounter.

We start with a step-by-step discussion of what is involved in building an effective bond. This is followed by discussion of how to avoid (or deal with) crippling relationship problems that can develop.

Although student teacher–cooperating teacher relationship issues are the focus of the chapter, the last section deals briefly with substitute teachers. The probability is high that during your student-teaching assignment the cooperating teacher will miss a day or more. As we explain, her absence can offer both opportunities for learning and new challenges to your problem-solving abilities.

## THAT FIRST MEETING

You knew the time would come eventually, and now it has: Finally you are going to be in a classroom on a daily basis. That is a big step forward, but you will have the necessary assistance to take it in stride. Your cooperating teacher soon will become the most important person in this first stage of your professional career. He or she can assist you in developing teaching competency and then, with a letter of reference, can aid you in securing your first position.

To take maximum advantage of your cooperating teacher's expertise and experience, you have to form a solid working relationship. If the relationship is a good one, the chances are that it will be much more intense than any that you formed with instructors during your college career.

*Don't Make Prejudgments.*   Before and after student-teaching assignments are announced, you will undoubtedly hear your classmates make some very subjective evaluations of different cooperating teachers: Hartman is good, but Hellman is a "loser." "I hope I don't get stuck with O'Shea down at Lincoln School," somebody will say.

If you hear your prospective cooperating teacher being so "evaluated," we advise you to ignore the comment. Without prejudgments you will be better able to enter your first meeting with an open mind and with the expectation that in due time you two will relate well and develop an effective teaching team.

*Psychological Readiness.*   That first meeting is important. You can do much in advance to make it a successful one. Prepare yourself psychologically. Come with confidence in yourself and your ability to succeed, and you will show that you are ready to accept classroom responsibilities.

Psychological readiness requires that you cope with your anxiety about your teaching assignment. You will want to harness the stress inherent in this situation. Let us assume that every time you think about the meeting you get nervous. If you deal with the situation by deciding not to think about the meeting, the worry will indeed go away for the moment. However, such a strategy also prevents you from planning for the meeting. Not thinking about a stressful upcoming event is a widely used defensive approach but, regrettably, it is also self-defeating.

The alternative, admittedly easier said than done, is to take the feeling of nervousness as an indicator that something important is about to happen and gear yourself accordingly. Such an approach reduces your tension. It also serves to increase the chances that you will plan for the important event, and be more successful.

How can this approach for dealing with nervousness work for you with regard to planning the first contact with your cooperating teacher? First, set aside some time to think about what you want to learn from your student-teaching experience. Jot down some specific skills you want to develop, content areas in which you want to prepare units, discipline techniques you want to test, and so forth. Then think about the first meeting with your cooperating teacher. Plan your part in it. What do you want to know from him or her? What do you want to tell him or her? You will find it helpful to rehearse the asking of certain questions.

*The Cooperating Teacher's Perspective.*   Reflecting on what to say is too difficult, you might be thinking now, because you cannot concretize a picture of the other party in the meeting (i.e., the cooperating teacher). But one way you can deal with this ambiguity is to imagine somebody who is both your boss and your instructor. Those are the cooperating teacher's roles. Now, imagine that you were in that position. What characteristics would you want in your student teacher? Would you be pleased to have a student teacher who conveys excitement and enthusiasm about what lies ahead?

While you are still in the cooperating teacher role, consider what else you would want. The instructor part of you would probably prefer a person who exhibits an appetite for learning as well as an eagerness to use you, an experienced teacher, as a resource person. The boss part of you, in contrast, wants a person who is willing to roll up his or her shirtsleeves to give what he or she can in doing the work of the classroom. If you have these characteristics, be sure to communicate them one way or another during the conference.

Although there is much you can infer about your cooperating teacher, you will not get the information necessary to substitute facts for assumptions until you meet. At that point you will get acquainted with some of his or her personal characteristics. For example, he or she is open and comfortable in the relationship with you, or he or she is restrained. You may learn about his or her orientation toward education. For example, he or she may stress mastery of skills and information as primary objectives or learning to raise questions. He or she may tell you the way he or she runs the class: for example, highly structured, following a well-defined schedule, or loosely structured and flexible.

When you are given your cooperating teacher's name, it is wise to telephone him or her and request an opportunity to meet. It is good to do this even if you have to first battle the normal, nervous feelings about making the call.

*Anticipating the First Meeting.* The ideal first meeting would be a leisurely one, held after school at a time and place convenient and comfortable to you both. Such circumstances would allow you to set a pattern of useful communication and thoughtful sharing of ideas. With time on your side you could also exchange ideas and feelings about education in general.

Unfortunately, the ideal is not always possible. Some student teachers will not know their assignment until the day before they are to begin. Others will have sufficient notice but a cooperating teacher who prefers not to meet until the term begins.

If the cooperating teacher seems to be putting you off in scheduling a meeting, remember it may not be for the reasons you assume. For instance, he or she could be slow in establishing relations or, at the time, very busy in his or her life outside the classroom.

So, for the reasons just given and a variety of others, conditions surrounding your first meeting may be less than ideal. Nonetheless, whenever and wherever it takes place, make that first meeting the first step in building a solid relationship.

Immediately after the meeting, and probably until your first full day in the classroom, you will be thinking about your cooperating teacher. You may feel fortunate in being assigned an effective and personable teacher, and that is fine.

On the other hand, if you feel the situation with the cooperating teacher will be disastrous, or, at best, much less than satisfactory, you still have plenty of reasons for hope. Often conditions improve as student and cooperating teacher become better acquainted and comfortable with each other.

## THAT FIRST DAY

Although it may not seem so at the moment, your first day in the classroom as a student teacher is really very special. You may be too busy to realize that it marks a milestone in your life as well as an important transition point in your professional career. That first day deserves special attention. Regardless of whether things go well or you end up needing two aspirins before noon, take a moment to become fully aware of your thoughts and feelings.

Alice, who was not able to meet her cooperating teacher prior to this date, described her first day impressions in her log. From her log entry you can see that Alice drew inferences that she expected would be useful to her when she assumed the role of teacher.

1/6: It was a pleasant day. I met Mrs. L., my cooperating teacher, who appeared to be friendly and highly concerned with her pre-kindergarteners. I was also introduced to the children, who seemed to be happy and most of them eager to learn.

I observed all day long and noticed how some of the children had very short attention spans. That should be useful to me when I begin teaching lessons. Since I was observing, I didn't have much interaction with the children. They tended to be a little shy with me yet.

Overall, I think I'm going to enjoy student teaching at Glen Avenue School.

Alice was obviously pleased. Some student teachers leave school after the first day in a state of ecstasy, whereas others are disappointed because the school, the cooperating teacher, and/or the children are not what they had expected. To some extent, Joyce felt this way, but she had hopes too, as her log entry shows:

1/6: This wasn't what I expected at all! I guess I'm really disappointed with the situation I think I'll be in at this school. Well, it's only for 10 weeks. With a big mental psyche maybe I'll make it. I like the other student teachers. And, if I'm not crazy, I feel an air of disappointment from them too. The staff seems friendly towards us all, but I receive negative vibrations towards me as a Black.

The class and I will get along fine. The school day in this classroom is so regimented! That's one thing I'd like to change. The kids are always in their seats. The fact that I'm Black may not upset them much, since I'll be the teacher. But, with the staff—things might be different. It's going to be hard working with Mr. P. . . . . He's so set in his ways and he seems to be against change. Hope I'm wrong!

To state the obvious, first impressions are not necessarily accurate, and it is a mistake—a very serious one in fact—to set your expectations on the basis of initial experience. Why? Expectations prepare us to act as if the "expected events" were inevitably going to occur. Then, without our necessarily being aware of it, by our actions we may help make them occur.

For example, if, on the basis of very limited experience, I expect my cooperating teacher to slap me down every time I utter a word, I will end up censoring myself and speaking only when necessary. Put another way, I will make my expectation come true and, at the same time, I will limit my chances to learn from my student-teaching experience. Instead of making premature judgments, I should go into the situation with a positive outlook.

## STAGES IN YOUR RELATIONSHIP WITH YOUR COOPERATING TEACHER

Our analysis of student-teacher logs indicates that the stages outlined in chapter 2 provide a good way to trace the development of the cooperating teacher relationship.

### Getting Started

#### Stage 1: The Early Days

The first time period is spent trying to absorb a great deal of information, quickly. So much is new and so much must be learned. You must channel energy into (a) becoming acquainted with the students and learning their names, (b) becoming familiar with the learning styles and personal characteristics of each class member, and (c) adapting to the pace of and atmosphere in the room. The "I'm overwhelmed" feeling inevitably develops, and, because of it, you will feel drained by the day's end.

You also will want to invest energy into building the student teacher–cooperating teacher relationship. As the logs we collected suggest, this relationship does not develop "automatically." Although some cooperating teachers will take the initiative, others do not. In such cases, it is in the student teacher's interest to begin building the relationship.

As days go by and you feel more comfortable with both the class and teacher, you will want to assume more responsibility. By then, your cooperating teacher will know you better and may be ready to have you teach. When you reach this point, a student–cooperating teacher planning-goal-setting meeting is useful. At such a meeting, you can speak about your classroom involvement to date and identify areas you would like to work in. Through give-and-take discussion, the two of you can develop a set of learning goals toward which you will work.

Sandra asked Darla, her cooperating teacher, if she would be interested in having a planning-goal-setting meeting. Darla thought it was a great idea, and it was she who suggested a luncheon. Much was accomplished, as Sandra described in her log:

1/26: Darla and I went to lunch. The first part of the meeting turned out to be more of a social situation than anything else. Later, we did discuss my position in the class and Darla was concerned how I was or wasn't enjoying the observation days. She informed me I could begin teaching lessons on Monday and we planned the procedure for the day. We also set up a series of long-range goals. These were for me to:
  a: rearrange the reading corner and that side of the classroom;
  b: plan a nutrition unit;
  c: fully acquaint myself with all materials in the room;
  d: design a unit on the senses;
  e: review the science manual and classroom laboratory kit and start science with kids;
  f: individualize with Stephen and Kevin;
  g: work on being a creative teacher;
  h: create a backlog of 5-, 10-, and 15-minute classroom activities;
  i: by the middle of March, see how much of the above has been accomplished.

For Sandra, building an effective working relationship with Darla was easy enough. And so it should be for most student teachers. All it should take is for you to call upon your social skills, and, with a full measure of determination, display what you have learned during your years of education at college. It should be much like forming a friendship with a willing person who shares common interests with you.

What if you cannot seem to build the kind of effective working relationship with your cooperating teacher that we have stressed is the key to a successful student-teaching experience? "Will he or she ever warm up to me?", you may be asking yourself as you puzzle over what you can do to improve the situation. First, reassure yourself by remembering that others have been in a similar position and successfully sorted things out.

Next, review the CONTROL-C method so you can think about the problem carefully and systematically. Questions to consider in analyzing the situation include: (a) Did you do or say anything the cooperating teacher might have thought was out of place? (b) Are you his or her first student teacher and, if so, could that account for the difficulty you are experiencing? (c) Is he or she a person who is by nature reserved and takes time to warm up to people? (d) Do you represent a threat to the teacher because of your personality, appearance, or some other trait or quality? (e) Is he or she an unwilling participant in the student-teacher program?

Follow the CONTROL-C procedure, which may lead you to discuss the problem with a classmate or friend. If matters fail to improve, approach your college supervisor, who may be able to help you consider alternative coping methods or, if necessary, may intervene on your behalf. If you have trouble mobilizing yourself to tell your supervisor about the problem, remind yourself that his or her job is to help as well as evaluate you. The supervisor knows that a poor relationship with a cooperating teacher deprives you of an optimal learning environment.

## Stage 2: Becoming a Member of the Teaching Team

A little more secure in the classroom, the student teacher now recognizes the cooperating teacher's substantial professional ability while also discovering that the halo has disappeared. Yes, the cooperating teacher is not perfect. He or she too makes mistakes, and does some things differently from the way the student teacher was taught. For example, he or she does not handle June's disruptive behavior head-on, and he or she ignores the fact that Harry who has so much potential will soon turn 16 and leave school unless somebody makes a concerted effort to convince him of the value of a high school diploma.

A frequently voiced concern during this time period relates to the cooperating teacher's classroom style and philosophy of education. For example, Ernest wrote in his log: "The teacher is so traditional. . . . She shouts at the kids all day. . . . Even an adult couldn't sit still for as long as those kids have to."

Student teachers airing such criticisms note the difference between their philosophy of education and teaching style and those of their cooperating teacher and often hasten to add comments like, "I'm not going to teach my class that way." But making such observations and declaring that one is going to teach in a different way does not end the problem. Some student teachers are deeply concerned about whether they can learn from a mentor whose approach seems so different, and that concern must be handled constructively.

Many student teachers have found that they can benefit from an experience with a teacher whose approach is very different from theirs. Richard is a good example. Although he first feared he would be unable to tolerate a semester-long relationship with his cooperating teacher, after several weeks he found that his classroom experiences were helping him crystalize his own thoughts about teaching.

2/5: School went well today. I have vowed to myself I will not teach in the same manner employed by Allyson. . . . My obedience to this vow remains to be seen. Also the question comes to mind, how will I teach?

. . . How? I am really not sure, but I will try to avoid shouting . . . and asking them silly or irrelevant questions when they cut up.

I will try to let them look at more books, have their work area less cluttered, and come up with more imaginative ways of introducing a lesson's learning objective. . . .

The reason we confidently state that you can learn in any cooperating classroom is that you are the key ingredient in what is learned. Regardless of your assignment, you can derive great benefits from your interactions with your students. It is true that with certain assignments you will have more extensive experience and more opportunity to experiment, but wherever you are, if you commit yourself, you can expect to see your own professional development.

At some point during Stage 2 you will probably compare yourself with your cooperating teacher. When you do, you will invariably find differences, some of which will affect your thoughts and behaviors in the classroom. Some of the most obvious possible differences are discussed here.

First, you two obviously differ in years of experience and perhaps in the kind of training you received. You have come upon the scene with fresh ideas from college that may contradict the experience that led him or her to decide what was best for him or her (although not necessarily for you).

Second, you have different roles and responsibilities in the classroom. Your main job is to learn from your student teaching. In contrast, although the cooperating teacher has some responsibility for instructing you, his or her first responsibility is to the class, that is, to see that certain instructional goals are achieved.

Third, the two of you may have different personalities, work styles, and so forth. You may be energetic and bubbly, whereas he or she may be quieter and steadier, or vice versa.

These differences, and others, may create divergences in the ways you approach students and in the preferences you have on how lessons should be taught, class order maintained, and routines conducted. As a person without the year-long responsibility for and task of maintaining discipline, you may be critical of aspects of your cooperating teacher's approach. For example, you might think he or she shouts too much, is too tied to routines, and is too whole-class rather than group-oriented. After you have drawn these mental conclusions, you may well be tempted to suggest changes to your cooperating teacher or to show him or her how you would handle things differently. Should you? Resist that temptation and consider these three issues:

1. Avoid being judgmental and assuming the cooperating teacher's way is wrong and yours is right. His or her approach and yours may each have advantages and disadvantages. When he or she handles a situation or teaches a lesson in ways that are different from how you would have handled it, enter that in your log and list the pluses and minuses of his or her approach and of yours.

2. You are in the classroom to learn. With an open mind, approach your cooperating teacher to discuss his or her approach. Ask "Why" questions and share your perspective. You may find that he or she is insightful and has well thought through reasons for selecting the approaches used.

3. Unless you have permission from the cooperating teacher to experiment with your own way, try to do it his or her way. Do so for several reasons, including the fact that you are an outsider in the classroom. If you give his or her approach an all-out effort, you can see how it works for you. With that experience,

the two of you can assess whether that approach works for you or whether another approach would be worth trying. For example, one of the authors was assigned a male cooperating teacher in an inner-city school. The rough-tough masculine approach to disciplining children did not work well for her. As a result of several discussions on this matter the two of them worked out a plan she could use for disciplining, which was comfortable for her but also consistent with his approach.

The log entries that follow show that differences in teaching approaches, which seem terribly important in the early days and weeks, generally get resolved satisfactorily as time passes. Discussions of methods, discipline techniques, and differences in style typically become more fruitful and comfortable as the student and cooperating teacher get to know each other as people. As far as being able to try new approaches is concerned, often what happens is this: After the student teacher wins the confidence of the cooperating teacher he or she is allowed to experiment. Marsha reported that that happened in her case.

2/19: When I first observed Mrs. H.'s split first and second grade class, I saw she was much more strict and traditional than I wanted to be. Her room was very orderly. She asked the children to raise their hands before they talk and tried to stress manners. I don't object to an orderly class, but it seemed to me that the children were too regimented. They all sat in their seats and were not allowed any paper or objects in their hands.

I think that they need quite a bit of direction to begin with. Also, they do need help in working quietly. But then gradually, they could work in groups, and be given a little more "room." Those are thoughts which occurred to me at the start. . . . Within a month Mrs. H. and I had a good relationship. She let me open things up more and try some of my ideas. She was surprised at how well they worked, even though I let the children go some.

When you get permission to try things your way, the results are not always satisfactory. Sometimes you are disappointed, sometimes your cooperating teacher is disappointed, and sometimes you both are.

Phyllis tried to give the students more freedom to be themselves and, when she did, she was pleased with the results. However, her cooperating teacher was not at all happy about what developed. The two of them spoke about their different views on classroom atmosphere and about what was tolerable in terms of control. Phyllis hoped they could define a middle ground between them, but they were not able to. Wisely, Phyllis accepted the fact that she had to run a "tight ship" for the rest of the term.

Many students are fortunate because they are assigned to cooperating teachers who give them opportunities to experiment. Not everybody will find this. If your cooperating teacher will not permit you to try your way of teaching, bear in mind that he or she is the boss. The relationship is not an equal one; the cooperating teacher has the authority and you have only that which he or she delegates to you. In any situation, when somebody must yield, and the cooperating teacher is not willing, then you must. Conflict between the two of you is self-defeating because, one way or another, you always lose.

In summary, if you are convinced that you are not getting the chance to use yourself effectively, try an approach like CONTROL-C and talk with your cooperating teacher and/or your supervisor. Then, if it becomes clear that there is no way of obtaining the teaching opportunities you feel denied, think about next year when you will have your own class. This should help you to accept this fate gracefully.

It seems appropriate to conclude our discussion of Stage 2 with a brief report of two studies that are very much related to the issue of student teacher–cooperating teacher differences over teaching (Harty & Mahan, 1977). The purpose of the first study was to examine and compare the orientations toward educational practice of these two groups of teachers (student and cooperating).

The instrument used, the Educational Preference Scale, assesses the values held on the nature of knowledge, the nature of learning, the nature of the learner, and the purpose of schooling. The total score shows the direction of the individual's orientation, whether toward conventional or emergent forms of education, whether against or for progressive education.

The Scale was given to 159 student teachers prior to and after their 16-week student-teaching experience. It was also given to the cooperating teachers halfway through the students' 16-week assignment.

The results were clear-cut. The student teachers were more liberal ("progressive" or "emergent") than their cooperating teachers before they began student teaching. By the end of the teaching their orientation had shifted in the direction of their cooperating teachers. And, in fact, a substantial number of student teachers actually ended up with more conservative scores than their cooperating teachers. The investigators concluded: "Student teachers tend to become more like their cooperating teachers with respect to their expressed orientations toward education as a result of a 16-week student-teaching experience."

This change occurs, we believe, not because cooperating teachers force it upon student teachers. Rather it occurs because of a bias toward conventional, custodial forms of schooling in our communities and in our society at large (Sarason, 1982). Student teachers discover this during their apprenticeship.

In the second study, 191 student teachers were compared with two other groups: students taking educational methods courses who would soon student teach, and students earlier in college preparation, some of whom were planning to be teachers (Hoy & Woolfolk, 1990). These three groups were compared in respect to the following orientations about controlling and managing a class of students: (a) The custodial orientation that calls for "an inflexible and highly regimented setting concerned primarily with maintaining order," and (b) The humanistic orientation that calls for "an educational community in which students learn through cooperative interaction and experience" (Hoy & Woolfolk, 1990, p. 281).

The results were similar to those of the first study: The student teachers became more custodial in orientation. (The other students remained unchanged in orientation.) These two studies indicate that the socialization process that goes on even during the brief period of student teaching seems to shift the student's outlook toward tighter control. "The ideal images of college preparation apparently give way to the instrumental necessities of maintaining order and running a smoothly functioning classroom" (Hoy & Woolfolk, 1990, p. 294).

## Overcoming Problems in the Relationship

### Stage 3: Soloing as a Teacher

This is it! Although student teachers learn much by immersing themselves in the life of the classroom and observing the process of teaching and learning, the heart of student teaching is in teaching itself. You will learn most when your teaching is accompanied by constructive criticism. Student teacher–cooperating teacher relationships often get rocky around the time that criticism is given and received. Sensitivity and fortitude, respectively, are essential to giving and receiving criticism, but more important, perhaps, is having practice with it so the process becomes second nature.

Few of us get much practice in being criticized, and that lack of experience can manifest itself in the student teacher–cooperating teacher feedback process, causing problems such as the following:

1. receiving no feedback from your cooperating teacher;
2. getting only negative feedback;
3. being criticized while you are teaching and in the presence of students;
4. having criticism of you publicized;
5. getting angry at the cooperating teacher; and
6. finding yourself in a difficult relationship with your cooperating teacher.

Each of these is dealt with, in turn.

*Receiving No Feedback.*   Perhaps the most frustrating problem is not receiving specific verbal feedback from your cooperating teacher. Without it, you do not know how he or she feels you are doing, leaving a gap you must fill by guessing and wondering. This hampers your learning, often forcing you to search for signs of approval from the cooperating teacher. Instead, in the interest of your own development as a teacher, you should be concentrating on your students.

Joyce had problems getting feedback and commented in her log on how that made her feel:

4/8: Today, I was supposed to take the class over for the entire day. The only thing I wasn't supposed to teach was history . . . (after lunch). And that is how it went.

The day went along great. Everyone got along and I feel my lessons were successful. The children really got involved with the math lesson. My first one! Boy, I was glad. Sometimes I wonder what Mr. P.'s bag is. He glares at me with approval (I think) but he'll never say anything. But then the glare could be envy or dislike. I wish he'd say something because as it is now, I don't feel at ease with him watching me. I just don't know what he's thinking.

What can a student teacher do if he or she finds herself in a situation like Joyce's? Here are general suggestions that may help:

1. When you have a good opportunity to talk (meaning that there are no students around and your cooperating teacher is not busy), ask him or her specific questions about your work, various class procedures, the functioning of individual youngsters, and so on. Remember to phrase your questions so they do not sound critical or threatening. Stress instead your interest in satisfying your curiosity or in learning about the art of teaching.
2. Ask about the possibility of establishing a regularly scheduled time to discuss your progress as a student teacher.
3. Receive any criticism you get graciously. If you appear intimidated, angry, or annoyed by feedback, you will make it harder for your cooperating teacher to criticize you and in fact may discourage his or her interest in giving you that kind of help.

At the core of these suggestions is the idea that you need to take the initiative. We recognize that the notion of asking directly for criticism is often anxiety provoking, even in cases where the student teacher and cooperating teacher have a fine relationship. Ed's log entry explains a concern he had for some time, about which he was afraid to ask his cooperating teacher.

4/4: Mrs. R. is fantastic. She spends so much time talking with me, suggesting, and giving me books to read. I also feel comfortable with her because I feel that we have ideas and beliefs that "mesh" and work together well, with the main objective being the benefit of the kids.

I still wonder if I am doing enough. . . . Does Mrs. R. expect me to do more? Does she think I'm lazy or afraid to take on more? I feel as if I am not asserting myself enough with her, that I should ask her more. I guess I am a bit afraid to suggest taking over more . . . than I do, and I can see that I am slowly doing more and gradually taking my place. . . .

Ed needed feedback from Mrs. R. about whether he was taking on enough work, but he was afraid to ask for it. As a result, he had needless worry and spent time feeling he was not meeting her expectations. When he finally asked, he felt reassured because Mrs. R. was very pleased with his work.

There are at least three ineffective ways to get feedback on what you want to know. Although they are widely used, we do not recommend these. The first is "dropping hints." Everybody knows how that operates. In a matter-of-fact way, you say, "Something just came to mind." Then you mention it and hope the cooperating teacher will catch on and tell you what you want to know. Sometimes hint dropping succeeds, but you cannot depend on it.

The second method is to start a conversation and "hope." This involves talking first about an issue related to what you want to know and hoping the teacher will catch on and move to your topic. Again, this is not a reliable information-gathering approach, as an entry from Vicky's log shows.

> 3/8: I made plans for today and informed Mrs. B. of them. But things didn't turn out as planned. I was very upset at one point when I told the children to go to their small groups and Mrs. B. decided they should have some exercise. Since I had already told some children (Group I) to get their books, there was a lot of confusion. ("Are we supposed to get our books now or get in a circle?" etc.) Besides the fact that she interrupted my plans and completely undermined my authority in the classroom, she chose to play an exercise song that half the children refuse to participate in because the other half of the children get so rowdy, I feel.
>
> Later, when I asked her if she had any comments about what I had done today (I was hoping she would bring up this part of the day so we could discuss my intentions), she only said she liked what I had presented, especially the "Bear Hunt."

Vicky started a conversation and "hoped," but the conversation did not turn to what she wanted to discuss. As a result, she went home frustrated and the air was not cleared. Whatever caused Mrs. B. to interrupt Vicky's plans was left unclarified, so a repeat of the incident at a later date was possible.

The third ineffective method is "mind reading." Mind reading is not a prerequisite for being a cooperating teacher! This method is unreliable because it assumes the cooperating teacher knows what you want feedback about — or that you want feedback at all.

*Getting Only Negative Feedback.*  A hazard of the student-teaching profession is encountering a cooperating teacher who gives you only negative feedback. What problems can this cause? First, people want to hear the good news about what was right as well as the bad news about what was wrong. When you hear one without the other, your opportunity for learning is accordingly reduced. Second, hearing only negative criticism can erode your confidence, even if you have the strongest of egos.

If you find yourself receiving only negative feedback, and getting very angry or frustrated about that, you should take action. A good initial step is to mobilize yourself so that you are able to determine exactly what your options are. Use CONTROL-C. Think the situation out systematically. Ask whether you need the positive words from the teacher to learn better, to build confidence, or as an ego boost in general. The information you generate in this way will help you plan your course of action.

In one log entry Leslie reported facing negative criticism and, after analyzing her situation, she concluded that she needed positive feedback to improve her teaching. She said to Mrs. R., "I need to know what I'm doing right so I know what not to change." Mrs. R. smiled and replied, "You are doing everything fine," but that was all the positive feedback Leslie got that week or the next.

More thought about the situation led Leslie to decide that Mrs. R. was not the "positive feedback" type, and that she would have to learn without hearing from her the positives that she craved. Instead, Leslie decided to get her own feedback by watching her students.

After each lesson she presented, she would ask herself, "What did I do well? Did they learn what I intended to teach them? Did they seem challenged and effectively stimulated by the material?" She also would look at their papers to document the reliability of her observations. Did a good many of the youngsters master the material taught, as evidenced by their performance on their homework and other material handed in?

Leslie also made good use of conversations with her supervisor and informal talks with her friends as a way of further determining whether her progress in student teaching was on track.

Although Leslie did not change Mrs. R.'s behavior, she did develop a plan that made things tolerable for herself. She still wondered, however, why Mrs. R. would not give her positive feedback. Of course, there could have been many reasons. Perhaps Mrs. R. had been taught to avoid complimentary comments. Perhaps, unknowingly, she could have been experiencing Leslie as a threat. Mrs. R. may subconsciously have been envying Leslie's brightness, alertness, and energy. It is also possible that Mrs. R. had been going through difficult times in her personal life or that she possessed a "negatively" oriented personality.

Without further speculation, Leslie made peace with the situation: She accepted Mrs. R. for what she was and learned to use the children as an indirect source of information to evaluate her work.

Lorraine's log entry shows how she worked at understanding possible hidden agendas in her cooperating teacher's feedback. Note how comforting it was for Lorraine when she sensed that it was a personal quality in her cooperating teacher rather than one in herself that had resulted in the flow of negativism.

> 3/4: Today went all right, and for the most part I taught for the entire (day). . . . I really like when Mrs. C. gives me corrective criticism or suggestions, but sometimes I feel as though she is stressing or pointing up to me that she has had much more experience. In a subtle way, at times she makes me feel inferior or not as intelligent, and I'm beginning to realize that this is just her personality.

As you might expect, when Lorraine came to this realization, she was much more able to profit from Mrs. C.'s expertness and also from her criticisms. Lorraine managed to deal with the negative-feedback situation without asking for help from her supervisor. As Leslie's experience suggested, however, this is not always the case. For example, there are times when the amount and intensity of negative feedback from the cooperating teacher is such that it is defeating to the student teacher. Kate's log entries describe what it is like in such an extreme case of being deprived of support while being on the receiving end of an over-abundance of criticism.

2/25: As I was leaving today, Mrs. N. said, "I can see by your face that you're not happy about today." I said, "I don't like the way things went." She answered, "Neither did I." I was glad she had answered me honestly. But at the same time, I think I was hoping more for reassurance.

Essentially my dissatisfaction came from the fact that whenever I tried to do something with the class today I never seemed to have their full attention—they wouldn't listen to me when I asked them to be quiet, etc. Mrs. N. said that I lacked control. (I don't know if I would choose that word. To me it connotes a dictator.)

On the way home I began developing a "fear of failure" feeling and I started dreading tomorrow morning. But after I sorted out my thoughts I realized my teaching strategy was not totally at fault.

2/27: As I walked out of the building today, the tears started pouring down my cheeks. I had held it all in for almost 3 hours, enduring the worst day of my life, and I was now ready for a good cry. When I got home I was crying so hard I couldn't even explain what had happened.

It took me all afternoon to sort out what had occurred, and I'm not sure now what brought about my noontime discussion with Mrs. N. She told me (the obvious) that I am responsible for the children or I will be when I take over full time. . . .

[Mrs. N's criticisms included,] . . . I tend to get engrossed in one activity and have trouble keeping track of everything else that is going on in the room (a character flaw, perhaps?). I am not disciplining the children. And she went on and on, the criticisms pouring out all over me. I tried to explain that I need time to get everything coordinated and that by the time I took over I was sure things would have improved.

I also tried to point out that because she always overpowered me I did not jump right into discipline situations. I would be standing there trying to talk with a child who had done something. Seeing it, she would be right behind me, with a "Stop it now!" directed at the child. Yes, the kid would stop, my discussion was over or I felt I might as well not bother. Anyway, our talk ended with her telling me that she didn't think I would make it and my numbly saying, "Don't worry."

I was so upset when the children walked in for afternoon classes. I don't remember how I taught my lessons. How could she do that to me? . . .

Hours later I'm still upset. I'm hoping that by morning Mrs. N. will be calmed down, the whole thing will be forgotten. Maybe she was having a bad day, because I think many of her comments did not take into account the fact that I am still learning and need time to absorb everything.

Kate went through a great deal of suffering with Mrs. N. for the next few days. During this difficult period, she sought and received support from her supervisor, who eventually spoke to her cooperating teacher. Within a week, Kate's persistence and the aid of Kate's supervisor began to pay off, as the following entry shows. Note that it concludes with thanks to her supervisor.

3/2: No more tears. Today was so much better. Mrs. N. liked my plans a lot. She was pleased with the way the day went and I was pleased too. The encouragement she gave me built up my confidence and I could teach again.

She told me that she could have cheered me up yesterday but that then I wouldn't have done the soul searching I needed to do. Strange reasoning, in my opinion. There must be an easier way than coming close to a nervous breakdown. But her words were, "Well, yesterday was worth it."

Now I realize that perhaps we just weren't communicating, and I really didn't understand what she expected of me. I just hope there isn't a repeat. Although I would know what to expect, I don't think I could go through it another time. Thanks for the hours you spent.

*Being Criticized While You are Teaching.* Two things we know for sure are: (a) you want criticism of your work but not while you are teaching a lesson, and (b) you want assistance in learning to control the class but not in the form of having the cooperating teacher step in during your lesson; nobody benefits from being contradicted in front of others. When this does happen, not only do you feel put down and worry that your authority has been undermined, but you also have to rebound from those feelings quickly so that you can overcome the interruption and maintain the flow of the lesson.

To some extent, you can take steps in advance to try to prevent your cooperating teacher from stepping in while you are teaching or handling discipline problems. The most important preventative measure is forming a healthy relationship with your cooperating teacher. If you are close, chances are good he or she will feel better about electing to withhold criticism until the two of you can have a private discussion. Realistically, however, you may be unable to build solid rapport, and even when that exists there are times when he or she may unknowingly countermand your directions.

Let us first look at an instance where the cooperating teacher, perhaps unknowingly, gives a set of directions that contradict the ones issued by the student teacher only moments before. Sheryl's diary entry describes an incident during her fourth day of student teaching:

1/8: The day didn't start out well. We were going to the museum and the bus was due at 9:00. I told the class to keep their coats on—why have them run in and out of the coatroom? Mrs. R. came and screamed, "What's going on? Take your coats off and hang them up now." She really laid it on and made me feel stupid and sorry for the kids.

The incident struck Sheryl hard because it seemed at the moment to halt the progress she was making toward achieving something important to her: establishing her authority and winning respect from the class. The episode resulted from lack of communication. Sheryl had not had a chance to tell Mrs. R. that she had told the children to keep their coats on. Of course, Mrs. R. could have assumed that or even inquired of Sheryl, but she did not.

Fortunately, the events of the next few days proved Sheryl wrong in thinking she had lost face with the children. Yet, at the time of an incident like Sheryl's, it is difficult to convince yourself that a single episode is not very important in a career.

When episodes of this kind are recurrent, however, there is reason for concern. Here are a few specific steps you can take to help prevent being repeatedly interrupted, contradicted, or countermanded.

1. Learn the class rules.
2. From the beginning, try to establish an early morning routine of speaking to your cooperating teacher about the day's plans. Besides what has already been scheduled for you to do that day, find out if there are any other specific tasks your cooperating teacher might want you to handle and what thoughts he or she has about these.
3. When you are observing, attempt to train yourself to know what your cooperating teacher is thinking and how he or she will react to events. For example, note at what point he or she speaks to a student who has been restless or disturbing, and how long after a group of youngsters becomes noisy does he or she put a stop to it.

Rose, who had been having trouble with in-class criticisms, reports how, by learning and applying class rules, she saved the children from criticism and herself from embarrassment.

3/3: Spring may be here at last. We went outside today for the first time. I really had the urge to slide down the sliding board with the kids, but I had the feeling Mr. N. would not approve. So I stood around with the other teachers on the playground and occupied my time by observing the large-muscle coordination of the children. I saw a lot more about their physical coordination out there where they were free to run around than I could ever have observed within the confines of the classroom. I also tried to absorb all their playground rules. Mr. N. has a lot of rules that I am unaware of until I let one of the children break a rule and he hurries over to correct the situation. (I, of course, always feel like a jerk.) So before we went out today I decided to learn as many as possible, so that I wouldn't end up embarrassed and the children wouldn't be needlessly confused. Mr. N. seemed pleased to list them for me.

Student teachers differ in what their predominant emotional reaction is when they feel their cooperating teacher repeatedly and inappropriately interferes with their lessons. Although some will be embarrassed or hurt, others will be angry or even infuriated. The least effective reaction is to slough it off, trying to convince yourself with an "I don't care—it doesn't bother me one bit."

No matter what the particular emotional reaction may be, such a situation should be confronted. This should not be done impulsively, because such action often leads one to talking about personalities instead of the situation, and to launching a diffuse, angry barrage. Instead, by using CONTROL-C, student teachers can get in touch with their reactions and use them as motivators to speak directly and firmly for their position. Having thought the issues through, they are more likely to stick to the incident, to how they felt during it, and to the relationship between the incident and their learning.

In the next example, we again focus on a situation where the student teacher was repeatedly criticized in front of the children. Although this example merits attention in its own right, here it illustrates how a student teacher can use his or her feelings to motivate a search for solutions. Note how Alice handled her problem over a 2-week period.

2/10: As I walked out of the doors of Glen Ave. this afternoon, I felt as if I had been a complete failure. Though I spoke with Mrs. L. about the day and accepted my criticisms well, I still felt something was missing.

Because I was 10 minutes late I was scolded by Mrs. L. for being irresponsible as an adult.

The children were restless throughout the entire day. I got very upset because Mrs. L. got angry because the day did not go smoothly—she criticized me in front of the children and before I had done my Valentine story. I told her that I would appreciate criticism after school. She said, "No, I'm going to tell you what you do wrong whenever I see you doing something wrong." I further explained that I could not function to the best of my ability if she did not save her criticism for later. "Well, that's the way I am," she said, "and besides if I said something to you after school, I would just blow up."

I told Mrs. L. that I am student teaching for the purpose of learning, and it seemed as if she wasn't allowing room for any mistakes. She neither agreed or disagreed but continued to talk about how I had done this wrong and that wrong.

This was a start for Alice and Mrs. L. Two weeks later they made further progress.

2/24: Each morning Mrs. L. writes assignments on the board. Today she put my lessons at the end, because yesterday I lost control of the group and she couldn't do anything with the children and had to punish them because of me. I asked her if she felt this was fair. "No," she said. When I asked why she punished them then, she said: "Because they must learn and learn to listen." I explained my feeling about having my lessons put at the end. I felt as if I was being punished for making a mistake. I asked her how I was going to develop control if she didn't give me a chance. Agree? She agreed. Then she put my lesson back on the board at the top, but she warned me, "The children must learn, and if you can't keep control I'll have to take them."

Mrs. L. didn't interrupt during the lesson, perhaps because Alice had handled the situation so well. Alice's success, in this instance, illustrates that forcefully but diplomatically stating your side of things can be an effective way of finding a solution.

*Having Criticism of You Publicized.*  Any real professional understands that criticism should be private, shared only with the student and the college supervisor. Yet that is not always the case. Remember a game called "telephone"? It was a favorite of Scout leaders and camp counselors. The way you play it is the first person whispers a secret to the second, who in turn passes it on to the next. By the time the story gets around, the last person announces the message as he or she has heard it. Typically, it ends up vastly different from the original.

Dorothy faced a situation in which she was not getting constructive feedback from her cooperating teacher. Instead, as with the telephone game, the cooperating teacher was telling another teacher who was, in turn, passing the information on to her student teacher. This student teacher was a friend of Dorothy's and kept Dorothy posted on how Dorothy's cooperating teacher was feeling.

Dorothy was never sure how accurate the information she heard was and, moreover, she wanted direct feedback. Dorothy's supervisor helped out, and Dorothy and she both agreed the college of education should add a workshop or course on "working with people" as a prerequisite for cooperating teachers.

*Getting Angry at the Cooperating Teacher.*  The student teacher's partnership with the cooperating teacher has the potential for being rather intense, as you have seen in some of the log selections. You will know rather soon whether the mix of your personality and your cooperating teacher's has the potential to lead you to uncontrollable anger. If you spot such potential early in the term, plan your method of keeping your temper under control. There is no reward for tantrums.

Certainly useful to you in preventing a volatile situation are the following:

1. Wait at least 1 day before you react to an upsetting situation.
2. Ventilate your feelings daily in your log and then, using the systematic thought process of CONTROL-C, develop suitable means of handling the situation.
3. Talk the situation over with your supervisor and with friends and get their reactions to your proposed ways of handling it.
4. Remind yourself that next year the class you will teach will be your own.

Becky was ready to explode with anger at her cooperating teacher, but she kept her temper, vented her feelings in her log, spoke to her supervisor, and let things settle into perspective. Here is how she sized up the situation.

3/9: Class-wise today was OK, but I had some problems with my cooperating teacher. She voiced her opinions on what I planned to teach when I take over the class. She told me exactly what materials I should use, rather than let me use my own plans, and exactly how I should go about it. I became annoyed, frustrated, aggravated, and just plain angry. But I kept my temper and said nothing and went along with what she said. I will be planning activities for all reading groups, as well as teaching them (these activities) to the individual groups.

 After my first week, she informed me, the aide will no longer help me. I will be completely on my own. I understood her logic of wanting me to have experience teaching without an aide, because, true, I might not have one. But for three weeks? I think that's a little ridiculous. I have to work by butt off while they are lollygagging in the teachers' room. Blah! I have decided I will try it for one week or 1½ weeks, but no more. After that, if the aide doesn't help I'm going to Mr. Y. and tell him he is paying his teacher and aide to smoke cigarettes and gossip in the teachers' room. I know I will "cause fireworks," but tough stuff. I have my limit too! Today was a terrible day. I was MAD!

Becky did not vent her anger to her cooperating teacher, which was fortunate because, as Becky's later two log entries show, her initial concerns and fears did not materialize.

3/10: Today was all right. My teacher came out of her witch act today. She was nice. She even offered to help me with my lesson plans for next week. And she gave me my very own plan book. Hurray! I'm going to let bygones be bygones because after all I still have to work with her and teach her class. And she has to give me my grade. I explained to her that I will be unable to stay for the afternoon tomorrow, because of a prior commitment. She understood. So I hope we are on the road to a better relationship.

3/14: Today was the first day I took over the class completely. My lesson plans are now done for a full week and my cooperating teacher is pleased. The day went pretty well. I came in extra-early to be organized, and it helped a lot. I planned the activities for reading groups, but we continued to teach as is. I taught my group, Mrs. C. taught hers, and Mrs. A. taught hers. I had trouble with the dittos at first but it was a minor problem. Things went smoothly and I was pleased. I left tired! But pleased.

***Finding Yourself in a Difficult Relationship With Your Cooperating Teacher.***   Ann was successful in building a relationship with her cooperating teacher despite an unhappy beginning. Ann experienced herself as a low-keyed person and presented herself in class that way. Unfortunately, at least as she perceived it, she was placed with Mrs. K., a vivacious "snappy" teacher, who wanted Ann to be a carbon copy of herself, even though intellectually she declared that every teacher should develop her own style.

Ann's success did not come easily. She had to work very hard to attain the good relationship she wanted. And she spent many long hours discussing her situation with her supervisor.

She found herself uncomfortable with Mrs. K. and unable, she thought, to talk with her. To complicate things further, Mrs. K. had already established a relationship with the classroom teacher's aide. This left Ann feeling like an outsider. The first time she was able to get the teacher's ear at all was the day the aide was absent. Ann took advantage of this situation, for she felt she had to grab at every straw.

The first day Ann asked for feedback on her science lesson the cooperating teacher responded with, "How do you feel about it? How would you mark yourself?" Ann's silent reaction to those questions was that she wanted Mrs. K.'s opinion, not questions. At this point Ann was not yet ready to evaluate her own lessons.

Ann and her college supervisor discussed the initiative she could take to improve communication. First and foremost, they decided, she had to be open and honest if she expected to establish a good relationship. She had to communicate her needs to Mrs. K. one way or another.

Ann knew that she would have to ask her cooperating teacher for time to discuss her feelings, time to discuss future lessons, time for feedback and suggestions for improvement. To get this she had to be flexible and willing to come in early or stay late. The situation, she came to realize in discussion with her college supervisor, was unlike social ones she was accustomed to, and she had to make a distinction between her personal and professional life.

When Ann's cooperating teacher turned down a request for a meeting, Ann had to ask again, although in her social life she would not have done so unless the turndown had been accompanied by an explanation and a request for a rain check. Instead, Ann persisted. She ended up treating Mrs. K. to lunch.

With support from her supervisor, Ann continued to arrange meetings and make progress with Mrs. K. About a month into her assignment she made this comment in her log, "I am starting to build up a very nice rapport."

Ann learned that she had to compromise on certain things while she was in Mrs. K's classroom; this included working with the children in a style that was acceptable to Mrs. K. She came to realize that sometimes you do things because your cooperating teacher expects it, but that you do not have to incorporate these things in your mode of teaching in the future. In fact she wrote, "One good thing I'm learning is exactly what I don't want to do as a teacher!"

The process for Ann was turbulent. At times her spirits were so low that she doubted whether she would ever succeed as a teacher—or even if she still wanted to be one. But Ann pressed on, saying, "I don't want to adopt her style. It isn't me. I'm not the snappy type; however, I probably do need to improve my voice inflection and I'm going to work on it." And so, out of persistence and effort, Ann built her relationship, won her cooperating teacher's respect, and received a top grade!

That is how Ann experienced the situation. As events came to pass, Mrs. K. asked to see the university supervisor after Ann's last day at school. The supervisor thought that Mrs. K. was coming to discuss Ann's grade, but instead, Mrs. K. opened a floodgate of feelings. This is the story as it unfolded:

Mrs. K. began apologetically, explaining that this was the first time she had had a student teacher. "I was very unsure of myself from the start," she said. During the early days she found it hard to relinquish her class to someone else—even the student teacher to whom she felt she wanted to give as much as she could.

When Ann tried her first lesson, Mrs. K. was shocked at her quiet but diligent style. "But she is so different from me," Mrs. K. thought. That observation led her to remember what had been said by the supervisors at the introductory tea: Each teacher has to be him or herself. So for the next few days, Mrs. K. tried not to impose herself as a model. Instead she tried to allow, indeed to encourage, Ann to do things her own way. However, that did not work. Mrs. K. saw the children changing under Ann's leadership. Discipline was loosening. The class was falling apart. She saw all her months of efforts "going down the drain." Eventually, Mrs. K. reached her limit and found it hard to refrain from imposing her standards on Ann and directly on the class.

Ann responded to Mrs. K.'s silent (and not so silent) impositions as harsh criticism of her teaching ability. It was then with the help of her supervisor that she undertook her campaign to improve communication and persisted until she set up the luncheon appointment. At that time, however, Mrs. K. explained during the conference, "I hadn't realized Ann thought I thought she couldn't teach. . . . I tried to interfere as little as possible. It was difficult to hold myself back. I thought my class, my children, were at stake, but I did hold myself back and much to my surprise it was not as disastrous as I had anticipated. Then when the end of the term came, and Ann began tapering off in her teaching and I began getting back into the act, I had another surprise. I didn't find teaching or disciplining to be a problem. Actually, I see it as a good experience: The children were exposed to both styles of teaching, and I think they grew and developed as a result."

In reflecting on the term that had just ended, Mrs. K. also mentioned with satisfaction that although Ann's style was different from hers, Ann had nonetheless acquired some of her ways. Mrs. K. mentioned that even the children noticed this, and had said to Ann, "That's the way Mrs. K. would do it."

The conversation ended with Mrs. K. and the supervisor agreeing about how important it is for the student and cooperating teacher to establish rapport and how the sooner they do it, the better it is for both. Mrs. K. said that unfortunately she and Ann did not have instant success, but at least they made it. Smiling, the supervisor said that in some cases it never happens.

We have seen both perspectives in the two-sided experience of forming the student teacher to cooperating teacher relationship. Basically, the essence of Ann's and Mr. K.'s problem is a universal one, and it reduces itself to the following conditions that always carry a potential for conflict: The student teacher must function in an established class and under the direction of someone who has over the years, developed his or her own way of teaching. On the other hand, the cooperating teacher must share the class with someone new, someone different, probably younger and more idealistic, and surely less experienced—characteristics that are likely to lead the student and cooperating teacher to have different perspectives.

We have now completed discussion of Stage 3, most of which centered on six problems related to giving and receiving criticism. We now go on to Stage 4.

### Stage 4: Feeling Like a Teacher

By this point, the major problems you will face during student teaching are probably behind you. With the end in sight, you will feel different: What was negative in your experience will seem more tolerable and under control; what was positive will begin to get the weight it merits. Hopefully, too, the present and future will seem bright and blend into each other as they did for Gerald:

> 5/17: Just a couple of weeks left. So much stuff to do and learn. Oh, well, there is always next year in my own class. My own class. I have to write that to believe it will happen.
> This is my second week of planning and doing the whole day. Before I couldn't imagine how I could [manage] the whole day. Now it seems so natural. Mrs. R. was gone part of the afternoon, and I felt like it was next year. I've learned so much from her—even the hassles we had now seem unimportant to me. I'll miss her, but I feel I'll be ready to do it on my own next September

### SOME "FEELING BADS"

As the term progresses and you take over more of the teaching duties, many thoughts will come to mind, including some that you may find surprising. We review a variety of these here, primarily so that you will know that they are normal and typical.

1. Feeling bad because you want the cooperating teacher to leave you alone in the room. This feeling is particularly annoying if you have had a good relationship with him or her, because in this case you may feel guilty "wishing him or her away." Vicky made the following entry in her log: "I can't believe it. Even after 3 months she (the cooperating teacher) still never leaves the room, and I wish she would every once in a while."

2. Feeling bad about having to teach a lesson you think lacks excitement or having to teach a concept using an approach you believe is ineffective. Laura provides an illustration: "The day basically went well. The one activity that I was

requested to do was pretty bad. It was a filmstrip on maps and globes. The kids were bored with it and so was I, but I had to do it. There are a lot more interesting ways to present maps and globes."

3. Feeling bad because you see time being used ineffectively in the classroom. Vicky complains about an excessive use of films: "I'm also getting a little upset with the practice of always going into another teacher's classroom when she has a film to show. I think it's great to get films but not necessary to see every one in the school. Just because the class next door may be discussing climate and is seeing a related film is no reason to take my class to see it when we could be doing other things that we never seem to have time for. . . ."

4. Feeling bad about being successful and worrying about whether your cooperating teacher will resent your success. Brenda shares: "I am beginning to feel more confident and I love the children. I really hope that Mrs. C. does not resent or mind my taking over sometimes, because I don't want to offend her. I decided that I wanted this to be a good learning experience, and I hope we can really make it one."

These feelings hardly deserve to be called problems. They sometimes develop during student teaching, and will not be problems if you reflect on them and put them in perspective.


## RELATING TO SUBSTITUTE TEACHERS

The chances are good that your cooperating teacher will miss at least a few days of school during your student-teaching assignment. Most likely on those occasions you will be teaming with a substitute teacher.

A day or two with a substitute usually provides a good learning experience for the simple reason that a new set of circumstances is introduced. Of course, the substitute's personality and skills as a teacher partly determine the kind of learning experience you will have, as do several other factors (e.g., whether the absences happen early or late in your student teaching and whether or not you have lessons ready on the day your cooperating teacher is out).

Also remember that in a sense you will be in a position similar to a substitute's in the near future. You will be as new to those in your first class as a substitute is to the children in your cooperating class. Be attentive to how the substitute introduces himself or herself and to the methods he or she employs. Assess how well his or her approach works and note whether it is one you would be comfortable with.

Before looking at problems you might encounter with substitutes, let us look at the bright spots in the picture. Whether you end up teaching (with a substitute observing) or watching a substitute teach is not as important to your learning as it may seem at the moment. In the latter case, if you are going to be observing for a good part of the day, you can often gain some otherwise unavailable insights.

Treat the substitute's replacement of your cooperating teacher as a quasi-experiment. The substitute is the one variable that has been changed while everything else has been held constant—the children, the physical setting, your presence, and so on.

Laura reports her gains from watching a substitute and seeing how the children reacted to a different teaching style:

> 3/19: The substitute today was fantastic. She was so bright and cheerful. The minute she walked into the room, you knew things were going to be good.
>
> In fact, Mrs. J. was one of the most enthusiastic teachers I have ever seen. After seeing how effective she was, I wanted to work on my own enthusiasm even more. . . .

Laura saw a style she wanted to try to emulate, and she was exposed to certain techniques that she might not have otherwise seen. By contrast, Stan had a useful day because he saw what he did not want to be as a teacher and what effect cynicism can have on a professional's performance. He entered the following in his log:

> 1/4: I worked with a substitute teacher who informed me that teaching was boring. It was evident he was not at ease or content, for his introduction of concepts was hastily completed, which led to impatience when (Jane and Blake and several others) . . . asked several questions. He failed to follow the lesson plans Mrs. H. had left for him. I can imagine how much damage a permanent teacher could do to a class if she or he didn't want to be there.

If you are scheduled to teach lessons on the day a substitute covers, you also could find yourself with an opportunity for constructive criticism from still another professional. If your initial contact suggests that the substitute is willing to observe, you could tell him or her how eager you are for feedback and how valued his or her opinion would be. With a substitute you may also get a chance to teach for an entire day, with him or her available as a backup on an "as-needed basis." Such an outcome can be exhilarating, as Irene reports:

> 2/26: Today was absolutely fantastic! Mrs. L. was out sick today and I felt I was the teacher and not just an assistant. She called me last night and told me about the things she had planned. She said that it was completely up to me whether I wanted to do them or give it to the substitute. I decided that I wanted to try to handle the entire . . . [day] and fit her plans into the ones that I had. The day went very well. The substitute was there but always in the background. I accomplished everything that I wanted to and . . . the day was over before I knew it. The more time that I spend in the classroom the more I dream about having a job in September doing what I want to do.

Finally in the substitute's presence, you might feel more comfortable experimenting and trying ideas you believe your cooperating teacher would not be comfortable with. Sheryl reports such a situation in her log, and what it meant to her.

1/21: Today Mrs. R. was absent and so we had a substitute, Mrs. T. The class behaved better for her than for Mrs. R., and I think it was because she didn't yell constantly over what I feel are unimportant things. She also put extra work on the board for them to do. All the children were afraid they wouldn't get done, which was a new twist. . . .

All afternoon the children were going in and out for reading and speech, so I postponed two filmstrips and read them a story instead.

At the end of the afternoon we had extra time, so we sang "Puff the Magic Dragon" and played two popular songs one of the boys brought. The kids really liked it. It took about 10 minutes and it was a nice way to end things. However, I don't think I would have done it if Mrs. R. was here.

Of course, any number of problems can arise between substitute and student teachers. Sometimes you try to solve them, other times you choose to overlook them, since the situation is a temporary one. An example of each is provided in the logs first of Carl and then Dorothy. Carl wrote:

2/19: Today we had a substitute. Was today ever horrendous! I had to raise my voice more today than I've had to in the past four weeks. It seemed as though their "routine" was broken by Mrs. B.'s absence. They behaved in ways they never had (i.e., acted dumb to the previously established rules and routines).

The substitute was a sweet person, but she constantly interrupted me and challenged my authority on several occasions. I only hope it really is for one day. I got the impression she wasn't working with me but against me at some points.

An example of this feeling of opposition . . . [was] her reinforcing behavior that was contrary to the established rules in the class, like talking, etc. . . . I realize that it was and is difficult for a new teacher to come into a class and take over; however, I would have rather had her completely take over . . . than [her having] me take over and then undermine my authority . . . I'm really thankful it's only temporary.

Carl wrote off the experience, knowing his cooperating teacher was returning the next day. He could have been more assertive, but at the time felt it was not worth the risk of causing friction. However, a few days later in a seminar he reported that if it were to happen again, he would have privately approached the substitute during lunch and said, "You know, while I was setting up the first lesson you interrupted me to discipline Brad. I felt the kids saw that as your challenging my authority. What do you think?" From there they might have had a useful talk.

Dorothy did take action, as she reported in this log entry.

> 2/8: Miss K. is gone for the entire week due to some illness. The substitute is an elderly lady. She is very sweet, but as she said, "The children are too much for me to control." The main problem was that she continuously sent students to the principal's office. This is not appreciated by Mr. R. (which I will hear about when Miss K. returns), and I don't think it helps the class. Therefore, I discussed the problem with the substitute. She said this was the last means of control and that she felt it necessary. After we talked, though, no more children were sent.

Dorothy took action in the interest of the class and also of herself and Miss K., because of the principal's anticipated reaction. The substitute did not welcome Dorothy's comments but seemed to respect her for speaking her opinion. Further, Dorothy's comments changed the substitute's behavior.

Sometimes you will get more than your share of chances to teach when your cooperating teacher is absent. This is what happened to Ruby, 2 weeks after she began student teaching, and to Carla, much later in her experience:

> 1/14: Today I came to school to find Ms. K. looking over lesson plans, and a note saying that Mrs. W. would be out and that Ms. K. would come across the hall every now and then to see how things were going. She would work something out if I couldn't be there in the afternoon. To this point I hadn't been alone with the class for more than 30 minutes. I knew that I couldn't handle the discipline effectively yet, but the seatwork and reading didn't frighten me. I was willing to try. My first thoughts were right. Assignments went well enough, but between 9:20 and 11:45 my discipline problems were so bad that I couldn't even try my two reading groups. After I left, I was exhausted and depressed but ready to do some serious thinking about myself and teaching. I decided that trying to do things as someone else does them—including making assignments—will not work for me. I must find things that work for me and the individual children.

This was a terribly difficult position to be in—having to take over the class for the whole day, without preparation and with only 2 weeks of student teaching under your belt. Yet Ruby was not thrown by it. Her experience led to reflection, good use of CONTROL-C, and a long and helpful discussion with her college supervisor late that very afternoon.

The situation is different if you have to take over later in the term, when you feel ready and willing. Here's Carla's reaction:

> 2/7: More adventures! Mrs. P. was gone today and they couldn't get a substitute. That's fine; I would rather have the class alone at this point.

We have been talking about problems frequently encountered during short periods of time working with substitutes. Occasionally student teachers find themselves spending substantial numbers of days with one or a series of substitutes. If that happens, the important concept to keep in mind is that these days represent a significant proportion of those you will have as a student teacher. Use these days as best you can for your own learning.

Elaine had experience with a lengthy absence of her cooperating teacher and wrote the following:

> 5/16: Mrs. R. told me today she has to go to the hospital. I know I can handle the [full] responsibility . . . because I did it the week she was out and part of last week. But I feel bad—I learn a little more every day from her and feel I'll be missing out. Besides, I'll miss her—I've gotten close to her. Well, the substitute they will be getting in her place will have much to offer on things too.

One final point. The presence of student teachers, especially after they are familiar with the children (and vice versa), is reassuring to cooperating teachers who face the need for a prolonged absence. Often, knowledge that the student teacher will be there to provide continuity is enough to sway the conscientious but ill teacher who might have otherwise come to school against her best interest. That she has that much faith in you will make you feel good.

## YOUR STUDENT TEACHING ASSIGNMENT AND THE REALITIES OF SCHOOL LIFE

By their very title, cooperating teachers are those professionals who cooperate with your college or university and with you for the purpose of providing you an approximation of a teacher's real-life experience in an apprentice–master type of relationship. The cooperating teacher is selected for the role because he or she is considered skilled. In other respects that person, like anybody else, possesses the emotions, idiosyncrasies, strengths, and frailties that go with being human.

By and large, in their role as cooperating teachers they want more than anything else to have a successful experience with you and to continue their work in future years with other student teachers. Their task, however, is a complex one and they must serve more than one master. Unlike other college and university instructors, whose responsibility is to a relatively homogeneous class of young adults, the cooperating teacher has a dual responsibility: To you as an apprentice and to a group of children.

Although your cooperating teacher wants you to have an excellent experience, he or she is subject to the policies of the school and under the direction of the principal. In a school that values teachers who maintain quiet and order and a structured teaching plan, the cooperating teacher is unlikely to encourage you to use a teaching approach that carries the risk of disorder. That does not mean that the cooperating teacher objects to the approach on intellectual grounds—or would prevent you from trying it under any circumstances. It means only that he or she accepts (even if begrudgingly) the realities of professional life in that school.

Realities like that will be very much part of your life, both as a student teacher now, and as a teacher with your own classroom in the near future. Perhaps the most helpful advice we can offer you about this is to make peace with the real limits you face in today's schools. Give yourself permission to function at your best within the boundaries of freedom of action available to you. Whatever limits are imposed upon you by your cooperating teacher, your supervisor, or your cooperating school, remind yourself that there is much you can learn, regardless.

Delight in the fact that you are a student teacher, and that you are teaching, not in some abstraction of a school, not in an experimental laboratory, but in a real community and a real school. That community may have social and moral values which are similar to or different from yours. That school may have educational values similar to or different from yours. Your cooperating teacher may have an instructional orientation similar to or different from yours. Whatever is the case, accept it and tell yourself, "this is my one and only student teaching experience—and I'm going to make the most of it."

Be good to yourself. Devote yourself to gaining confidence in teaching in ways that circumstances permit. Except for those your cooperating teacher permits you to try, save your innovative ideas for your own future class. Write down in a notebook those good ideas that come to your mind that you know your cooperating teacher would not want you to use in her class. That way you will have them available when you can use them—next September or in the years ahead.

In summary, from the very first meeting with your cooperating teacher recognize her or him as a potentially helpful person. Understand at the same time that that person will be affected by your responses. If you show that you are eager to benefit from advice, you are more likely to have good rapport. If, instead of learning to seek, manage, and grow from criticism, you always react annoyed when it is given, you will make life difficult for your cooperating teacher. And you will probably discourage her from offering you helpful suggestions.

If you feel resistance within you when your cooperating teacher begins to offer criticism, try to tell yourself, "Here's an opportunity for me to learn how to be a better teacher. She is not evaluating my worth as a human being. . . . She is simply suggesting how I might be more effective in one realm of functioning."

Even with the best of intentions and the greatest of efforts in the relationship with the cooperating teacher, there are always occasions that call for problem solving. And that was the focus of this chapter. When you encounter problems, remember that your supervisor and a method of problem solving like CONTROL-C are invaluable resources.

# 4
▼▼▼▼▼▼▼

# Relationship With the College Supervisor: Learning From the "Third-Party" Mentor

College supervisors are a special group of people. Most likely, of all the faculty members in the field of education, they have the greatest involvement in the schools in your community and pay most attention to the problems of daily life in the classroom. Their scholarly and practical knowledge of the field of education and relationships with various school districts are a great advantage in connection both with your student teaching and with your obtaining a regular job as a teacher.

Who are the people who serve as supervisors? All of them have had experience as teachers, some for many years. Having themselves been student teachers, they understand the difficulties of being an inexperienced teacher. They know the problems as well as the benefits of working with a cooperating teacher.

Some are educators who have chosen this activity as their specialty, their area of professional concentration. Others are professors who take this assignment to keep in touch with classroom activities. Still others are graduate students working toward advanced degrees in education.

Supervisors differ in experience, personality, educational background, approachability, and the capacity to be helpful. Although these differences may shape the nature of your relationship, they need not significantly effect your opportunities to learn. Your supervisor will be a person who is interested in your professional development. You will want to develop an effective working relationship with that person, whoever he or she is.

## HOW YOUR SUPERVISOR CAN HELP YOU

Supervisors, like student teachers, often feel overwhelmed by work. This is understandable, given the heavy loads and the set of responsibilities most of them carry.

Their tasks range from the obvious, such as:

1. scheduling and holding observation sessions for each student teacher, including meetings with the cooperating teachers and principals involved;
2. writing reports on the observations they make; and
3. conducting a seminar for student teachers; to the less obvious, which include:
4. planning and hosting professional-social activities, such as teas for students and cooperating teachers;
5. striving toward maintaining cordial relationships with the principal, department heads, and other school personnel (this for its own purposes but also as the college's "ambassador");
6. serving as a confidante, problem-solving aide, resource person, and supporter to student teachers, usually during office hours;
7. record keeping, including supplying information to the placement office and to the registrar for official school documents;
8. keeping informed of position openings for teachers;
9. composing letters of reference for student teachers; and
10. evaluating the student teacher by providing an official letter grade for the student teacher's work (often this is done in conjunction with the cooperating teacher but sometimes it is the sole responsibility of the cooperating teacher).

The supervisor is very much a middle person, an agent of the college but working toward the satisfaction of many people's needs. We look now at issues that arise as the supervisor performs his or her duties.

*As a Classroom Observer.* Your college supervisor will observe your teaching at least several times. On those days you can "put your best foot forward," by approaching the classroom much as you would on any other day. Most supervisors want to observe you and your students under typical conditions in the natural setting of the classroom. That is reason enough to function in the ways in which you have become accustomed.

But do this for another reason too. To differ greatly from the normal routine adds new dynamics that may lead both you and your students to feel uncomfortable. This, in turn, may invite the unpredictable to emerge. The accustomed routine puts both you and your students at ease and increases the likelihood that you will teach at the same qualitative level as on other days when the supervisor is not present.

Although the observation days themselves should be treated like others, the days preceding them should be treated differently in anticipation, because your supervisor's presence is another factor for which you want to prepare. In doing so, bear in mind that your supervisor's several visits allow you to demonstrate the diversity of your skills.

As at other times, prepare your materials and plans thoroughly and well in advance of the observation day. Prepare yourself psychologically. This can be done by mentally picturing the day unfold. In effect you will be previewing the events you expect.

Imagine yourself entering the room in the morning with carefully planned lessons well suited to your abilities and the students' needs. When your supervisor arrives, picture yourself handing him or her a copy of your lesson plans for the day, including your aims and behavioral objectives for each lesson. Then, because your classroom has an accepted procedure for introducing classroom guests, imagine clearing your throat and making the introduction. Your cooperating teacher smiles and so does your supervisor.

If, at any point a negative thought comes to mind, banish it. If, for instance you start thinking that you have chosen the wrong lessons, reassure yourself immediately. Remind yourself that the class has previously responded well to lessons like the ones you have planned. Remind yourself that you are well prepared, and so forth.

Return to the fantasy and picture yourself remaining effective throughout the observation period. Imagine the supervisor asking, "Do you have time for your critical feedback now?" The words "critical feedback" ring in your ears: You remind yourself that this is the evaluation your supervisor promised to give you after his or her observation. You are alarmed again but only momentarily. You remember that your supervisor has your development as a teacher at heart. He or she wants you to have a successful experience, to help you become the best possible teacher.

Playing out the imagined scenario of a forthcoming observation is an effective preparatory mechanism. It helps you deal with the feelings of anxiety and stress evoked by thoughts about your supervisor's scheduled observation. These feelings of uneasiness are natural ones under the circumstances. Your supervisor is there to evaluate you: You alone are in the spotlight and you want to excel.

Returning to the preparation of your materials and plans, try to do this well enough in advance to discuss them with your peers. Then, after benefiting from their input, you can discuss them with your cooperating teacher. The consultation will help you gain confidence. However, keep in mind, you may do this and find you are still nervous. That is the time to again remind yourself you are well prepared. Phyllis wrote:

3/8: I was tense about the observation at the beginning . . . in the back of my mind I was hoping that the children would be easily managed and my lesson would go all right. As it turned out, an early part of my lesson failed but everything else seemed to go well. Afterwards my supervisor gave me some good criticisms which I have really thought about, and now even the failures of the day seem unimportant.

Because Phyllis prepared extensively, much of her nervousness passed once she began her lesson. Further, she was well enough in control of herself so that she was not devastated when—early in her lesson—things did not go as planned. Under the pressure of being observed, that minor misfortune would have upset many a student teacher. But Phyllis had prepared for contingencies and thus was able to handle the situation.

Although Phyllis' nervousness was short-lived, Stephanie was never able to free herself of anxiety. This was true even though Stephanie's supervisor had worked especially hard to make her feel comfortable while being observed. Stephanie wrote to her supervisor in her log after two successive observations:

2/25: Today I must admit, I was a little edgy and nervous. It's funny, but I feel very comfortable and relaxed speaking with all of you in college, but I felt nervous just knowing that I was being observed by you, Mrs. S. Also, the lesson I had planned did not go according to my plan, though it went pretty well. . . . I was very glad that you spoke with me immediately afterward and gave me many interesting suggestions.

The next month, she still experienced substantial anxiety about being observed, although she was becoming a more confident and able teacher.

3/30: Today I must admit again I was a little nervous. As I explained to you, Mrs. S., you're one of the nicest people I have ever known and I feel very comfortable talking outside the classroom, but I guess that just knowing I am being observed can throw me a little. Well, anyhow, my day was planned and everything went pretty smoothly. Afterward, I felt very comfortable speaking with you, because I felt by criticizing and making creative statements about how I could improve certain things you were helping me. One other thing that I felt very pleased about was when you told me that you thought I had good control and was doing a good job teaching. As you once said in a seminar—a little praise never hurts anyone!

Stephanie, although able and sensitive, could not manage to fully free herself of anxiety about being observed. But that was fine because she managed to keep it at levels that did not affect the quality of her work.

Not everyone is fortunate enough to build a profitable learning relationship with his or her supervisor. Although Bev taught in a situation similar to Stephanie's and Phyllis', because her level of anxiety was higher and she was unable to control it, her student-teaching experience was less satisfactory. After describing high-quality work she had done, Bev wrote about what she thought the stress of being observed did to her:

> 6/2: . . . I'm a high strung person . . . the presence of my supervisor and at times my cooperating teacher made me uneasy, and unsure of myself. I had the most faith in myself when no one was there, and I feel that's when I did my best work.

Bev assumed that because she was high strung, the presence of adults observing her in the classroom would inevitably affect the quality of her teaching. Once Bev "bought into" this assumption, she handcuffed herself. Instead, she should have used a logical problem-solving procedure, like CONTROL-C, to tackle her anxiety.

Although Bev performed adequately as a student teacher over the course of the term, she did not develop in a most important personal way, that is, in terms of her confidence in working under the observation of others. Our profession is a public one. Our classrooms, in sharp contrast to the offices of our fellow professionals—lawyers, physicians, and dentists—are always open to the scrutiny of others. Next year Bev will have to work at making herself more comfortable with her principal and with parents who come to observe her own classroom.

If you find your stress level uncomfortably high during an observation and that this continues in second and third observations, we advise you to take action. First, apply CONTROL-C. Try to identify factors related to your anxiety. Second, as part of the CONTROL-C process, talk about your difficulty with a friend or, better yet, with your supervisor. This is what Nancy did, initiating contact with her supervisor through the following log entry:

> 1/20: I feel very loving and warm today. I like myself. I was thinking about our talk last week: You must think I'm immature. It's really weird that I can't talk with you. I'm usually pretty open. I guess I'm intimidated by roles. Nope, that's not it, because I basically feel that you deserve no more human respect than anyone else. I respect the fact that you have gone to school a lot longer than I and are valuable and helpful as a resource person. But I'm not in awe of professors. I wonder why I am uncomfortable, uptight with you. I'm sorry.

When Nancy discovered that she had considerable difficulty in dealing with the student teacher–supervisor relationship, she treated her problem in an effective way. Although some might have been tempted to delay taking action, Nancy immediately raised it with her supervisor and the two of them together were able to help Nancy resolve this difficulty successfully. As a result, Nancy was able to capitalize on the guidance and insights her supervisor had throughout most of the weeks of her student-teaching assignment.

Carole, in contrast, never built a relationship with her supervisor and, in fact, never gave her a chance to be of any help. The problem arose early in the term when Carole had a direct conflict with her supervisor. Unlike Nancy, Carole did not foresee the value of tapping her supervisor's resources and took no steps to resolve their differences. Instead, she simply let things drift, trying without enthusiasm to please her supervisor by her behavior in class.

Let us follow events that took place in Carole's relationship with her supervisor, starting with comments in her log about their first meeting.

> 2/8: Wednesday was the first session with my supervisor. . . . I brought up the question of the role of the student teacher in the classroom, giving my opinion that it is a dual role: (1) the cooperating teacher aided the student teacher by contributing to his development and guiding him, and (2) the student teacher contributed to the cooperating teacher by bringing new approaches and developments that were being introduced in university classes. My supervisor stated, "But most teachers and principals would not agree with you." I answered, "But ideally this is what we want." Her response was, "But ideals don't exist in city public schools."
> This is a 7-credit course and I have already antagonized the supervisor. That's all I need to do!

One month into the term Carole had already been having a difficult time with her class. Frustrated by classroom conditions she had no power to change, Carole seemed to release her frustrations in her first session with her supervisor by defining the student teacher–cooperating teacher relationship in a "radical" way. She did this without forethought about how her comments might be perceived by her supervisor, a person charged with the responsibility of maintaining good relationships with the cooperating teacher and school.

Carole would have been better off if she had recognized what was really going on inside of her. She was frustrated by her mixed success in the classroom and could have benefitted greatly if she would have asked her supervisor to observe the class and then discuss with her how best to approach the situation. Fortunately, Carole's supervisor returned to her school the next week. This time Carole handled the situation differently.

> 2/17: Mrs. W. stopped in briefly for a conference with the other three student teachers and me. We had an interesting conversation. She'll never really see things my way, but at least I used my head more today in the discussion. That helped us to be more open with each other.

The relationship between Carole and her supervisor had taken a step forward. She knew that her supervisor would be making four visits to her classroom and that her grade for student teaching would be based on the outcome of these. Carole wrote about the next visit:

> 2/29: My opinions about my supervisor have changed somewhat. At least I must admit she's a well-meaning person. I also must realize that she had a rather strange first encounter with me. The things I was saying weren't things one would normal-

ly say to a supervisor just like that. . . . As far as Mrs. W.'s actual observation went today, there is nothing particularly exciting to say. My lesson went well. . . . I spoke to her briefly right after the lesson. She commented that I should be more dramatic. Things should be gre-e-e-e-at and w-o-o-o-o-onderful when kids get them right. Mrs. W. was surprised (and she said so) at how well things seemed to be going in the class. She mentioned that after our first talk she was a little disturbed and had prepared herself for the worst.

Carole's classroom assignment was not an easy one. As the weeks went by Carole realized that her cooperating teacher, although considerate, was not overly committed, what with holding a second job and going to graduate school, and being a parent. Carole's learning experience would have been richer had she learned more fully to tap what her cooperating teacher had to offer. But Carole did not mobilize herself to work at this personal learning objective.

Carole's second observation went poorly. Her supervisor arrived early, the class had been having a bad day, and in teaching her lesson nothing seemed to go right. Although the third observation was better, the final one, she felt, was a great success:

5/9: Today was my last observation. I must admit that it was a relief to have it over with. I learned my lesson well. I put on a show for her, and she obviously liked it. The kids really enjoyed the African folk dancing lesson. You can tell. It just shines all over their faces.

Each time Carole had been observed she went through severe anxiety and tension, made worse, most likely, by her doubts about her relationship with Mrs. W. Had she at the outset employed a logical problem-solving method like CONTROL-C, she would have spared herself unnecessary pain and gained more from her student teaching assignment.

Carole's experiences offer many lessons. One of the first is this: The student-teaching experience is brief (although at times it may feel endless). When you identify a problem in your relationship with your supervisor, try to correct it as soon as possible. Carole knew a problem was brewing after the first meeting with her supervisor, and she expressed her concerns in her log. If at that point she had obtained information about the purposes of student teaching, she would have learned that they did not include providing continuing professional education to the cooperating teacher, even if that sometimes is a by-product.

If Carole had used CONTROL-C and sought this information, she would have confronted questions such as the following (all related to her February 8 log): Where did you acquire the concept of the dual role? What did you mean when you responded to the supervisor, "This is what we want?" Whom did you mean by "we"? What motives were involved in confronting her? Why do you think you antagonized her? What will you do now? Presumably, faced with those questions, Carole would have evaluated her motives of challenging her supervisor and would have acted to correct any damage done.

Why do you think Carole allowed herself to remain alienated from a professional whose help and support could have been greater than it was — which was considerable under the circumstances? We ask you to give thought to that question. By supplying your own reason you can alert yourself to motives that might hamper you in making full use of your supervisor.

Three further points are worth noting. First, Carole had moderate success in overcoming the initially poor relationship. Although this improvement was partly due to her supervisor's professional behavior, Carole's efforts were helpful too, even if they were primarily driven by concern about her course grade. Although that is an understandable motive, it is just not enough for anyone who wants to make the most of this unique experience.

Second, an important aspect of professional development is strengthening one's skills of communication with peers and supervisors. During a successful experience, the student teacher learns from interactions with the supervisor and cooperating teacher as well as from those with students. In this regard, it is important to remember that because the student-teaching assignment is of such short duration you must immediately work to make the best of it, even if you are not happy with your supervisor or have a difference of opinion about educational issues. See the relationship as a significant one and learn an important principle about working with others; recognize and utilize their strengths and learn from their weaknesses.

Third, Carole's supervisor, like yours, wants her student teachers to meet with success and to have the kind of experience that will help them become effective teachers. Besides caring about students, supervisors take pride in the quality of their own work and are concerned about their professional reputation, both of which depend partly on the success of their student teachers.

*As a Problem-Solving Resource.* The logs we collected contain hundreds of examples of supervisors making suggestions that aided student teachers in solving a variety of problems (developing materials, timing lessons, coping with different kinds of students, and so forth). Although the assistance they provided was similar to that offered by the cooperating teachers, supervisors had the advantage of different perspectives: first, of seeing many teachers at work in different schools and school systems and, second, of bringing to their observations in any given class the fresh outlook of the outsider.

An important specialty area of supervisors is in helping student teachers deal with difficulties in their relationships with cooperating teachers. Here we explore three examples that illustrate this supervisory role.

Brent, whose student-teaching experience seemed to be going well, came to see his supervisor, unhappy about the grade his cooperating teacher had given him for the first marking period. He thought that he had established good rapport in the classroom and that his work had been well received by both the class and the teacher. True, he might have been a little weak in disciplining, but Mr. H.

had never expressed any dissatisfaction; in fact, he had praised Brent often. So why the mediocre grade, he asked.

The supervisor supported Brent's questioning of the situation. After some discussion it was agreed that the supervisor should take the initiative and set up an appointment with the cooperating teacher. This was done and, after the usual niceties and a general discussion of Brent's classroom work, they turned to the subject of Brent's grades.

It turned out that this was Mr. H's first experience as a cooperating teacher and he had decided it would be wise to mark Brent low on the first grading period and then on each successive marking period to grade him progressively higher. Mr. H. felt this would be advantageous because it would show Brent's growth during his student-teaching experience. After a constructive discussion during which the supervisor explained to Mr. H. the consequences of his well-intended actions, he decided to change Brent's grade to one that reflected his actual performance.

The supervisor intervened directly in Brent's case. More commonly, he or she will help you solve problems by sharing his or her ideas or perspective on problems you face. Ann's cooperating teacher wanted Ann to work with the whole class, but Ann felt she could work only with groups. The supervisor could see that Ann's protests and worries were not consistent with observable fact, even reported fact, for Ann herself had written:

3/10: I also had quite an experience reading a story to about one hundred children while they waited for the film to be ready. I'm not sure how I did. They were all quiet, so I guess I must have been doing something right.

Ann's cooperating teacher kept urging her to "feel self-assured." Ann insisted that this feeling would come to her only with time. The supervisor scheduled a series of appointments with Ann to discuss this difference and what was involved in being self-assured.

The supervisor argued against the position that you were either self-assured or not. She explained the meaning of a continuum and applied it to self-assurance, noting that compared with others, one might be below the midpoint on a distribution from very low to very high. The supervisor noted, however, that Ann was hardly devoid of self-assurance, reminding her of the previous log entry, although it was written as if Ann were reluctant to admit her assurance. The supervisor then explained that efforts in teaching the whole class would bring Ann success that, in turn, would yield greater self-assurance.

A supervisor can also help you better understand relationships in the school and adjust to the realities associated with them. The example we use is a poignant one, illustrating as it does the harsh fact that it is not only students who are victims of stress when the college supervisor comes to observe. Unfortunately, but understandably, some cooperating teachers feel that they themselves are being observed and assessed. As former college students, some assign a more prestigious status to college professor visitors from your higher education institution than to themselves.

Following are reports written by Leslie about two of her observations and her cooperating teacher's reaction to them. We have also included in brackets the comments the supervisor wrote in Leslie's log.

> 3/9: I was quite anxious to see how Mrs. J. was going to react with my supervisor in the room. After the assembly program, the kids were very excited. Mrs. J. was getting nervous because they weren't being quiet. She kept giving me these frantic looks. I don't know what she wanted me to do, because I certainly didn't expect them to sit like angels after having attended such an exciting program. [Supervisor: I thought the kids were great.]

> 3/31: Mrs. J. was so hyper when I reminded her my supervisor was coming tomorrow. It really bothered me. She told me to make sure I had control. I don't know whether she expected them to sit around like silent bodies or what, but I didn't like the idea that she wanted them to be little angels just because there was going to be a visitor in the room. At lunch Mrs. J. suggested I tell the children to be extra quiet to help me out during my observation. I told her I didn't want to do that and she assured me that she used to do it and it worked out well.

> [Supervisor: her reaction — it is a pity, but I see it time and again, though usually not carried to this degree. I think it's basically a lack of security which I can understand in a student teacher but not in an experienced one. You handled the situation well. I hope you will not allow these experiences to interfere with your learning from her. She does have much to offer.]

Only pressure of great intensity would lead professionals to be so concerned that instead of being a source of strength and security for the student teacher, they add to their anxiety. Because these cooperating teachers see the success of their student teacher as a reflection of their own ability, they unknowingly create unrealistic expectations about what their student teachers should achieve.

Granted that some cooperating teachers have to contend with their own problems, we urge you to concentrate on the strengths of those assigned to help you, even as you recognize their frailties. Leslie had been incensed by her cooperating teacher's suggestions about asking the children to be "extra quiet." She made an appointment with her supervisor to discuss her annoyance with the cooperating teacher. When they met, the negatives poured out. As Leslie talked and, through her supervisor's help, understood her own attitudes, she became less self-righteous and more understanding of Mrs. J. as a person. She was able then to recall the various ways Mrs. J. had been very helpful to her and could accept and even appreciate her despite the inappropriate advice in this instance.

*As a Source of Emergency Help.* "May I phone you at home?" supervisors are often asked by their student teachers. If your supervisor makes no mention of that possibility early in the term, ask about it, and if the supervisor approves, obtain the home number and the preferred calling hours. If a telephone number is given, unless you are instructed otherwise, use it very sparingly: Only for genuine emergencies, by which we mean that you are very troubled and cannot resolve a dilemma or reach a decision necessary for the next day.

In an interview, Tracey, who worked in a center city high school, reported the following:

> I came home late one afternoon and spent several hours over-organizing my kitchen and wrestling with the question of whether to call my supervisor. Finally, at 10:00 p.m. I made the call to Mr. A. The teachers are meeting tomorrow to discuss unionizing—and my cooperating teacher invited me to come. In fact, it seemed more like a request than a polite invitation. She said, "You might as well learn now about what teachers have to put up with in terms of bureaucracy." I have mixed feelings, however. I would like to get a job in this district next year. My husband works downtown and I don't want to alienate the principal who I want to write a letter of recommendation.
>
> Mr. A. and I had a long talk. When he finished he said, "I'm glad you called me about this decision. It's the kind of thing teachers must think long and hard about." I do have one question, he added. "If you knew about the meeting for a week, why did you wait so long to call me?" I didn't have an answer for him then. But after a little bit of thought, however, I figured it out. I was hoping the issue would just disappear, so I wouldn't face the decision at all.

*As Seminar Class Leader.*   In many colleges the supervisors conduct a seminar for student teachers. This seminar, designed to supplement the practicum, differs from other college-level classes, including other seminars, in several important ways. First, there are typically no exams and sometimes no letter grades. Second, all the students are having the same kind of preprofessional experience, although their learnings may be very different. Third, student teaching, and that alone, is the major focus of the class. Fourth, the major objective of the seminar is to give the support (professional, academic, and psychological) that will help student teachers be most effective and profit from their experiences. How can you best use this resource?

First, use it as an incentive to organize the thoughts and feelings you have about your classroom. Prepare for your seminar beforehand by reviewing the classroom events of the previous days. The process of making such a preparation may help you gain fresh insights into what you have been experiencing and may also ready you to participate more actively in the group's discussion. With the help of the seminar group, you will be able to see that the barrage of stimuli you experience every day in class with your students are not just a mass of unrelated events. They fit together and relate to theories that you have studied.

Second, use the seminar to discuss problems you are confronting. Be open with your thoughts and feelings. Some student teachers are hesitant to be frank, feeling that such disclosure will reflect badly on them. However, the fact is that if they are experiencing a particular difficulty, the probability is high that other student teachers are too. They will be pleased with your mention of it and perhaps relieved, as will the seminar leaders who want active participation by the group in order to have useful sessions.

Third, the seminar provides an ideal forum for exchanges. Participants in this sharing can benefit not only for the present but also for the school years ahead. You can share and trade ideas, lessons, methods and materials, and teaching strategies (e.g., finding a way to involve students in a science experiment, or to help manually awkward pupils in industrial arts or to encourage handicapped students in physical education).

Mark spoke of the benefits of sharing in his seminar: "The second period English class is awful. Four senior girls sit in the back corner and giggle. I know one or two of them have a crush on me. I brought the matter up during a group supervision and found that several other students, both male and female, faced the same difficulty. Together we figured out several ways to tackle the problem."

*As a Support Figure.*   The college supervisor also functions as a support figure, sometimes through providing "tea and sympathy" (much as headmasters' wives did in years gone by and in the classic film, *Goodbye, Mr. Chips*). Student teachers may need such support because the experience has the potential for arousing disillusionment. Why? Some begin with grossly unreal expectations about their chosen profession in general and their student-teaching assignment in particular. This is to be expected. They have been working toward this gateway to teaching for years and may have exaggerated notions of what they can accomplish.

Fortunately, most student teachers replace wishes with facts. They find themselves satisfied soon after beginning to teach more lessons and to participate more fully in the classroom. Those who do not make this exchange, however, are often disillusioned. Anthony, for example, first had hopes of changing his cooperating teacher's class in ways he felt were pedagogically superior. He comments:

> 3/3: I have become aware of something, that is, that any changes that are going to be made in the class are only going to be incremental.

Anthony expected Ms. V. to change in his direction, and he expected to be able to teach exclusively in his own way, not Ms. V.'s. His next comment suggests that he felt there was something inherently wrong or undesirable about trying out the cooperating teacher's "routine."

> 3/10: I'm a little worried. I seem to be getting the idea that I will be following Ms. V.'s routine when I finally take over. I realize the children need some type of a steady schedule, but frankly there are times when I'm bored with her routine.

With help from his supervisor Anthony came to understand the following:

1. the class routines had been established before he arrived,

2. Ms. V. and the class would have to work together after Anthony finished student teaching, and

3. he should try to accommodate himself to fit her teaching style.

Anthony had an "aha" insight. To be an effective teacher he had to develop his skills in recognizing and taking the perspective of others. His supervisor explained that from Ms. V.'s perspective, he was a guest. From the perspective of the students, the issue was not whether Anthony was bored by Ms. V.'s lesson, but how they, the students, were reacting. She may have read the same story half a dozen times, but they kept asking for it and still had the same transfixed expression of delight on their faces when he read it to them.

## WHAT SUPERVISORS LOOK FOR

Take a moment right now and put yourself in your supervisor's place. Ask yourself what you would do with your student teachers if you were he or she. Hopefully you would assign yourself an active role of constructive criticism about the professionalism, the curriculum decisions, and instructional practices of your student teacher. Your student teachers would wonder exactly what criteria they would be evaluated on and to what standards they would be held.

Your supervisor probably will inform you of his or her expectations at the outset of your experience as a student teacher. If he or she does not, it would be appropriate for you to ask.

Even without asking, you can be sure of some important dimensions that will be taken into account. Your college supervisor will want to see you develop as a true professional. You do that by establishing the basic qualities of the professional—qualities that all educators value. Promptness, for example, is essential. Reliability in other matters is also of vital importance.

If you are ill and cannot work or if your car breaks down and you will be late, phone the office to inform the principal and your cooperating teacher at the earliest possible time. If you are scheduled to prepare some material for school or to give a report at the college student-teaching seminar, have it ready by the due date. If you are annoyed with the cooperating teacher or the supervisor or both, do not allow your anger to build silently; on the other hand, do not resort to angry outbursts. Bring the matter up directly and professionally.

Absences should be reduced to essentials. A person who phones in ill repeatedly is not one who is going to be wanted or recommended for a position. A person who tends to schedule medical and business appointments during school hours is going to leave an indelible impression on the supervisor and cooperating teacher, and not the kind that leads to good ratings when grades are due or when reference letters are written.

Natural and normal appreciation of what others do for you should be expressed. Supervisors, being human, get satisfaction from knowing that advice they gave you about some home economics equipment or about a more effective way to use a machine-shop tool really meant something to you. They also like to be appreciated when they help you understand that your cooperating teacher, although perhaps lacking a diplomat's tact, is nonetheless pointing out a way for you to improve the questions you raise in class or to make better use of science equipment. And if their interpretations and interactions with you are just not rewarding and their critiques not penetrating, they want to know that too, and early.

The final section of this chapter is on evaluation of the student teacher. Before turning to that we want to elaborate on some of the conditions in your student teaching that are beyond your control, especially the classroom climate established before you arrived.

## THE CLASSROOM CLIMATE YOU FIND SETS LIMITS

As we have said before, there is no one right way to teach. Each of us formulates a personal approach. It is based on our beliefs, experiences with teachers in schools and college, interactions with students in our classes, and the influence of the school system in which we teach. How we teach may also depend on some factors beyond our control. For example, the physical structure of our classroom or the school's rules may limit us. Further, important limits are imposed by the class climate already established by the cooperating teacher and others in the school.

Here we review the results of three studies that speak to other limits that exist in cooperating classrooms. These studies are valuable because they point to subtle factors that are often overlooked by student teachers.

As a rule, student teachers have been exposed to many different kinds of teacher behavior. As elementary and secondary students themselves, they have experienced diversity, and as college students they have learned about varied instructional techniques. They have a right to wonder, in advance of their beginning to take over the class, whether there is some way of knowing if certain kinds of teacher behavior are likely to be more effective than others.

A study by Copeland (1978) addresses that question in particular by examining the use of one skill — asking probing questions. Such teacher questions, following a student's verbal statement, are based on the substance of that statement. The questions are intended to encourage the student to go further into the thought previously expressed. Copeland wanted to find if there was support for either or both of the following:

1. The cooperating teacher, by asking probing questions, encourages the student teacher to use the skill.

2. The cooperating teacher, having accustomed the students to the skill by using it prior to entry by the student teacher, fosters and supports the use of that skill by the student teacher.

Copeland used 32 student teachers who had been trained to ask probing questions, and 64 experienced teachers (Grades 2–5), 32 of whom were high users of probing questions and 32 low users. Of the student teachers, 16 were assigned to high users as their cooperating teachers and 16 were assigned to low users. That means that half the student teachers had cooperating teachers who served as models of teachers using probing questions and the other half did not.

In the meantime, the other 32 experienced teachers (16 high users of probing questions and 16 low users) were teaching their own classes without having any student teachers. Here is how they entered the study. After 3 weeks the student teachers were asked to spend 30 minutes each day for a week teaching reading groups in another classroom, classrooms taught by those other 32 teachers. The question now was: Which student teachers will ask probing questions during those 30-minute sessions with the reading groups? Will it be those student teachers whose cooperating teachers had served as models or will it be others?

The findings were as follows:

1. Student teachers who taught reading groups in classes accustomed to hearing probing questions used them themselves – whether or not their cooperating teachers in their regular student-teaching class used them.
2. Student teachers who taught reading groups unaccustomed to probing questions did not utilize them extensively whether or not their regular cooperating teachers provided models of the use of that skill.

The conclusion of the study is that the ecological system in the class (what the students are accustomed to) has a large influence on what skills and practices a student teacher will engage in. Students become accustomed to behaving in a certain manner in a certain class and are likely to respond to their student teacher much as they do to their teacher. This important study demonstrates that a limit to your ability to experiment in your cooperating class relates to the style and approach to which the students are accustomed. This finding makes sense at an intuitive level. Keep it in mind early in the term when you are trying to establish yourself as a disciplinarian. To hold their attention and to maintain the necessary order for learning, find out what practices they are accustomed to.

The second investigation (Hearne & Moos, 1978) is about a subject of much interest to teachers and certainly to student teachers – classroom climate. The researchers went to 19 high schools (11 general and 8 vocational-technical) to study the relationship between subject matter and classroom climate. To do this they gave the 4,000 or so students and their teachers in the 207 participating classes a 90-item questionnaire designed to measure the extent to which the following nine dimensions were present in their classroom:

1. Involvement: assesses the extent to which students have attentive interest in class activities and participate in discussion.

2. Affiliation: assesses the level of friendship students feel for each other.

3. Teacher Support: assesses the amount of help, concern, and friendship the teacher directs toward the students.

4. Task Orientation: assesses the extent to which it is important to complete the activities that have been planned.

5. Competition: assesses the emphasis placed on students competing with each other for grades and recognition.

6. Order and Organization: assesses the emphasis on students behaving in an orderly and polite manner, and on the overall organization of assignments and classroom activities.

7. Rule Clarity: assesses the emphasis on establishing and following a clear set of rules, and on students knowing what the consequences will be if they do not follow them.

8. Teacher Control: assesses how strict the teacher is in enforcing the rules, and the severity of the punishment for rule infractions.

9. Innovation: assesses how much students contribute to planning classroom activities, and the extent to which the teacher attempts to use new techniques and encourages creative thinking in the students.

As you examine Table 4.1, note that the researchers grouped the participating classrooms listed in Column 2 into the categories listed in Column 1. The climate they expected to find in each category is listed in Column 3 and what the students reported in Column 4 and 5. As you examine the table you will see that in some cases, but not in all, they found the climate as they expected.

These results illustrate several important points:

1. Each class has its own climate;
2. students tend to describe it similarly;

TABLE 4.1
Classroom Categories and Expected and Observed Characteristics*

| (1) Classroom Category | (2) Classroom Subjects Assigned to Each Category | (3) Expected Characteristics of Classroom Climate | (4) Characteristics Rated High by Students in Each Classroom Type | (5) Characteristics Rated Low by Students in Each Classroom Type |
|---|---|---|---|---|
| Realistic | Auto repair, carpentry, electronics, general shop, machine shop, power mechanics | Asocial, conforming, frank, genuine, materialistic, persistent, practical, stable, thrifty, uninsightful | Involvement, affiliation, competition, rule clarity, teacher control, innovation | Task orientation |
| Investigative | Algebra, biology, chemistry, geometry, mathematics, physics, physical science, science | Analytical, curious, independent, intellectual, introspective, introverted, passive, unassuming, unpopular | Task orientation, teacher control | Involvement, affiliation, innovation |
| Artistic | Art, band, composition, drama, English, French, German, Italian, literature, music, Spanish, theater | Complicated, disorderly, emotional, imaginative, impractical, impulsive, independent, intuitive, nonconforming, original | Innovation | Competition, rule clarity, teacher control |
| Social | Civics, economics, government, history, political systems, social studies, sociology | Friendly, helpful, idealistic, insightful, persuasive, responsible, sociable, tactful, understanding | None stood out in the analyses | Task orientation, rule clarity, teacher control, involvement, affiliation |
| Conventional | Bookkeeping, clerical office practice, retailing, shorthand, stenography, typing | Conforming, defensive, efficient, inflexible, inhibited, obedient, orderly, persistent, practical, prudish | Task orientation, competition, rule clarity, involvement, affiliation | Innovation |

*Portions of this table are from Hearne and Moos (1978, p. 113).

3. classes offering the same subject matter tend to have similar classroom climate;

4. the class you enter for your student teaching will already have a climate of its own;

5. studying the dimensions of classroom climate described in the table will suggest the kind of climate you might find in your student-teaching class;

6. bearing in mind the results of the previously mentioned Copeland study, you will probably find yourself working most effectively if you operate within the limits of the classroom climate already established by your cooperating teacher.

*Student brinkmanship* is another behavior to consider in connection with classroom climate. The term has been defined as behavior that students engage in to resist school authority, in other words, to resist you, the teacher.

The concept of brinkmanship, of being on the brink or on the edge, has been used because the behavior involved—for example, clowning, giggling, chalk-squeaking, book-dropping, and enthusiastic hand-waving instead of hand-raising—is not really punishable. They can use it to release their hostility to authority and get away with it.

Newman and Licata (1986-1987) studied the relationship between such behavior on the one hand and teacher and classroom climate on the other. Their subjects were students and teachers in 122 classes in a large, urban–suburban school district in the midwest. Both the teacher and student samples were representative of the diversity seen in today's schools.

The findings of this carefully designed study suggest the following useful hypotheses:

- Students are less likely to use brinkmanship if they feel positive about the teacher as a considerate person and about the classroom climate, in general. In other words, they tend to be less hostile and not engage in brinkmanship if they find the teacher is friendly, respecting, and warm, and if they find the classroom climate favorable (cohesive—students interact and feel friendly with each other; satisfying—students like their class and work).

- The frequency of student brinkmanship is inversely related to classroom routinization. Teachers can reduce the incidence of brinkmanship by increasing the amount of time given to following well-established, orderly routines. Initially, to establish routines, the teacher sees to it that students know what work is to be done and when it is to be done.

Implicit in Newman and Licata's study and their discussion of their findings is this advice to student teachers: While you are developing a positive teacher–student relationship (based on "consideration"), rely heavily on routinization. Once the relationship is established to your satisfaction, you can then give routinization its proper place and use it consistently within your own teaching philosophy and approach.


## HOW YOU WILL BE EVALUATED

Evaluation will be important in your professional career. It is an enormous and complex subject. Understandably, at this point in your life you are mostly interested in the evaluation that will be made of your student teaching. Therefore, our comments about evaluation focus on that. Nevertheless, the general principles of evaluation that are discussed apply equally to those assessments made by your cooperating teacher and those you will make of your students' work in your classes this year and in the future.

Evaluation involves the process of making judgments. Your cooperating teacher and university supervisor (with different degrees of influence depending on institutional policy and individual differences) will make judgments about your student teaching.

Those judgments will be of two types. The first, which is known as *formative,* will be made for the purpose of advising you. They will advise you, not grade you. Your mentors, as a result of their observations, will indicate to you, perhaps through questions or direct comments or a combination of the two, some of the ways in which you could be more effective. They may, for example, suggest how to arouse more student interest in classroom activities, or how to manage the class with fewer discipline problems. Their aim will be to help promote your development as a teacher—or, as we might say, to help you "form" yourself professionally.

The second type, which is known as *summative* evaluation, will be made to indicate by means of a grade whether you have successfully completed student teaching. This will be a judgment of your all-round effectiveness, taking into consideration your strengths and weaknesses. This type of evaluation can be thought of as a form of "summing up" your current level of performance.

One of the greatest gifts you can give yourself is the belief that the evaluation you get at this time in your career is worth a fortune, and that it would be good to lower your defensiveness. Two experts are going to share their time, observations, and advice "for free," something you are unlikely to get to this extent at any other time in your career.

If you find in yourself a feeling that you want to avoid their observations and hide your usual practices from them as much as possible, then think of the following example: A young singing artist, hopeful for a career in opera, goes for a lesson with an expert teacher who will listen, advise, and listen again. Can you imagine that young singer thinking: "I pay that teacher $100 a lesson, but I want to hide my usual style, and when I get advice I won't take it because I think the teacher is wrong." Student teachers should not allow themselves to get either that uptight about being observed and evaluated or that close-minded about another person's point of view, even if they believe the observers hold a different philosophy of education.

As we said, you may never again get this quality of evaluation (based on multiple observations by two experienced teachers). A leading expert (Raths, 1982) explained that claims are made that evaluation of teachers is an ongoing process all through their careers. They are told that it is a joint activity intended to strengthen their instruction. In practice, he pointed out, this is more rhetoric than fact. Unless there are major changes in the future, you are likely to be evaluated in your career by administrators who will have observed you infrequently.

Sometimes the chief purpose of the evaluation will be to decide if you should be tenured, given an increment, or reassigned. The administrators will in all probability use a rating scale that may include many dimensions. The assumption in constructing these scales is that they are tapping the important criteria of effective teaching. Presumably, good teachers get high ratings on most or all dimensions.

So far as *student teaching* is concerned, several researchers set out to investigate how they were evaluated on the national scene (Fant, Hill, Lee, & Landes, 1985). By drawing on prior studies, they identified 8 factors. We are describing each of the 8 factors because you may well be evaluated in terms of them and also because you may find them useful.

*Clarity:* Objectives clear and understandable to students. . . . Content well organized. . . . Important points stressed. . . . Reviews and summarizes.

*On-Task Behavior of Students:* The percentage of time students are involved in learning, in contrast with time spent in trying to keep order or discussing unrelated topics. (This is not an argument against discussing the circus coming to town or the World Series, but for managing a high proportion of on-task time.)

*Use of Feedback:* This is formative evaluation. This involves giving your students high-quality feedback about their work.

*Task-Oriented:* The class climate is task-oriented, meant for learning not entertainment. Learning objectives and tasks are clear, class starts and ends promptly. (A business-like atmosphere does not exclude humor and lightness.)

*Warm, Supportive Environment:* Respect and acceptance of all. Teachers are kindly and available to help.

*The Flexible, Adaptable Teacher:* Can change as situation demands it, and can adapt plans as student responses dictate.

*The Enthusiastic Teacher:* Excited about learning and students know it. Believed to be important to motivation and students' tendency to concentrate on learning tasks.

*High Expectations of Students:* High expectations are believed to result in higher achievement. (Few teacher education programs included this criterion. For reasons already discussed, we consider it important.)

As a student teacher, one of the great benefits of evaluation is the opportunity to learn how to evaluate yourself. A format described by Hanhan (1988) is conducive to that kind of learning. In advance of a mid-semester conference with one's supervisor, the student teacher is asked to reflect on 13 questions. Some of them are about the times of the day and/or week that are the easiest and the hardest, areas in which one feels pressured and those that are smooth-running, a description of some of the students, and a view of one's role as teacher. The student teacher is asked to prepare a question about an area of personal concern about teaching which is to be discussed at the conference. The self-knowledge from the conference is believed to breed self-confidence. It also helps to establish a mode of dealing with problems.

Those reported gains are, in the final analysis, two of the major objectives of supervision: self-confidence and problem-solving skill.

# 5
▼▼▼▼▼▼▼

# Relationship With Students: Challenges, Pains, and Satisfactions

As a student teacher you are not a powerless force in the classroom. True, you do not have the authority to unilaterally modify the curriculum or to experiment extensively with teaching styles. Despite these limitations, however, student teachers can and do make substantial contributions to the education of their students.

Because students are unquestionably the central characters in the classroom, your objective is to give them the best possible opportunities for learning. Despite limits within which you must function, you are still free to do meaningful things. Most importantly, you are free to develop a relationship of trust with the students. You can do this with the class as a whole by acquiring a reputation for fairness and with individual youngsters through conversations about their interests and concerns.

You are free to strengthen these relationships by establishing the practice of making comments to individual students that give them recognition and a feeling of self-worth—and not just to the most able learners but to all students. You are free to demonstrate your interests in them by making their classroom experiences exciting, that is, by relating learning to their lives. In all, you have many opportunities to come to know and help your students, and, in doing that, you gain confidence in your ability as a teacher.

## KNOWING YOUR STUDENTS

Because your time as a student teacher is limited, start looking at individual students from the outset, preferably on your first day at school. Guard against having your attention predominantly focused on the obvious ones, such as the attractive, the bright, the vocal, and the belligerent. The quiet, restrained, disciplined ones (some of whom may also be bright) need just as much attention. All students, fast, average, or slow, have something that interests them. It is worth discovering that something, whatever it may be, in order to make use of it in your teaching.

How well you know a student partly determines how much he or she will achieve in your class. When you know the student's current level of development, then you know what assistance he or she needs to make additional progress. Just as in the work of the physician, diagnosis is needed before you write the prescription (i.e., plan of action). That plan will enable you to help a student take the next step in his or her intellectual and social development.

Here is Ruby, in her first week as a student teacher, working at getting to know the students so that later she can more effectively assist them in learning. Her log entries are instructive for another reason too.

1/6: Kids—I'm getting to know them better, to know their names and personalities. A lot of them have problems or unusual home situations that they want to tell you about; questions aren't necessary, they just want to be listened to. Felicia likes to tell about her family, and even though it doesn't seem ideal, she seems happy about it. Stan is supposed to be in a primary special class, but because there is no room he is in a regular third-grade class. Mrs. W. says that he cannot do a lot of the work, so a lot of it isn't assigned to him. He seems bored.

My first impression was that Stan needed personal attention. I didn't question the idea that Stan has learning difficulties, but he does a lot of the work that the other children do and with just a few minutes of personal attention he has done work for me that wasn't expected.

Daniel is another child that I am concerned about. Mrs. W. says that he consistently receives Fs on his work and has expressed her dislike for him because of his attitude. She says his family is on welfare and his mother is a real "slut." My first impression of Daniel was that he was a nice boy who needed a good one-to-one relationship and a lot of motivation. Today on the multiplication test Daniel missed 5 out of 12. After the test he asked me his score. I showed it to him and he said, "I had both of my fingers crossed hoping I'd get a hundred. I haven't got hardly any hundreds all year."

1/7: Mrs. W. seems concerned about my interest in Stan and Daniel, and I'm afraid she feels that by showing concern for them I'm questioning her success in teaching them. Today in the lounge the principal mentioned a chance at getting help for some of the kids. Mrs. W. told him Daniel had already been tested and still no outside help has been made available to him.

After going back to the classroom Mrs. W. and I talked about Daniel a little more. Mrs. W. explained that there wasn't time for her to give Daniel 15 minutes of personal attention each day. I agree. But Stan and Daniel need that attention and help, and the school system has a responsibility to provide it for them.

Yes, Ruby made the kinds of observations an effective teacher makes, but she was not being helpful to herself by her self-righteous attitude. Sensing that her cooperating teacher felt threatened, by approaching her in a sensitive manner, she could have made this a more successful learning experience for herself and more helpful to the children. Because it was early in the term, for example, she might have asked Mrs. W. for suggestions on how she could help Daniel and Stan or, alternatively, developed a plan and asked for Mrs. W.'s reaction and approval.

Another matter worth attention is that we sometimes get a false sense of self-worth because we are able to recognize something another person has missed. By "false" we mean that it is not coming solely from our own perceptiveness but from that, combined with a good feeling over another person's errors.

Ruby should feel good because she got to know her children and learned about needs they had, but not because of what may be seen as another's (her cooperating teacher's) inadequacies. As Ruby and all teachers come to learn, when there are 20 to 30 children in a classroom, even the best of us cannot single handedly be aware of everything that is important, not to mention attend to all that needs to be done.

Returning to the subject of understanding the students and their classroom needs, skill in making accurate diagnoses does not come automatically. The classroom is an active and busy place. So much is going on that our mind tries to adapt by unwittingly stereotyping the students and treating them according to certain expectations — one child is responsible, another a doll, this one the quiet one, that one the bully, the troublemaker, or the dull one.

Juan's comment addressed this point:

My day brings me into contact with over 120 different kids in my classes and 1,000 more in and around the building. During my first few days I formed impressions about many of the kids — and the impressions tended to stick. I was really surprised yesterday when Jacki — who I thought was a "tough too cool lady" — came up to me after class and asked for extra help. Was I surprised! I had to revise my thoughts about her and now I'm wondering about all those early impressions.

Let us look at how other student teachers experienced stereotyping and what they did to correct it. Making a last entry in her log, immediately after her student teaching ended, Patty reflected on her experiences:

6/6: In the beginning, I watched the children closely, finding that certain ones appealed to me more than others. I guess this must be quite a natural, automatic feeling, but I knew these feelings shouldn't influence my attempts to reach all the children. To deal with this, I tried to talk more with the children I thought would be harder to handle. I would ask them questions on an interpersonal level, and in handling discipline, I talked to the child individually, hoping to build some rapport. In doing this, I hoped to let each child know that he was equally important to me, and that his feelings and behaviors were given my attention. I found incidents where, because of my attempts, children began to respect my feelings too, and a rapport grew. However, I also saw some of the children could have been given more of my support.

I found getting to know the needs of each child to be quite difficult. In order to find a child's level of maturity or ability, I once again related to each child on an individual level. Observation is another technique I used to see the development of the children socially. I'm quite sure that sometimes I interpreted, underestimated, or expected too much or too little from some children. I feel that if I would have had more time with them, I would have understood more.

Anyway, I was very conscious of showing the children that I did care for each as a person. In group activities, I tried to build confidence in certain children by allowing them to perform successfully. When I showed them my pleasure, they became pleased with themselves.

Rita recognized a tendency in herself to attend to certain types of children to the neglect of others. Her log entry is unusual in that she found herself paying special note to shy children, an uncommon and valuable practice when not done at the cost of other youngsters.

1/28: I have a tendency to attract and pay more attention to the shy and introverted children. . . . Since both of those girls [referred to earlier in her log] are extremely outgoing, I think I might have been passing over them. I'll have to correct that.

Today seemed destined to "prove" to me the difficulties of finding a balance in your relationships with children in the classroom. How can you accept, without rejecting, those children who want to almost cling to you so that they can learn to be independent and yet also friendly and at ease? How can you relate to the child who seems to be afraid of you, without intruding? Perhaps the answer is just to be friendly and at ease to all and let time and their individual personalities decide the outcome.

Elaine, a talented young student teacher, took the problems she faced in stride. No wonder she did, the way she saw the children as individuals. In reviewing her student-teaching experiences she reports:

5/25: My feelings about my children and my profession are fantastic! Each of my children was beautiful in a unique way. Each was capable of a certain amount, and I made each know that I believed in that capability. I always tried to include all of them, especially those who were less secure about themselves. They all knew that I liked them, and I've no doubt that they all liked me. Being with them was a great ego trip.

My greatest faith in myself as a teacher concerns my ability to love and understand each child equally, and deal with them accordingly. I enjoy very much, and am proud of, the profession that I have chosen. There is something very special about working with children.

It is because of all this that I want to teach. I value myself, and what I am doing, and I have faith in my abilities. Student teaching succeeded in backing up my confidence.

You can guard against stereotyping students by being alert to instances when this might occur and actively working to circumvent it. For example, at the end of the first few days of your student-teaching assignment, note which students you observed and about what percentage of the day you spent watching each. After a few more days note whose names you know and whose you do not. Every half-day or class period single out one student for your attention, go to him or her, say something supportive, have a conversation, and/or ask a question.

Every week or so develop a list of strengths and weaknesses of several students and a program to correct a weakness of those in most immediate need of remedial help. For example, the pupil who daydreams during class assignments could be helped with occasional positive reinforcement when he or she is concentrating on work: "You are really coming along, Chris," or "Good work." These ideas are a start. Add to them any plans that suit the needs of your class.

## STUDENT TEACHER AND CHILDREN:
## FEELINGS ABOUT EACH OTHER

Expect certain thoughts about the children to cross your mind, some of them troubling. For example, when we are having difficulty with a student (or for that matter an adult) we may use him or her as an excuse for failures we are encountering, or we can even have fantasies (or dreams) in which we eliminate the person. If you tend to be excessively self-critical, you may condemn yourself for thoughts such as these. Remember that such transient thoughts are natural and widely experienced.

The other side of the coin is being troubled about how the children feel about us. A student teacher who has an excessive need to be liked by the children is at a great disadvantage. Stephanie appears here in the first of two log entries to be expressing warm feelings about the children.

2/17: Today was my first day back in over a week. I really missed the children, and it made me feel good knowing they remembered me. Since I had written out their Valentines before I got sick, I brought them in and the children liked the late surprise. I was sorry that I had to miss their Valentine's Day party, but they told me all about it. I even got some Valentine cards from the children. It was nice.

Almost 2 months later, however, Stephanie's log puts her behavior in a different light. Her report suggests that her need to have the attention and affection of the children was excessive and not constructive.

3/9: Yesterday when I met the afternoon class for the first time I walked around, spoke with them, and by the middle of the session, a few of them were even fighting with one another to hold my hands.

We all want to be accepted and liked, and if this happens, it makes the student-teaching experience that much more pleasant. The problem here, of course, is not Stephanie's gratification from the children's apparent feelings about her, but that she could report with obvious satisfaction that she was so liked that they fought over her. This is not a teacher devoted to the needs of the pupils; it is, instead, a teacher inducing the pupils to satisfy her needs. Needs like this that dominate our classroom functioning interfere with the kind of clear thinking we, as leaders in the classroom, must engage in if we are to see to it that the students have the necessary opportunities for learning.

That very kind of clear thinking enabled Erin, then about 2 months into her student teaching, to use a child's ordinary drawing as a projective technique. By doing that, and by avoiding self-centered temptation, she gave a child an opportunity for emotional release. She herself was able to get important insights about the child that would otherwise have been difficult to obtain.

> 3/19: Today went great. I had the children draw something they like to do and then tell me a story about it. Some of the children were very creative and I gained a lot of insight into how well they express themselves. This one little girl did two pictures, one with me in it and one about home. I wanted to ask about the one with me, but I decided I'd learn more from the other one. Her story about that painting was amazing and I felt it reflected a lot. In it she had different objects and whenever she went to play with one, her mother would yell at her or beat her. It was amazing how well she could tell me a story about this picture, and it probably reflected her home.

Erin's supervisor praised her for creative use of the pictures and for developing hypotheses about the meaning of the girl's statements. However, she urged her to treat it as no more than a hypothesis and to discuss her observations with her cooperating teacher.

## CLASSIFYING STUDENTS

Students are classified in many different ways. As you are aware from personal experience, IQ tests, achievement and aptitude tests, and vocational interests measures are widely used in schools. Less widely used, but valuable to teachers in understanding children's abilities is Piaget's system of stages in cognitive development (Piaget & Inhelder, 1969). We discuss its usefulness, along with other practical theories, in chapter 7.

Another classification scheme that can be helpful to teachers is that on temperament. Research psychiatrists Chess and Thomas (1987) defined *temperament* as the behavioral style of an individual. It is the "style" of behavior, not the "why" (what motivates them) or the "what" (the content and abilities that go into behaving). They found that normal children from early infancy differ in nine categories of temperament, some examples of which follow:

1. *Activity level* refers to motor functioning. Even from infancy some children tend to be active in their behavior, whereas others show this trait to a low degree. Teachers will see some children wiggle continually as they work, whereas others sit still.
2. *Approach or withdrawal* refers to the individual's initial reaction to any new stimulus, be it food, people, places, toys, or procedures. Teachers will see some students stand back, not ready to respond to a new stimulus until they have grown accustomed to it, whereas some of their peers go out eagerly to meet a new situation.
3. *Rhythmicity* refers to the regularity of the individual's behavior. Some children, from early infancy, eat, sleep, eliminate waste, and socialize almost by the clock, whereas others, the arrhythmics, at the opposite extreme of normality, do these irregularly.

Some students will settle in for the class period, grow restless toward the end of the lesson, and show other signs of being influenced by their "internal clock," whereas others will behave in a "studious fashion," regardless of what the schedule is or whether lunch time is at hand. Attention span and persistence are two more categories of temperament with educational significance.

Knowing about some of the ways in which people differ is important. It explains, for example, how perfectly normal children who are arrhythmic but assigned to rhythmic teachers can become behavior problems without anyone's realizing that at the root of the situation is a difference of temperament—perhaps present from birth.

The teacher has all of these types in the classroom, and the teacher is also one of these types. He or she will find it useful to be aware that different behavior—very active or very inactive, impatient or leery about meeting new experience, very rhythmic or the opposite—is still normal and may be more or less unchangeable in some students, even into adulthood.

You may want to do what Barb described in her interview: "After learning about temperament in class I went to the library and read more. Then I mentally classified myself and several of my students. I saw where I meshed with some of them and where I didn't. Then I developed plans to deal with what I call the 'temperament gap.' "

During your professional career you will find it helpful to become acquainted with a variety of modes of classification and especially the theory and rationales behind them. Also, you will want to learn how to put these systems to work. For example, students vary on how much control they feel they have in social situations. A study of junior and senior high school students has shown that those who feel "they have some degree of control over what happens to them" tended to exhibit prosocial behavior in the classroom: that is, they were rated by teachers as being task-oriented and considerate in contrast to distractible and hostile (Bradley & Teeter, 1977).

What is the practical value of such a finding? If a disruptive student believes that luck almost totally controls how he or she makes out in school and other social situations, then changing this belief may modify his or her behavior. How could a teacher change this belief? Would setting up a contract that rewarded him or her for his or her own successful performance help the student learn that he or she can have some control over the outcome of situations? Would involving the student in decisions about his or her punishments help him or her develop a feeling of control and decrease misbehavior? These are effective measures although they do not always succeed in changing every student's behavior. Only by trying them can a teacher know whether they will work in his or her classroom.

## DEALING WITH TROUBLING AND TROUBLED STUDENTS

For your needs as a student teacher during your brief stint in the classroom, we believe the most useful classification system is one that is practical and useful to you. It should help you become aware of troubling and troubled students. The troubling students are those whose behavior creates difficulty for the class and the teacher; their actions distract or disrupt the ongoing teaching–learning process. Troubled students are those who are unhappy with themselves and who often have great difficulties in interpersonal relations.

Troubled children can go unnoticed in the classroom for a long time. Carla told about an experience 2 months after she started that made her first realize the nature and something of the depth of the problem of one troubled boy, Christopher.

> 3/3: One thing happened today that did upset me. When the kids were lined up waiting for the buses some punching occurred. I asked the children to stop, saying that I thought we were all friends in our class and that I was upset they were doing something that might hurt a classmate. At this point one little boy, Christopher, said that nobody liked him. I said that I didn't know why he said that—that I really liked him (he's really a very sensitive and likeable child). I was hoping that some of the kids would also contradict him, since they could all hear him, but nobody spoke up.
>
> Christopher always sounds as if he has a cold and does not enunciate any sounds well. I feel this is a big factor in his lesser communication with classmates and maybe a reason why he feels "unliked" by his peers. I feel bad for the kid. I really do like him and would like to make him feel more comfortable with his peers. I'm not sure how to go about it, however.

Although Carla applied her common sense knowledge of human behavior, she did not understand that: (a) She was indeed on the correct road of helping Christopher in the classroom by her interest and sensitive understanding; (b) This kind of problem is not quickly remedied. Her supervisor, after rightfully complimenting Carla for her handling of the situation, explained that Christopher did not need pity or sympathy. He needed understanding and the kind of creative teaching that would give him some experience of success.

Troubling children and adolescents vary in how troubling they are. Some discussed here might be considered tame compared with those who act out their anger and frustrations in overt acts of aggression against classmates and even the teacher. These "tame" examples are useful, however, partly because they are much more frequent than the very serious cases, but also because their greater simplicity facilitates learning the principles involved in acquiring effective coping techniques.

For example, what principles are present in Mrs. S.'s management (described here) of a situation in which one student tells you that another one called her a "bad name"? Jean described the following:

1/19: Through observing Mrs. S. handle an emotional incident today, I learned how to handle it. The incident consisted of Margaret telling Mrs. S. that another girl had called her a bad name. Mrs. S. asked Lauren, the accused, to apologize to Margaret. Lauren walked over to Margaret but couldn't say that she was sorry; and then Mrs. S. said to her (very effectively), "Lauren, it's so easy to say nasty things, but very hard for us to say we're sorry." I thought that the lesson was well conveyed and made a positive impression on the child. Had the situation been mine to handle, I'm not sure I would have been able to do such a good job. Now, however, I feel that this can be incorporated into my way of thinking.

Before you read further, consider how you would have dealt with the problem. Did you wonder why Mrs. S. did not first ask Lauren if she was "guilty as charged"? In all probability Mrs. S. knew enough of the students' behavior to assume the report was correct. Furthermore, Lauren did not deny it. Mrs. S. was effective because she was not riled up by the use of a "bad name" and was not vindictive. Being clearheaded, and in command of herself, the adult was able to express matter-of-factly the kind of human wisdom that hits home, no matter what age group it is applied to.

Besides having the desired impact on the children, Mrs. S.'s behavior, when followed consistently, has long-term consequences. With regard to this episode, Margaret had the satisfaction of knowing that her teacher would protect her against abuse in the classroom. She would not have to accept abuse and internalize it (i.e., "swallow it," which is never good for mental health) or carry on some kind of a fight in the class and suffer bad consequences.

Lauren learned that antisocial behavior was unacceptable and also that her teacher was a human authority figure who did not condemn or humiliate her but could actually understand and reflect her difficulty about apologizing. Also the rest of the children, or those within earshot of the incident, learned all of these lessons, although at lower levels of intensity than the leading characters.

The troubling child can be the bane of the student teacher's existence. Because your effectiveness in the classroom depends on your success in coping with troubling children, we deal further and concretely with this in chapters 8, 9, and 10.

Whatever the age group or class level, coping with the troubling student requires an attitude of respect combined with clear and unrelenting firmness. That is why a basic principle of this book is that success for you really means fostering your own development, so you can feel and react like the adult authority figure and class leader you are perceived to be by your students. If you are like most student teachers, it will take you time to make a transition — to move from the relatively passive and subordinate role of student that you have had for years to the active and superordinate role of teacher. That change is probably the most crucial professional adjustment you will face during student teaching.

## AVOIDING PROBLEMS

We refer again to Jean's log about Mrs. S.'s handling of the situation involving name-calling. Besides reaffirming her position as a fair, humane, but forceful teacher, Mrs. S. avoided unnecessary confrontation and subsequent damaged relationships and negative attitudes. She did not threaten: "Now, Lauren, either you apologize to Margaret this minute or I'm sending you to the principal." Never — yes, we use the absolute here — compound problems by creating unnecessary confrontations. They do nobody any good.

Student teachers must also guard against whatever vestige remains in them of a childlike grudge (e.g., She did it to me, now I'll get back at her). Once the offending student is punished, the episode is terminated, even if he or she shoved you or used an obscene word to describe you. For the sake of your professional effectiveness the experience of such unpleasant interactions should be the occasion to think more about preventing them.

There are many ways to prevent avoidable problems with students no matter what their age. A few are mentioned here, first by Roger:

> 5/18: Mrs. M. feels it is more beneficial to reward good behavior than to reprimand bad behavior, and I agree with this. While this is something I try to keep in mind, and remember to do at times, it comes more naturally to me to ask a student to stop an inappropriate behavior than to praise another for an opposite, acceptable behavior. However, I will continue to work on this.

Bored students find ways to stimulate themselves. Sometimes they do it by provoking classroom trouble. Laura found a creative way to deal with one boy's boredom.

> 2/15: Leonard is extremely bright: for the most part, the group activities are below his level. Today when we were going to have a story I decided to let Leonard read

it for the class. He did great. It solved the problem of his being bored, and the kids enjoyed it too.

At the end of her student teaching, in a discussion with her college supervisor, Dorothy said a most valuable lesson for her was learning to listen to the children. She discovered this principle after the following incident:

> 3/25: I felt so bad today. Actually I felt like an ogre. Tracy asked me to go to the bathroom twice while she was doing seatwork, but she had just gone to get water. I said, "Wait till you finish coloring." Well, a few minutes later she peed in her pants and gave me this look. I told her I was sorry. I just hope Tracy doesn't hold it against me. I took her aside and said that I was really sorry.

From her experience, Dorothy learned the value of listening and trusting as problem-preventing tools. From hers, Nancy learned how, in the future, to avoid the kinds of problems that develop when a teacher has unrealistic expectations.

> 2/2: The kids put on their plays for the other ninth-grade English classes today. We explained that these were works-in-progress, not finished productions. The second-period group's play was a fiasco, but fun. They were disappointed and mad at themselves. Definitely a learning experience.
> I'm more relaxed and accepting again now that it is over. I think I was taking these plays too seriously and expecting too much. The "mad" notes the kids wrote me, after I asked them to, said I was asking too much, and I think they're right. We went into these plays with the idea of having fun and learning to work together. I got too hung up on technical things. I guess it's been a learning experience for me, too. I hope so.

## HOW FRIENDLY IS OK?

One question that comes repeatedly from student teachers is, "How friendly should I be with the students?" Our answer is: A teacher is not a friend. Teachers and students have different roles in the classroom and different responsibilities: Being a close friend with students conflicts with being a teacher. Contrast friendliness — an attitude of interest in the students' welfare and support for their efforts — with that of being a friend, which means being a peer, a co-equal involved in the personal lives of others.

Some student teachers deal with their uncertainty in the class by seeking approval from everybody and anybody. If they have a great need to "win" the students' favor, and if they work toward this goal, they may find themselves unable to manage their class. Arnold wrote about his cooperating teacher's warnings:

> 4/11: . . . I asked her about my control over the fifth-period class. She told me that I was getting too close and that the guys may soon treat me as a friend more so than a teacher.

Beth talked with her cooperating teacher about being a friend with the children. Here is how she thought about it and what she did:

1/9: Ms. W. discussed with me the issue of being too much of a "friend" with children. Ms. W.: "If you become too much of a friend, the children will run over you." I agree, but where is the happy medium. I feel she is too extreme, but, how do you handle discipline problems? For example: Alice said Donna took her black crayon. Donna denied it. How do you handle this? I responded by saying, "Donna, Alice said you have her crayon. Will you please give it back?" Donna said she didn't have it. I asked her again, very nicely, but Donna continued denying it. When I told her to clean out her desk she immediately returned the crayon. Looking back, I can see that I was too cautious, still talking to Donna as if she was a friend of mine rather than a child. Maybe Ms. W. isn't too far off. I'll have to try her way.

## LOGICAL PROBLEM SOLVING

It is true that teachers are sometimes expected to accomplish the impossible. Take presenting a lesson, for example. Imagine finding material and an approach that will hold the attention of 20 or more youngsters long enough for you to get key points across, to have them understood, digested, and made part of their body of knowledge. Teachers have to do that several times daily with children and adolescents and, as Amy reported, it does not always work:

3/2: I began a unit on space today by reading the children a short story about a mouse and what happens when she sees the moon's reflection in a puddle of water. I also hung up a skylab poster. I was pleased with the poster because the children took to it right away. The story however had its ups and downs. At one point the children seemed really interested in the story. Then a few of the children became very disruptive and the whole class began to lose interest.

I think the whole problem with the lesson though was when I stopped to speak to the disruptive ones and when the story was interrupted by an interesting but lengthy point. Some children lost interest then. I also think the interested children began to mimic the behavior of the disruptive ones.

One good aspect of the lesson was that it gave me feedback in the sense that I now know what direction I need to go to hold all the children's attention. To prevent some children from becoming disruptive. . . .

Amy continued her analysis of the situation in her log, as she explored the many parts of that experience. She approached the problems in a logical way as a rational adult.

You will want to analyze problems you face in your class in this way, using a logical problem-solving approach, like CONTROL-C. You will also want to devote time to understanding the students in your classroom and to reflecting upon the kinds of relationships you have with them, individually and as a group. This is a helpful way to learn about yourself and grow as a professional.

As you examine your work, do not be hard on yourself, no matter what flaws or mistakes you identify. No teacher, not even a masterful teacher, has a succession of perfect days, a fact your cooperating teacher will certainly validate.

As you are analyzing your classroom work, bear another fact in mind. If school curriculums were designed mainly around the interests of young learners and if those learners were conditioned to a less authoritarian system, the student teacher would not have to be so cautious about maintaining his position of authority. Anthony found that out. After a particularly difficult day with his class, he asked his students why they "listened" to Ms. V., and not to him. He raised this question to the whole class. With the frankness that students can be depended on to give, they told him that Ms. V. gets angry and shouts. Anthony wrote:

> 4/19: I have found it hard to raise my voice and to keep from smiling. But I began to see that I had to try and see what would happen if I did. It worked, I'm glad and sorry to say. It sure made life easier, but it left me with a dilemma. Maybe when I have a class of my own I will be able to condition them to respond to me as the teacher without my having to shout. But it won't work here.

We agree that Anthony's hope is justified. It is possible to teach and control a class in that way. Some teachers do. A teacher can be the complete leader with a smile and without shouting. But a student teacher may not be able to do so in a class he or she was assigned—especially if the children have been trained to respond only to scolds, reprimands, threats, and other forms of intimidation.

We work with an imperfect educational system. Doing so is simply an everyday feature of life. Our present educational system is all we have. Although it is being improved—at a snail's pace—we must make the best we can of it. That means we use it as effectively as we can to help the children and adolescents of our country receive the best possible education under the prevailing circumstances.

# 6
▾▾▾▾▾▾▾

# Relationship With Parents, Principal, and Others: Figures in the Background

In fantasy and in real life absent characters sometimes play important roles. Hamlet's father, offstage except for his lone, ephemeral appearance as a ghost, plays a central part in that great drama. In a one-woman play about the poet Emily Dickinson, members of the audience sense that they are witnessing a drama involving many characters. Yet, all the other characters, some of them very central to the story, are "offstage."

How much that is true in the classroom! Neither parents nor principals nor department chairpersons are physically present, but each has a voice as to what goes on in class. Together, they determine some of the important limits within which we work: the size of our class, the curriculum we teach, the standardized tests we administer, the values we stress, the topics we may or may not discuss, and often even the mood children are in when they arrive at school. Other important absent characters include members of the school board, vice-principals, and fellow teachers.

## THE PARENTS

Most teachers have personal contact with parents in several different circumstances: Parent–teacher meetings and parents' night, individual parent conferences for special needs as well as "conference day," and informal parent visits during the school day. Selected groups of teachers such as teacher-coaches, band directors, drama coaches, and so on, may work closely with parents particularly when parents provide support groups for these activities.

*Parent-Teacher Meetings, Parents' Open House Night.* These school events are settings where you are most likely to meet the parents of the students in your classroom. These contacts will probably be brief, perhaps little more than a simple introduction. Nonetheless they can be meaningful, both to you and to the parents.

This introduction serves an important function for the parents. Now they can greet the person who had been but a name spoken by their child and perhaps repeatedly mentioned over the dinner table. Having met the parents once, even briefly, it might be easier to invite them for a conference about their child, should that be necessary, or to solicit their participation in some classroom or extra-curricula activity.

In most school systems, parents' open house night is scheduled once each academic year. Parents come to this event to learn about the year's curricula, to visit their youngster's classroom and to meet the teachers. For this reason and because parents will be in the classroom itself, parents' nights call for more preparation than school-wide meetings. If you are fortunate enough to begin student teaching in the fall when most meetings of this nature are scheduled, carefully observe how your cooperating teacher prepares for this event.

At the elementary school level most teachers decorate their rooms in such a way to represent curriculum and work produced by the youngsters. Curriculum materials are made available on (or in) the children's desks and the teacher often presents either orally or on charts the curriculum content for the school year. Equally important is a presentation about rules and student behavioral expectations.

Frequently teachers give an overview of homework guidelines and projects that will be expected during the school year. Many teachers talk with parents about developmental characteristics of children in their age group—basic information about bedtimes, stress, and how to help the child develop a positive sense of self and responsibility.

At middle and high school levels, parents are often given the opportunity to follow (in a much abbreviated time frame) their children's daily schedule. A teacher may have only 10 minutes to present him or herself to each group of parents. Teachers (and student teachers) must make the most of this by preparing in advance and putting their best foot forward. Parents of older students often seek information about grading procedures as well as homework assignments.

Open House night is not the time for individual parent conferences, but it is the time to let parents know you welcome the opportunity to meet with them. A brief word to an individual parent on parent's night will open doors to future opportunities for an in-depth meeting.

In most school systems, 1 and frequently 2 days/evenings of the school year are set aside for individual parent-teacher conferences. Parents are encouraged to come and discuss their youngsters' school progress on an individual basis. Often the success of such a day is dependent on how teachers approach this opportunity.

Observe carefully how your cooperating teacher notifies parents of this upcoming event and makes other preparations.

Although the process of preparing the classroom, and collecting work samples representative of recent classwork and student progress are important aspects of one's readiness, these tasks are relatively easy to carry out. More difficult, and perhaps more important, for both you and your youngsters, is to prepare *yourself.* That involves giving consideration to each student with respect to his or her progress to date, his or her status, what you would like to find out about the student from the parents, and the information about the student that you deem appropriate to share with them. To maximize your learning and effectiveness and to avoid embarrassment or causing harm by saying something that should be left unsaid, share your thoughts with your cooperating teacher.

Susi discovered that by reviewing each of the children with her cooperating teacher, she learned a great deal about them and a great deal about herself.

3/30: Beginning of this week I helped Mrs. C. write out conference slips indicating the strengths and weaknesses for each of the children. I found this to be really enlightening insomuch as I discovered my reactions to the children on a one-to-one basis.

I was hit rather hard by the realization of my own bias regarding each of the children. I discovered in a few cases I have been reacting toward certain children as extremes. One boy, for instance, is a constant discipline problem. I had no trouble listing his numerous weaknesses, so many, in fact, that there wasn't enough room. The surprise part came when I couldn't think of a single strength—not one positive attribute. This was very upsetting to me. I had horrible visions of stereotyping and self-fulfilling prophecies. Not trusting myself to make a mental note, I immediately started an observation sheet on the boy and have listed some positives. Also I have made an effort to provide him with positive experiences.

I also discovered difficulty noting weaknesses for the superlative children. I felt this was also a stagnant attitude inasmuch as it impeded pathways for new exploration. My attitude about them has been something like, they are so fantastic there can't be anything they need to improve on. I think in this case I need to reevaluate just how challenging school is for them.

Consider Susi in a parent conference prior to the insights she reported in this log entry. Parents would have been misinformed. The parents of the unruly boy would have become defensive ("You just mean you don't like our son?") or worse yet they would have accepted the version of him as "all bad." The parents of the "superlative children," as Susi called them, would also have been given a distorted portrait of their offspring. Susi's preparation made a big difference for her, as it will for you.

A good way to prepare for a parent conference is by being empathetic. By putting yourself in the parents' shoes you will understand that they want to hear about their child's strengths, weaknesses, progress, and problems. Further, because they want the best for their children, most will be willing—perhaps even delighted—to listen to suggestions you make about homework procedures, supplementary study materials, and so forth.

A difficulty many teachers and student teachers face in preparing for parents' nights is in mobilizing themselves to overcome their fear of meeting parents. Another problem is in taking the initiative in directing informative and useful discussions with them. Young and inexperienced people, in particular, have difficulty thinking of and presenting themselves as professionals to parents (who generally are a few years older and perhaps well established in the business world). But teachers and student teachers have something valued by parents: information about their children.

If you face excessive anxiety in thinking about parents' night, apply CONTROL-C. Discuss your concerns with your friends, cooperating teacher, or supervisor.

The best way to deal with any hesitancy on your part and to ready yourself for next year is to talk to parents while you are a student teacher. If your cooperating teacher provides you with this opportunity, you will see that most parents will take you seriously and will respect your training. More to the point, they will appreciate your helpful, constructive appraisal of their child.

In sharing knowledge with parents remember that you have a right to feel confident (you have been trained as a teacher), and you should remind yourself of that. If an occasional parent is unjustly critical of you, questions your behavior in the classroom, or even gets angry at you without provocation, put that in perspective. Remember that some adults (parents among them) lead lives of great frustration. They may not even be reacting to you personally but rather to their feelings about school, their difficulty in coping with the child, or their own reaction to authority.

After having actually been involved in your first parent conferences and assessed what they produced, you, like Laura will probably be relieved to find that they were helpful to you in understanding the children, easier to conduct than you expected (even if you had to deliver bad news), and a boost to your morale when you heard from parents about the positive impact you were having on their children. Laura expresses this in two log entries:

2/19: The parents I met were concerned about how their children were doing in school. After talking to the parents it became very obvious that the children whose parents worked with them at home were the ones who did best in school.

2/20: There were more parent conferences this afternoon. I had my first and second experience in telling parents that their child was most likely going to have to repeat unless they made tremendous progress by June. Both parents received the news better than I had expected. The conferences have been a very enlightening experience. A few parents complimented me and some said their children had spoken about something I had taught. It made me feel good hearing that.

*Individual Parent Conferences for Special Needs.* There comes a time when a student is so troubled or so troubling in class that a teacher decides it is both wise and necessary to meet with the child's parents. When the important people from a student's two worlds come together, a great potential for aiding the student is developed.

The motivation for conferring with the parents is often to exchange information—"to brainstorm." From this joint venture new understandings can develop that could assist both parents and teacher in planning a program to aid the student. Such a meeting is often useful in helping teachers understand what is happening to a child outside of school that could be contributing to problem behavior or to recent behavioral changes evident in class. For example, an increased need for attention might be related to an imminent divorce of the student's parents. Mo's comment during an interview is relevant:

> I couldn't believe it. Janet fell asleep during my presentation last week in mythology. She's such a great student. I got so angry. Her head kept nodding and finally she put it down on the desk. I tried raising my voice. Finally, I moved right in front of her as I spoke. Only her mom came for the parents' day appointment. It seems that her parents have been having serious marital problems. So Janet's taken on many domestic tasks as well as a part-time job and has not been able to get her usual amount of sleep. I guess that's why she fell asleep in my class.

So far we have noted how information from the parents can aid the teacher. There is the other side of the coin. A teacher may feel he or she can aid a student by making a concrete practical suggestion to parents and seeking their cooperation. For example, to encourage confidence in reading aloud, he or she could recommend that parents and student take turns reading a portion of a story to each other.

To aid a student hoping to attend college, the student teacher can assess whether the parents are familiar with the process—speaking to the guidance counselor, writing for information about several possible schools and about financial aid, studying vocabulary and math formulas before the SAT or ACT tests, and so on.

Following are some additional examples of student teachers' involvement in parent conferences. Although the cordiality and results of the conferences varied, as did the extent of the student teachers' involvement, in all cases the student teachers acquired new insights into students' behaviors. They felt better able to devise strategies to help them.

In the first example, Ginny was able to use information acquired during a parent conference in developing a plan to change a pupil's problem behavior. First, before creating a behavior change strategy, she had to consider how the boy's home and school environments differed and the kind of treatment he might get in each setting in the future.

> 2/20: I talked to Mrs. M. about Geoffrey today. She said that when she had a conference with his mother she discovered that his mother devotes all her attention to her children. She said that Geoffrey's family has financial problems and his mom

feels that the best thing that she can do for her children is to shower them with constant praise and attention. This helps to explain Geoffrey's attention-seeking behavior. So, with this in mind, I tried to reinforce Geoffrey's positive actions today and ignore the negative ones.

As a result of what I did, he was much more at ease and calmer. However, I'm concerned with the end result—I am giving more attention or praise than he will most probably receive in another classroom situation. Although I noticed a change in his behavior today (he was even more sociable with the other children), I really wonder if it is good to do this. Am I just preparing him to be a behavior problem next year? On the other hand, if I continue as is and then gradually taper off the amount of reinforcement, then Geoffrey might adjust. Only time will tell, but this seems reasonable.

Circumstances did not work out as well for Stan as they did for Ginny. Stan's parent conference with Theresa's mother, as we see in his log, left him with a greater understanding of a troublesome child's behavior but also with the knowledge that he would receive little or no support from the child's home.

1/10: Mrs. H. told me Theresa has been taught to punch people if they call her a name and that her mother spoils her and stands up for her constantly. Also, Theresa's mother's attitude is belligerent and she lacks warmth and understanding, possibly the understanding and attention Theresa needs.

I saw today that Theresa shows her need for attention by being aggressive, sarcastic, and distracting in the class. I don't know what the best solution would be, whether to ignore her or to keep her busy and make her feel important.

1/14: Today Theresa pushed a book off a boy's desk and cursed. She was also hitting Maria.

1/21: Last week Theresa said she didn't have to answer a teacher "yes" or "no." We had her mom in for a conference today. Her mom didn't smile or extend her hand as I introduced myself. During the conference, she, Mrs. H., and the principal agreed that Theresa should be forced to have respect for her elders. "But I'm still going to tell her, 'If someone kicks you, you kick him back,' " Theresa's mother said at the end. I thought, like mother, like daughter.

Stan looked for civility in Theresa's mother's behavior and found none, except perhaps in the agreement that Theresa "should be forced to have respect for her elders." But that "agreement" solved nothing, as Theresa cannot be "forced" to respect others. In assessing the meeting, Stan realized that to enlist this mother to help change Theresa's behavior would take time. It might also require conferences, dealing first with her mother's negative attitude toward the school. If a problem like this would arise next year, Stan thought, he would develop a year-long plan and enlist the aid of the principal, and of the school counselor in working with the child and his or her parents.

Mia felt both overwhelmed and excited after attending a conference with her cooperating teacher, Mr. H., and the parents of one of their ninth-grade history students, James. Her experience in this conference left such a powerful impression on her, that at seminar the next day she asked the help of her supervisor and fellow students in sorting out her thoughts.

> 10/20: During our "free" fourth period today, Mr. H. had scheduled a conference with James' parents. He asked me if I would like to sit in on the conference. I thanked Mr. H. for inviting me—and said yes, I would very much like to meet James' parents.
>
> Now, for some background info. I really like James. He seems personable, always ready to answer questions in class and to participate in class discussions. But I can't quite figure him out. He seems bright—but he's barely carrying a "C" average. I helped Mr. H. grade the tests from the last unit. James did well enough on section I, true-false. The fill-in-the-blank section was adequate. But he lost the most points on his essays. He never even got to the second essay and I could barely read the first essay. His handwriting was atrocious. He couldn't spell a thing—used the word their instead of there, our for are. You would have thought he was in fourth grade.
>
> Anyway—James' parents arrived, test in hand, as well as a book and pamphlets on the learning disability, dyslexia. They were well prepared—to say the least. They explained that while James was quite bright, he had difficulty reading, taking class notes, and in spelling. I couldn't believe it. They had a copy of his history textbook on tape and James could (and did) listen to the tape as he read along in the text each night. They asked if James could tape our class lectures—in order to help him study, because he had difficulty in note-taking. They didn't want us to "take off" for misspelled words in his essay and explained that James needed "extra" time in taking tests because it took him longer to read and process the questions. They offered us lots of material to read on dyslexia.
>
> Mr. H. seemed almost overwhelmed, but thanked them for the information and said he would take this information into consideration. He would also need to talk with the school's psychologist and the chairman of the history department. He would get "back to" the parents after that and thanked the parents for coming. We had classes for the rest of the afternoon and didn't have time to discuss it later. Tomorrow in seminar I'd like to discuss this problem. I don't know what to think.

Mia, with the help of her seminar leader and one fellow student teacher in particular (who had a dyslexic brother) felt enlightened. Bolstered by the reading of the literature James' parents had given her and the support of her fellow student teachers, Mia felt she could successfully accommodate James' disability by making minor changes in her lessons.

Mia's experiences show that alertness to parents' ideas pays off. Student teachers also have to be alert for less directly expressed ideas parents may hold. For example, student teachers need to watch for the possibility that parents feel that they are being blamed for their child's problems, groundless as such a feeling may be. If parents feel "accused," it will be difficult for them to work with school personnel. Blair was involved in trying to convince a parent she was not being held at fault.

2/27: Kevin cries on the average of once or twice a day. Mrs. T. and I spoke with his mother. She took it very personally, as if it were her fault. We assured her it wasn't, over and over again. Still she didn't believe us. There was little we could do for Kevin since we could not get his mother to do anything other than blame herself.

Student teachers often experience mixed emotions about calling a parent to set up an appointment to discuss a youngster's difficulties. They want to help the child, but a parent–teacher conference seems too grave a step. The mixed emotions sometimes stem from their own feelings of inadequacy because they have not been able to cope effectively with the child. Sometimes they come from the student teacher's hazy and unlabeled feeling that he or she is "telling on" the child and as a result the child is likely to undergo harsh punishment at home. Such feelings typically emerge strongest when the student teacher has had a problem with a youngster or if the youngster's behavior has special meaning to the student teacher.

With her cooperating teacher's permission, after seeing eighth-grade Tanya smoking a cigarette on school grounds, student teacher Denise called Tanya's mother. The call was difficult for Denise because she herself had experimented with cigarettes in high school and because, after having trouble with Tanya earlier in the term, Tanya was now responding well to her. After making the call Denise felt guilty, but she knew she had taken the right course.

A few days later Tanya began smiling at Denise again. More importantly, she stopped "hanging out" in the smoking area. This reinforced Denise's conviction that she had acted professionally.

Typically schools have either a formal or informal procedure about contacting students' parents. Early in your student teaching discuss your school's procedures with your cooperating teacher. You may learn that when a student is involved in a physical dispute, an immediate phone call is placed to the parents. Many teachers find that an early phone contact prevents a larger, more complex problem.

*Parent Visits During the School Day.* Parents visit their youngster's classroom both on their own initiative and also at the invitation of the teacher as part of programs to familiarize them with their schools. They come to meet the teacher, to see the class in operation, and most of all, to watch their child in action.

With both a student and a cooperating teacher in a room, one of them can take time to welcome an arriving parent and to describe the scheduled activities of the day. This should be done unobtrusively. A parent's orientation should include specifics about the content of the lesson, its objectives, and how they fit into broader goals. A copy of the materials the students are using should be provided the parent so he or she can follow the activities.

After the lesson is explained, the parent could be told that in watching the activities he or she might be interested in noting: (a) how attentive the child is,

(b) what his or her work habits are, (c) how the child follows directions, and
(d) how he or she relates to classmates. Parents also should be told that their
presence might cause their youngster to act a bit differently than usual. For instance, their child may be more or less hesitant to raise his or her hand and answer a teacher's question with a parent present.

You might well find yourself presenting a lesson with parents observing. What
is that like? Joanna reports what happened to her:

> 3/2: With three parents in the room I knew that the kids would be distracted, but
> not to the degree that they were. I was very surprised to see . . . [them] act ex-
> tremely opposite of what they had ever acted before.

The students were not only inattentive but they couldn't sit still. Joanna was
first disturbed by the disruption, but quickly regained control of the class. She
accomplished this by introducing the parents and then immediately setting the
students to work, assigning them material that, although not scheduled, generally held their attention. When she saw the slightest sign of disorder, she redirected their attention to the work firmly and in her usual manner.

Joanna's approach of requiring the same disciplined behavior as on any other
day was sensible. Postponing the scheduled activity and substituting another was
also wise. The only other deviation she made from regular classroom procedures
was to concentrate on giving the students whose parents were visiting ample opportunity to participate actively. Providing such opportunities makes parents feel
good and the youngsters happy, all without harm to the other children.

Juanita, near the end of her assignment, was scheduled to teach a difficult social studies assignment the last period of the day. As she was about to begin,
the principal and several politicians walked into the room and asked if they could
observe. Juanita's cooperating teacher said sure and privately offered to teach
the lesson. Juanita said "no," she was prepared. Much to her surprise the children sat, listened and then participated in discussion. Later, Juanita said, "They
behaved like angels."

*Parental Reactions to a Student Teacher's Work.*   From time to time an
action by a student teacher, perhaps an expression of warmth or caring toward
a child, will be brought to the attention of a parent and will move the parent to
react. Most frequently the student teacher gets an oral compliment or a note of
thanks from the parent. No matter which, it is a much appreciated boost to the
ego that should be enjoyed. Charlene reports the following:

> 2/11: Morris had been a terror at home and at school since his sister was born.
> That was 4 months ago. I had tried all kinds of ways of dealing with his aggressive-
> ness in class. Taking away privileges failed, the principal's office failed, and be-
> havior modification failed. Then I used role playing to show him that he had been
> behaving like a 3-year-old. We role-played for a week and it made a difference

at school and at home. Morris' mother called my cooperating teacher and wrote a beautiful, most flattering letter to the principal.

On rare occasions, the note you receive is not one of thanks. Dorothy shares an example of the infrequent critical messages parents occasionally deliver to student teachers. Negative though it was, it set off a chain of events that ended positively.

2/12: One of the girls handed me a note from Leona, who was waiting in the coatroom at the time. The note to me was from Leona's mother threatening that I "better let Leona have the Valentine party." The reason for the note was that on Wednesday, due to discipline problems, I informed the children that if their name occurred on the board with three marks after it, then there would be no party privileges for them. Well, Leona would not stop talking, therefore, I put her name on the board. But she had no marks after it and didn't lose her privileges. Leona misunderstood and according to her mother she cried all night because I wasn't going to let her share in the party fun and trade Valentines. Well, I got on the phone and explained what had happened. I told her mother Leona would be at the party as would everyone in the class. I also said, "I'm sorry that I upset Leona so much." After talking to my cooperating teacher I reported the incident to Mr. R. (the principal). He said I used a poor means of discipline, but to forget it.

*Parents in Non-Traditional Families.* Some years ago several self-proclaimed experts on America's future made the followed announcement: "The family's dead. Long live alternative life styles." The writers, newspeople, and social commentators of the time were wrong—very wrong. The family has not died, but rather has remained the keystone institution in the United States.

Over the decades the shape of American families has changed, adjusting to the times. It is not likely that the parents of the children in your class will be like Ozzie and Harriet Nelson, the Andersons ("Father Knows Best"), or June and Ward Cleaver ("Leave it to Beaver"). Although the families of the 1950s are gone (dad works, mom stays home and paints the white picket fence in front of their suburbia home, wearing a flowered dress and apron), family life will be as important to your children as it was to those in school a few decades ago.

However, the children in your class will probably come from families of varied make-ups. Statistics indicate that close to 10 million children now live in step-families and millions more dwell in single-parent homes. Thus, in the average class you should expect several students who have experienced the divorce of their parents and the subsequent change in their family unit and perhaps one or more whose family is in the midst of this kind of emotional upheaval. You might also have students in your class whose biological parents never married and those who have lost a parent.

Some children may come from intact homes where only one parent works outside the household, whereas others will have both parents working and may be latchkey children. Others may be living with aunts and uncles, grandparents, foster parents, or adoptive parents. Still others may shuttle back and forth between households, or live with one parent and regularly visit the other, who may live out of town or be incarcerated. The variety in family life is almost endless. Small towns, suburban areas, and the wealthiest communities are not immune to such variety.

Whatever familial arrangements you yourself may have experienced growing up, now you are faced with the need to accustom yourself to looking out on the world with a different perspective. For example you face the challenge of looking through the eyes of a child whose parenting comes from a mother who was 15 at the time of the child's birth, or from one who is an only child and unaccustomed to sharing toys and turns with his or her peers.

In their approach to issues like one-parent families — or other potentially sensitive areas such as religious and ethnic differences — teachers consider the particular learning needs of the classroom group. No matter the age of the students, teachers can contribute to their awareness of the diversity of backgrounds and ways of life of all people. This is not to say that one should discuss the advantages of one way of life over another; a teacher's responsibility is simply to build awareness and respect of such differences. This is particularly necessary if the textbooks included in the curriculum always refer to intact families and a way of life detached from one or many of the students in his or her class.

When classroom activity calls for making projects or cards for parents, or writing parents or guardians, you want to consider all the students in your class. For instance, if your art activity is to make Father's Day presents, it would be wise to individually approach the students who do not live with their dads to see what their preferences are. For one student the solution might be to make two father's presents — one for her natural father and one for her stepfather. A second student might elect to make a father's present and give it to a grandfather. In other words, what we are suggesting is to take such action that will give you the feeling that you have made things right for all your students.

Elementary school teachers, who deal with smaller numbers of students, are more likely to know about the stresses and strains in the children's families. By contrast, high school teachers, dealing with many more students in their classes, are unlikely to have that knowledge. They need to be sensitive to the possibility that a marked change in the performance or behavior of students may be due to difficulties in their family.

You may have personal contact with parents or parent substitutes in nontraditional families during conferences. The *process* of conducting conferences with parent substitutes, young parents, single parents, stepparents, and so forth is not different from that with traditional (dad works, mom stays at home) parents. The teacher is empathic, that is, he or she shows in what he or she says and does a genuine interest in the parent's concern and a sincere attempt to recognize and appreciate the feelings of the parent. The teacher listens carefully to get a broader picture of the life of the student.

The teacher may learn that the 12-year-old boy, who is a serious disrupter in class, is a source of anguish to the parent who feels helpless in controlling his aggressive behavior at home and in the neighborhood. Or the teacher may find helpful information indicating that the disinterested, turned-off 15-year-old boy in class is a joy at home where he maintains all his family's farm vehicles and those of the neighbors'.

The *content* of conferences about students from nontraditional types of families often is different and that is to be expected because some of the problems are related to familial status. For example, the son or daughter of a single-parent family is more likely than others to get less after school supervision, to have available fewer parental hours of help with school work or of advice about friends and behavior in general. Of course, in some single-parent families, the child is not at all deprived, but the probability is greater in those circumstances. As a result, teachers try to be sensitive to the special needs of students and parents. They try to be knowledgeable about resources in the school, school system and community that can be called upon for assistance, given their particular circumstances.

*The Absence of Parent-Teacher Contact.*    It would be difficult to imagine anyone disagreeing with the principle that parents and teachers can and should be powerful and effective allies in the education of youngsters. Between them they have the information necessary to develop a solid understanding of a learner's behavior and needs. Between them they can plan and carry out effective programs to foster the student's development. Because the potential power of a parent–teacher team in stimulating growth in an individual and in solving or ameliorating problems is substantial, why does it so often go untapped?

Even in your student-teaching period you will probably learn about parents who shy away from school. Their reasons are many and varied: Some feel they are too busy; some feel the teacher would be unhappy to receive them; some feel intimidated by the teacher; some feel that school visits are restricted to problem occasions; and some feel anxious in school because of unhappy or frustrating experiences during their own student days. As a group, working-class, minority, and immigrant parents have been found to be less likely than others to come to their children's schools.

A 1988 national survey by the U.S. Department of Education tells us about parent visits to schools. Parents of eight graders had the following contacts: 50% attended school meetings; 52% contacted the school about the child's academic performance; 35% contacted the school about academic programs; and 29% visited classrooms.

If we examine those facts in another way, we see that 50% *did not* attend school meetings and 48% *did not* contact the school about the child's academic performance. What can we do to encourage contact with *those* parents?

Some cooperating teachers are hesitant to make parental contacts, because of busy personal schedules or in fear of a bad experience. Those in the last group may be reacting to principals and department heads who get upset when an angry parent, perhaps irrationally, accuses the school of a perceived injustice to their child or objects to an assigned book. They also know that some administrators get disturbed—not simply upset—if the complainer is a powerful figure in the community who threatens to take the problem to a higher authority.

Because one angry parent can injure a teacher's reputation with the principal much more than a pleased parent can help it, some teachers steer clear of parents whenever possible. Why risk it? Of course, there is a fallacy in this logic. Parents who have had contact with a teacher are less likely to complain to the principal than those who have not.

If your cooperating teacher has minimal contact with parents, in all probability you will have little opportunity yourself, unless he or she finds it convenient to encourage you to handle meetings. In either instance, next year as a teacher on your own, the job of relating to parents will be yours. Because you, like generations of teachers who preceded you likely received no formal training in this area, cultivate whatever opportunities you have during your student teaching (Sarason, Davidson, & Blatt, 1962).

## THE PRINCIPAL

Your first contact with your school's principal may be the day you visit the school to meet your cooperating teacher. In fact, the principal may show you the school and be the one who first introduces you to your cooperating teacher.

As its administrator, the principal's role is to maintain the smooth functioning of the school. His or her job includes supervising and evaluating teaching and related services, playing a role in hiring teachers and staff, and administering all of the operations in the building. Most principals strive to operate their schools in an unobtrusive manner. They prefer to grant teachers the freedom within well-defined limits to conduct their classes as they wish, so long as the curriculum is followed. For the most part, principals operate in the background at least so far as the day-to-day life of the student teacher and his or her classroom is concerned. An important exception to this rule, however, is that student teachers are frequently observed and evaluated by the principal, whom they may call upon to write a reference when they are applying for a full-time position.

*As Classroom Observer.* Many student teachers quiver at the thought of having the principal as an observer. It is comforting for them to recognize that generally the principal is a strong advocate of providing the best possible learning experience for all people in his or her building, including the student teacher. That he or she should be concerned about you and your welfare is not surprising. Without the principal's support the school would not be involved in a relationship with the college of education and offer opportunities for student teachers.

The emotions aroused in some student teachers by a forthcoming observation by their principal are not unlike those associated with an observation by their supervisor. The student teacher can cope with them by preparing him or herself in the same way recommended earlier for a college supervisor's first visit.

Jane, whose school had an autocratic principal, found that teaching during an unexpected observation could evoke uncomfortable feelings. Early one morning late in her student teaching the principal walked into the class and saw the children out of their seats. Jane wrote:

> 6/5: Mrs. C. walked in and said "What are all of you doing out of your seats?" I explained to her about my "senses table" and how the children recorded what sense they used to guess what was hidden daily in a box. She said, "That's a terrible way to start the day. You kids sit down." Then she walked out. I was so mad. If she had a comment to make she could have said it to me in private and she shouldn't have told the kids to sit down when I said they could be standing.

Although Jane was understandably upset, she wisely avoided a confrontation, responding only with her explanation of the children's activities. She recognized that there was nothing to be gained by an argument. Although Jane's experience was negative, many student teachers have positive ones. That is, their principals provide them with insightful criticisms and sometimes with innovative ideas and a fresh perspective. In an interview, Molly reported, "The vice-principal had observed me, but not the principal, Mr. C. I had heard about how harsh he was, so I was glad he hadn't come in. Last week, in the middle of my lesson—in he walked—unannounced. Class went OK and afterwards he congratulated me. Turns out he was a science teacher and he gave me several good ideas. I actually told him that I hope he comes back again."

*As School Leader.*    Both as a student teacher and as a beginning teacher, you should find out as much as you can about the principal, his or her philosophy, and mode of school operation. Ask your cooperating teacher about the principal; tactfully ask other teachers too. If the principal is the kind of person who encourages teachers to talk with him or her, then you should do so. You will enhance your understanding of the school if you find out about the principal's educational beliefs and goals.

It is definitely to your advantage to have a good working relationship with the school principal. For one thing, he or she may be an excellent reference and the source of a letter of recommendation. For another, the principal may have some influence in who will be hired in his or her own school system in the next year or may have friends who are school administrators to whom he or she can recommend you.

Working under a principal whose educational philosophy and mode of interpersonal behavior are very different from yours need not be a problem. "And there sat Mrs. Z., probably the fastest paddle in the west," wrote Sheryl in her log. Even if you cringe at the thought of the paddle (or whatever is the ultimate discipline measure used at your school), and it is clear that you and your principal differ greatly about classroom control, you should see to it that the difference does not lead to open conflict.

Generally, it is only when a classroom is being so noisy as to disturb other classes, or a parent has complained about something that a principal regards as a serious problem, that he or she focuses on a particular classroom. In such instances the principal should not be faulted; it is the principal's responsibility to assure quality education to all students.

If you have your cooperating teacher's approval, when you are doing something that you feel might interest your principal, invite him or her in to observe. One of us recalls working with a principal who, unlike the cooperating teacher, believed children should have limited opportunities to leave their seats. One day when the class was making silhouette pictures of themselves, the student teacher invited the principal in to have his silhouette drawn. His picture was proudly hung on the classroom wall along with the children's.

In spite of the differences between this student teacher and principal, they worked effectively with each other because (a) the student teacher did not flaunt her different style and did not try to convert him; (b) the principal was tolerant of others and believed that if teachers maintained adequate control over their class, they were entitled to teach in ways consistent with their philosophies.

Because the school principal is the chief officer in the school and the final authority, he or she is the school's ultimate disciplinarian. A teacher sends a child to the principal's office when the teacher has exhausted all possible measures in the classroom and the student's presence is disruptive to the class. As a student teacher you will learn from your cooperating teacher the practices in your school about the use of the principal for this purpose. Occasionally sending a child to the office may be just the emergency measure you need at a particular moment. If your principal is supportive, do not hesitate to have him or her help you control your class in this way. However, as you may also be told, overuse of this measure is likely to lead the principal to believe you have problems controlling the class.

It is also possible that you may be placed in a school in which the principal is a valuable resource person. For example, he or she may be helpful in the development of a lesson or he or she may have specialized knowledge or skills to contribute to a unit. The principal in a school in which one of the authors worked was noted for his knowledge of the plants and wildlife in a park adjacent to the school property. This otherwise conservative, authoritarian principal could easily and most happily be prodded into conducting fascinating nature walks in the park, providing an excellent foundation for a science unit.

Sometimes, as in Bob's case, a principal may set a theme for the school. Bob complained, "I'm not happy spending 3 weeks on the town's anniversary, but the principal insists on it." The principal felt strongly that this date was an important one, to be recognized by the students in all grades. He did not indicate how the teachers were to plan their activities but only instructed them to absorb the students in the upcoming event.

During discussion at the seminar for student teachers, Bob came to see that the principal, as school leader, was in his right to set such a theme. (Ideally a principal involves teachers in the decision making.) In the seminar meeting Bob also learned the important lesson—important to all teachers but vital to student teachers—that they must operate under constraints of one kind or another in this real world. They must find what those limits are and, within them, come as close as they can to doing what they feel is best.

As you student teach and again when you have your own class, carefully sort out your feelings toward your school's principal. Do not allow yourself to be caught up in feelings that will prevent you from building a useful working and sharing relationship.

## THE OTHER TEACHERS

It is true that most of your hours in school will be spent in the presence of your cooperating teacher and students. However, you will encounter other teachers in the faculty lounge, the cafeteria, and the restrooms. At the elementary school level you may interact with art, music, and/or physical education teacher specialists who work with the children in your class on a weekly basis. Some children in your classes might see a speech or reading teacher specialist.

Many middle schools are organized into teaching teams in which two teachers are responsible for a major portion of the students' classes (e.g., one in math and science and one in the humanities). At the secondary school level you will meet other teachers in your own department, and also some from other departments, especially at meetings and in the faculty lounge. At all levels, if you have a desire for collegiality, and to learn from others, you will have frequent chances to build it. Many student teachers take advantage of these opportunities during their short stint in a school. Clearly there are benefits from experiencing more life in the school than that in one classroom in one corner of the building. More specifically, you can learn a great deal from the perspective of others in the school and from asking about their techniques of handling the problems you find difficult.

There are many ways, of course, of utilizing the resources of fellow teachers. Discussions and exchanging lessons come to mind quickly, but if there is flexibility in your school, the possibilities could also include observing and being observed by your co-teachers, teaching lessons at other grade levels, and so on. Furthermore, other teachers can be helpful in your hunt for a job. They may have information that is not yet public, such as the plan of Mr. Doe to leave his position to move to another area in the country or of Mrs. Doe to take a year-long maternity leave.

One of the important lasting results of the interactions with the other teachers is the professional identity that it helps develop. Previously, in the many courses that preceded your student teaching, yours was the life of the student, your thoughts were about courses, assignments, and grades. That is not the case now, at least not in the here and now, in your student teaching classroom and in the teachers' lounge. And it will not be the case next year either when you will likely yearn for a break to converse with other adults.

## THE STAFF

Armies, it is said, survive because of the soldiers behind the front lines, and elementary and secondary schools survive, we believe, because of the work of the staff. Although you as a student teacher will probably have infrequent reason to call upon the services of the secretaries, it is good to get acquainted with them, if for no other reason than to appreciate the totality of the school's operation.

Although the secretaries do the obvious tasks of an office, such as handling correspondence, phone calls, and supplies, some of their work is unique to a school. For example, they schedule rooms and special events, help check teachers' registers, and make many contacts with parents both by phone and by mail.

There are at least two reasons to develop good working relationships with the school support staff. First, on this as on any job, the work day is more satisfying when one has pleasant relations with co-workers. Compared with most other occupations, this point is in some ways even more crucial to the teacher, who needs good moments with adults because he or she spends so much time with children or teen-agers. Amy, commenting on her experiences as her student teaching was coming to an end, had this to say: "No matter how bad things were going, I could always be sure of a cheerful smile from one of the secretaries in the principal's office and somehow that helped make it easier to go back the next day."

The second reason is a more self-serving one. You may have an occasional need for assistance from the staff. For example, you may need to write or phone a parent or a community resource person and will want the help of one of the secretaries. It is much easier to ask such aid from a friend or acquaintance than from a stranger.

## THE CUSTODIAN

Professionals in most fields of endeavor have rare occasion to work with a building custodian. For a teacher, however, the custodian is an important figure. A classroom, even in a senior high school, is more likely to require extensive cleaning than a lawyer's or doctor's office. When your class leaves the room in a messy state it is reassuring to have confidence that the custodian is friendly and understanding.

Generally, custodians have long tenure on their job and acquire status and influence not usually associated with such a position. Their acquired authority is shown in the following excerpts from Dorothy's log. We want first though to stress that Dorothy's experience is an atypical one. Nevertheless, the report of it shows that the custodian, blue-collar worker though he is, has a quasi-professional standing in the school and often a sensitivity to the needs of the students as well as the teachers. We want also to stress our consistent point of view that the student-teaching experience is a prologue to your teaching position. This period is a good one in which to practice building relationships with the kinds of workers you are going to want to know on the job the following year.

> 3/7: Today I made another mistake. I used enamel paint in the classroom. Well, the children got it on their hands and just a little on some of the desks. Ms. K. had not been in the room all day so she didn't know what was going on. But when she found out I had used enamel paint she wanted to know why in the world I would use that.

> 3/8: A good thing did happen today. Mr. G., the janitor, came in the room during lunch and I was cleaning off the desks. He said, "What are you doing?" I replied, "Cleaning off paint." Ms. K. then said, "Enamel paint at that!" I explained the whole thing and said, "I know I should have used my head." Mr. G. looked at Ms. K. and said, "What are you for?" She did not reply, so he then said, "I mean isn't it your job to help her learn and give her guidance?"
>
> I must admit he picked up my ego and how thankful I was that someone finally told her what her position was supposed to be. All quarter I've wanted to ask what her job as a cooperating teacher meant to her.

> 3/9: Well, Ms. K. has been much nicer since Mr. G. made his comment yesterday. In fact, she even said to me today that it was too bad she wasn't in the room when we started the painting.

## A NOTE ON NEXT YEAR

We have, in Part II of this book, devoted space to the persons in your student-teaching life, very much in accordance with their significance to you. The students, the cooperating teacher, and the college supervisor were each given a separate chapter, and most of this chapter has been devoted to the parents and the principal, with lesser portions to other teachers, the staff, and the custodian. When you become a teacher in your own right the allocations will change in the following way: By then, you will have incorporated as part of you the guidance of the cooperating teacher and the college supervisor. You will no longer have a professional connection with them. However, next year, you will have a direct and more involved relationship with the parents, principal, and staff members at the school where you will be teaching.

# What and How
# You Teach

# 7

▼▼▼▼▼▼▼

# Curriculum: How to Stimulate Interest and Learning

By the time you begin your student-teaching assignment you will have studied the principles of curriculum, observed in a classroom, and perhaps participated in an early field experience program. During your student teaching you will enjoy that intense experience of witnessing your readings and studies come to life—in your very own hands, so to speak, with you as the central figure.

Our objective in this chapter is to examine the curriculum from the point of view of the student teacher. You will find the following topics:

1. curriculum guide/course of study: what they are, what they contain and how to use them;
2. the textbooks and curriculum of your student-teaching class(es);
3. observation of curriculum at work;
4. resources to help achieve the objectives of the curriculum;
5. your teaching and the curriculum, including the use of the arts, technology, and individualizing instruction;
6. assessment—looking back to help you in the future; and
7. next year—collecting material.

## CURRICULUM GUIDE/COURSE OF STUDY

You may recall from your study that the word "curriculum" is derived from the Latin verb *currere* meaning "to run." The noun *cursis* in Latin means "race" or a "course." In essence, we as teachers conduct a group of children or adolescents on a course; we head them down one pathway or another.

Those using a pathway or road generally have a destination. True, we could wander aimlessly, selecting roadways quite randomly. That can be an appropriate choice during a vacation, especially when we want to be totally carefree and can afford to arrive no matter where the path leads. It is totally unacceptable when we are responsible for the education of our students.

No dallying? But of course. We can dally only after we have chosen our objective (e.g., the basic concepts of decimals or of the American Revolution), made the important decision about the route we will traverse to get to our destination (e.g., chalkboard demonstration, drills, worksheets, laboratory experiments, games, drama), and set ourselves a reasonable timetable, taking into consideration all of our destinations during the term or year.

Then we will have a clear idea about how much time we have to dally. And dally we must, at least if we mean by that spending some time following the interests that arise quite naturally (and sometimes unexpectedly) out of the planned and scheduled work.

You will not be involved in selecting the curriculum objectives for your student-teaching class. That will already have been accomplished, probably carried out by a team of teachers and administrators, maybe under the aegis of the school district's curriculum council. These individuals look at a curriculum in its totality and build continuity in material from one year to the next.

Once you are established as a regular teacher you can play an active part in reviewing and revising the curriculum and in selecting textbooks. But for now, as a student teacher, the course of study that you are to be guided by is fixed. Still, that allows you considerable imagination in leading your students through it.

The curriculum objectives you must work toward are spelled out in detail in the school's curriculum guide. Typically, these guides explain the significance of a particular subject to the total educational experience of the student, and also detail the specific importance of each particular concept and skill.

After specifying the subject's importance, guides move right to the heart of the matter, that is, to the measurable, behavioral objectives, such as the specific skills to be learned in connection with decimals or the concepts to be understood in connection with radiation. Those objectives must be clear and concrete if by the end of a unit's work we are to reliably determine whether or not the students have mastered them, which is another way of seeing the extent to which our instructional plan has been effective.

To illustrate, one fifth-grade course of study in mathematics includes the following among its objectives: reducing fractions to the lowest term, defining "equilateral triangle" and "right triangle," rounding decimal numbers to the nearest whole numbers, 10ths, or 100ths, and then 70 other objectives. In the next section of the guide these objectives are correlated with the textbook selected for use in the fifth grade. Then suggestions are given for resource aids and materials on the given objective.

Filmstrips, audio recordings, kits, instruments, books, computer software, and other educational aids, as well as suggestions of visits, resources in the community, television programs, and other educational experiences, are listed. Also included is a section on lessons and exercises that the teacher may use to reinforce the learning of the concepts.

Finally, in some guides there are tests that can be given periodically to evaluate learning during the study of a given objective. Preferably these are tests that are diagnostic in nature, enabling you to pinpoint the particular concept or skill that each student has or has not mastered. With that valuable information you will be in a position to provide very targeted instruction.

College students in education, appropriately excited by the prospect of conducting a class as a student teacher, have a large supply of creative ideas. Upon seeing the school's curriculum guide, some of them become resentful, as if an overwhelming power were at work to force them into a lock-step kind of teaching. This is not so. The curriculum guide is intended to be just that, a guide, or a map. It will select a road for you to take and provide many helpful signposts and resources to use as you wish. But what you "see" on the road, at what stream or wildflower you pause, what berry you taste, what hare or fawn you photograph en route is for you and the interest shown by your students to decide.

The course of study or curriculum guide is an extremely useful resource. In all probability you will find sample course of study/curriculum guides in your college library. If you are not yet acquainted with them through assignments made in your education courses (and if you have not yet begun student teaching), you may wish to familiarize yourself with their contents now. See how they are written, their general format, their valuable content and the ways in which they can be helpful to you in your teaching.

## TEXTBOOKS AND YOUR CURRICULUM

If your cooperating teacher has not shown you the teacher's editions to the textbooks for your class during the first week of your student teaching, ask him or her about them. Ask how much your cooperating teacher uses them, how much he or she refers to them, how much he or she deviates from them, and what are his or her expectations about your use of them. Similarly, ask to see the complete set of textbooks used during the year and their accompanying teacher's editions. Study the volumes and get to know the objectives. Familiarity with these will help you become better acquainted with the program of the class and more ready to assume teaching responsibility.

The teacher's editions usually include the entire content of the students' text. As you explore yours, you will most likely find it contains information similar to that in a curriculum guide, although in greater detail. In addition to an overall description of the material and a list of objectives, you will find information on the following: the specific objectives of individual chapters or units, the instructional materials and vocabulary needed for each unit, estimates of how much time should be devoted to each lesson, and suggestions for handling evaluations.

Within each lesson of the unit there are detailed suggestions on ways of introducing concepts and instructing students in the material at hand. Frequently follow-up activities, evaluative tests, "challenge" activities and references for further study are also included.

Considering the need for large amounts of lesson preparations during the course of student teaching (not to mention during a full school year), commercially prepared textbooks and the accompanying teachers' editions are of great value. With their use you need not devise every single exercise, assignment and test that you will need. Instead you can save precious time by using those that they provide, in the original form or in an adapted form, altered to serve your specific purposes.

## OBSERVATION OF THE CURRICULUM AT WORK

Observation, as you have surely heard many times, is more than simply looking or watching. It is purposeful and focused.

There are few skills that will be as useful to you as observation in so many different ways throughout your career. Observation can be used for the purpose of learning your cooperating teacher's implicit objectives in a given lesson, the subject matter he or she teaches, the methods and techniques he or she uses, his or her own personal behavior (both initiatory and reactive), the reaction of the students, and the evidences of the success or failure of a lesson.

And observation can be used to help you gain a fuller understanding of the students. You learn a great deal by observing them in different settings, such as in the homeroom before activities begin, in the corridors between periods, or at certain transition points in a lesson. There are other uses, a great many in fact, that you might want to apply in order to acquire insights about the students — all in the interest of understanding and, therefore, teaching them more effectively.

We have several examples of observations made by Linda Kozusko, a full-time secretary who was attending evening college prior to her student-teaching assignment. Although the quality of her presentation of her observations is enhanced by her literary talent, one need not be an English major, as she was, or possess her facility in composition, to train oneself to make keen observations.

The first is a report of her observations in the school cafeteria, beginning at 8:30 a.m. We present Linda's log entry as an example of purposeful observation that leads to a deeper understanding of the students and of the learning environment provided by this school.

The room was enormous, especially with the added space of external landscape provided by the floor-to-ceiling windows that composed one entire wall of the room. It was very quiet; students moved to seats and either just sat, or pulled out frazzledlooking notebooks and small books to peruse. No one seemed in a hurry, either to talk or to study. The day was beginning for these students who had the pleasant expectation of a soon-to-open kitchen where breakfast would be available.

The students were all White in that room. They were as friendly as half-awake people can be expected to be, and they seemed not unhappy with the fact that it was Wednesday, they were in school, and the books in front of them had to be read. This sense of contentment was present throughout my day at Franklin High School.

Lunch hour was more hurried, laughter and calling replaced the silence and shuffling of the morning, but the lack of consternation, the smiling and the eating remained constant. Teachers ate among the students, talking with them, stopping on their way to tables to follow up on plans for some project, basketball news, play problems, etc. The classroom was not a set of walls; teachers and students coexisted on easy terms throughout the day's schedule (even during the fire drill in the afternoon) and in every hall and room that I entered.

It was nice seeing that school could be so open, so cheerful. I went away kind of happy that there are kids lucky enough to be in a free atmosphere in which to learn. I also went away feeling that the school was somewhat unreal – too White, too friendly, too campus-like, too disruptive-free. Perhaps this is an overreaction, but I can't help feeling that Franklin High may be just a little too "West" of cities, of hatred, of dirt. All that contentment may not be functional in the future world of these kids. I hope that this feeling is wrong and that the school is not so much an incubator or isolation ward as it appeared in a one-day glance.

This report and those that follow show the quality of observation that penetrates beyond the obvious. It shows what you as student teacher should look for. One notes physical attributes ("the floor-to-ceiling windows") and more so the human attributes ("friendly as half-awake people"). Going deeper, Linda generalized about relationships ("teachers and students coexisted on easy terms throughout the day's schedule"). Even further, she weighed what she had seen and speculated about its meaning ("all that contentment may not be functional").

Now after having made these wide-ranging observations, and after checking their validity, she would be in a better position to develop and teach lessons for these students. The same qualities, interpretive as well as descriptive, are evident in the following report.

The cold remains of what was at one time a form of ravioli sat on the cabinet. Next to it, a young man sat with a teacher, Ms. P., to whom he had come for advice on a project for another class. She was very informal with him, her language was that of an adult talking off-handedly with a kid, no pompousness, no "let me tell you how." They were talking about music, about themes present in the songs on a new album of folk music, and she was throwing in some names of appropriate research sources for a paper on one theme. They were involved with one another, eager to talk through the idea, eager to understand each other's feelings about the singer, the theme, music in general. It was good talk, profitable, I felt, for both. I didn't have any sense that Ms. P. had given up her free period to help a kid who was not her own student—all of which, in fact, she had done.

On several occasions during the day, teachers in the department of English identified their goal as being a "Renaissance Person." The creative drama teacher is a musician; he has studied dance. Ms. P.'s off-time activity revealed how thoroughly open to new ideas, new avenues of art and knowledge the teacher should be ready to pursue, how thoroughly open to interruption and brain-picking a teacher must be. I felt so very challenged: my 10 years of staunch secretarial avoidance of questions and interruption hung in the air of that room like tight-lipped gauze that will have to be torn down if I'm ever to teach successfully. All my narrow studies in literature cracked under me — what else do I know, am interested in? Ugh! What a challenge.

Linda's observations have brought her face-to-face with a problem a good many student teachers eventually confront: Even after all my courses, do I know enough to teach a meaningful lesson? Will I be asked a question I cannot answer? These natural doubts are usually soon overcome.

Moving on now to observations more directly related to curriculum, we have Linda's report on the behavior of a teacher in a course on fiction. The course was designed to encourage an interest in and habit of reading.

It is second period of the day and I hurry along a laughter-filled students' corridor toward Room 303 where I am to witness Franklin High's answer to the "uninterested reader" disease. On my way, I note a shortish teacher, zooming along with an enormous cart of books, stopping here and there to talk with students. I eavesdrop long enough to learn that the topic of one of his chats is girls' basketball scores. Upon entering Room 303 I find the energetic cart pusher is the man I've come to observe, Mr. W. His zeal for basketball news is immediately redirected into the students in his room, "What book you reading? Who needs a new book? Got a great one on. . . ." I'm reminded of the hospital aide who turns the inertia of illness into active interest through the appeal of a seemingly innocuous Milky Way [candy bar]. It's salesmanship I'm witnessing, high class, very sophisticated, salesmanship.

The buyers are ordinary-looking teens. Males predominate, and I'm told by Mr. W. that the course's appeal is that a free period in which to read is an opportunity valued by the blue-collar sons who spend post-school hours pumping gas or loading supermarket shelves. T.V. has become a drag for most of these guys, and the day's long hours of school and work make a second-period breather for silence and reading a pleasure to be sought. The students are not college bound. The goal for the course, one with which Mr. W. is enormously in tune, is to make reading a free, happy, and worthwhile experience.

He succeeds. A slight girl passes in two index cards (one is required after completion of each book) on which she has written her concise appraisal of the books she has read. Pinned to the cards is a poem, unexpected creative writing from a student moved to write her thoughts on the theme of one work. A huge, young football-type senior rolls over to our section of the room (desks and tables are in wonderful disorder; Mr. W. and I are sharing two seats dead center of the room near the cart) to display with great displeasure a large paperback. "It's boring." "Why?" "Same stuff all the time." "Why not write a parody on it?" "What's that?" "Mock it." Mr. W. uses every student comment and yawn to teach something – and it's so painless, this teaching.

He and I chatted at length. Kids inspire Mr. W. He loves their energy, their zest. (I'm afraid it's catching – 9 a.m. is a ridiculous hour for zeal.) A dedicated teacher, Mr. W. is working on his doctorate in education. His most important task as teacher: Make them write. He expects very little of each student: Read and respect the right of others to read; write a critique of each book, and whenever possible, write some original stuff on the works – a different ending to a novel, a better dialogue within a scene. The course is an elective; within this elective is complete choice of material. His cart is not the world – anything the student chooses to read is acceptable. He sees the writing of the students improving every week. He also brings films to class. *Of Mice and Men* is on the cart, and he will bring the film in soon for the students to see.

All the while that he and I chat, students read, write, approach the cart, bring a problem or thought to Mr. W. for straightening and also at times for simple sharing. Silence and sun prevail. My initial fear that Mr. W.'s zeal might overpower, making him the sole motivator for activity, dissipates as I realize that he's only an arm to the cart. The students are using him.

I'm excited to see this – a human teaching machine – push a button and your next novel is suggested, your misunderstanding of a word is sent to *Roget's* for qualification, your disgust with pornography's repetition is shared. I wonder how this happens. I hated the class I was in in high school whose purpose was similar. Perhaps the difference was that silence was mandatory; or perhaps it was the want of choice of material. More likely, though, is the fact that we never "did" anything with our reading. You read *Jane Eyre* and that was that. The requirement to place the reading experience on the page surely is an important character in this course's success. I'm excited by this realization. I share it with Mr. W. – he agrees. My first observation is worth coming here for – I've learned something. Translate an inactive, receiving experience into a communication, out of solitude into sharing, active writing from inactive reading, unconscious reaction to conscious, specified feelings. Read and write.

In the next report Linda relates what she witnessed and experienced in a course on creative dramatics. Her observations are worth taking note of, no matter what grade or subject you teach.

The course is open to juniors and seniors and is an elective. In its description (which is available to students when registering), the following focus is identified:

"In addition to a study of the structure and types of drama, the course provides acting experience, critical judgment, and a deeper enjoyment of drama through the total development of the student in a group activity that demands constant adjustment to other people."

The period which I spent with the class certainly demonstrated the characteristics identified in this description. In the first place, I was not permitted to observe – students and teacher hoisted me on stage and initiated my creative drama career right there in Franklin High School!! Did I fail, succeed? No. No one either fails or succeeds. We had fun, and that fact is something of a phenomenon in the face of stifling heat in the room and the lateness of the hour (it was nearly time for the close of school).

The teacher was there, but not there. Mr. S. focused our thoughts on a task and then withdrew, after a demonstration, to sit—all attention—on top of a couch to observe the class in the act of carrying through the task. For example, after assigning us into groups of three or four, he quickly identified to each group an activity to perform as a group (one of ours was to move a set of living room furniture into an awaiting moving van), and then become a member of the audience—the remaining class members to attempt to guess what we were doing.

During our act, he called out changes—"it's a piano"—to which we had to adapt and respond appropriately. This teacher's physical and mental agility, performed with ease and a cheerful manner, had no aggressiveness in it and surely moved this tired old student to find a new relationship with space, students, and objects. Bravo! My group changed three times during the period; in each new set of students, I found the students warm, happy, and as excited about the class as I. Discipline problems? No way. The kids supported each other through teasing, suggested improvements of activity, and applause. One devastating way that creativity came into play was through the presence of a student in a wheelchair. When this group was "playing ball" the ball (imaginary) had a way of getting caught in the spokes of the chair and he and the others had the devil's time freeing their "toy" for action.

Does the course "provide . . . the total development of the student in a group activity that demands constant adjustment to other people"—you bet it does. And through such a freeing, happy method!

The final observation took place in an atypical class, in that it was composed of only five students. We have included it, however, because of the characterization of the teacher, so different from Mr. W. and Mr. S. and yet excellent in achieving the curriculum goals. There is, as you know, no one correct way to be an effective teacher, or to teach content effectively.

By the time I had reached Ms. P.'s room, the heat and newness of the day had won. The class (in home economics) was tiny, five students, I believe, in all. The room was a combination lab and study; this day the students were at desks (large tables shared by more than one student) attempting to plan a menu. They also seemed a bit dried out and tired. Lethargy smacked from each of us in the brightly lit, pink and white cooking lab. All of us, of course, except Ms. P. She was as bright and comfortable-looking as the room. I saw my grandmother in her, so quiet was her way as she moved next to the students to encourage each one's search for recipes. No mean task apparently, since the young girls are terribly diet-conscious and planning meals to be eaten is a struggle against calories.

Of those teachers whom I had observed during the day, Ms. P. seemed the most at ease with her students. The "grandmother" image I think was not peculiar to me. She was genuine in her interest in why I was there, and I felt that sincerity. I'm sure others, for example, these hot, tired kids, also feel that sincerity. She worked the entire period, always aware of what each was doing (not doing), turning her attention to each of them to help. Watching her competent, friendly manner turn a dull period into a nice experience was, in a way, the highlight of my day.

By making these observations in the classroom, lunchrooms, and halls of Franklin High, Linda had learned a great deal about the students that would help her in planning lessons. She also "saw" three different teachers using very different styles of teaching to achieve the curriculum objectives of their respective courses.

It is true that some courses are more amenable to certain methods than to others (e.g., the controlled experiment in the physical sciences and role playing in the humanities, rather than vice versa). However, the differences among these three teachers were not due just to the subjects they were teaching but also to their general styles of relating to their students, their temperament as people, and the particular teaching strategies they employed — individual reading and critique writing by the first teacher, participatory dramatics (role play) by the second, and encouragement and support combined with an individualized research approach by the third.

As we said before, there is no one correct or effective way to implement the curriculum. As you become skillful in observing, you will be able to analyze the styles of different teachers. The best time to start doing that is when you observe your own cooperating teacher.

Answer questions like these in your log: How does he introduce a new unit? In what ways does he make the topic relate to the lives of the students? What else does he do to make it interesting? What activities does he initiate? How does he get the students involved in activity? What resources does he use? Diagnostic tests? Follow-up instructional methods?

If you were a student in his class would you have found a particular lesson interesting? Would you have learned? If you were the teacher, what would you have done differently? What assessment would you make of the effectiveness of the unit? After you have answered these questions, list issues you want to discuss with your cooperating teacher in order to get fullest benefit from your observations of his or her teaching.

## RESOURCES

It is no exaggeration to say that teachers' resources are unlimited. They have access to the universe. However, we restrict our discussion here, looking to materials close at hand to you as a teacher and to your students. For almost every subject in the elementary and secondary school there are teaching aids or other useful stimuli accessible without cost. Through the school window or in a walk around the block, teacher and students can find pictures to paint, objects to sculpt, and themes for poems, stories, essays, plays or narratives.

For early childhood and primary school arithmetic, there are the pebbles to provide the concreteness so important to learning number concepts and arithmetical skills. For science, there are birds to see and hear, trees to study, a collection of random items picked up from the sidewalk to classify or to analyze in a laboratory, and clouds and the wind to observe and study. For sociology and economics, there often is diversity of population in the area (if not in the classroom) and indications of historical change in the buildings in the surrounding blocks. Granted that in some suburban and rural areas, some of these resources are absent. To compensate there are probably others not available in a city school district.

Our stress on what is "in front of our eyes" if we will but see it is not intended to discourage the use of materials especially designed for the classroom. We favor their use. We believe, however, that you will be a more effective teacher and a more confident and independent professional if you can rely on your own imagination in choosing additional materials to incorporate in your teaching.

Essentially, we are asserting that resource usage should not be limited to what is listed in an attractive catalog (and then ordered) or by what is available in the school's storeroom. Usage should be based, first and last, on what kinds of concrete and illustrative or stimulating or provocative resources or experiences you think will help your students learn.

Once you set goals and identify your resource needs, by all means use the storeroom and the colorful catalog and any commercial materials available to you, but choose them to serve your purposes, by which we mean the needs of the children. The following outline conveys the diverse resources that may be available to you now and in the future.


## AVAILABLE RESOURCES

A. In classrooms
   1. Reference books
   2. Supplemental textbooks as alternates to assigned text or for group study
   3. Trade books, records, cassette tapes, compact disks, and videotapes
   4. Specialized equipment for science, mathematics, art, geography, music, physical education, etc.
   5. Computers and software packages
B. In schools
   1. Professional library that may include books, journals, magazines, pamphlets, information on reference sources
   2. School library, with accompanying borrowing privileges; the services of a school librarian
   3. Audiovisual aids including opaque, film strip, slide, overhead and movie projectors, videotape cameras and machines and a library of materials to be used with them

4. Specialized equipment as in A4, with larger and more expensive equipment
5. Writing paper and general school supplies
6. Art materials
7. Copying machines, typewriters, piano, computers, kitchen equipment
8. Space availability including auditorium with stage, gymnasium, kitchen
9. Specialized personnel including nurse, physical education, art, music, remedial reading teachers, guidance counselors, tutors, etc.
C. In school systems
1. Central library with accompanying borrowing privileges and the services of a reference librarian
2. Central resource center (with accompanying borrowing privileges for specialized curriculum materials)
3. Specialized personnel (as in B9) including the services of a drug and alcoholism prevention specialist, psychologist, speech therapist, and teachers of physically, emotionally, and educationally handicapped students
4. Buses for approved school trips
5. Central office curriculum departments (i.e., math, science, reading) to aid with advice and in acquiring needed teaching materials
D. In communities
1. Parents
2. Community library with accompanying borrowing privileges, the services of a reference librarian, and possibly lists of books for particular grade levels or subjects, books for classroom use, loans of artwork, films, videotapes, records, compact disks, tapes, and computer software material
3. Government agencies, as sources of speakers, printed materials, charts, pictures, equipment, audiovisual materials, and software
4. Businesses and industries, as sources of speakers, field experiences, and materials
5. Local universities, as sources of speakers, field experiences, and specialized resource centers for student teachers
6. Museums, historical societies, and national, state, and local parks

Of special long-term benefit to you during your student teaching will be learning to use audiovisual and other available electronic equipment. It is also useful to develop the habit of reading one or two professional periodicals in which you are likely to find timely and practical suggestions about curriculum.

## YOUR TEACHING AND THE CURRICULUM

We suggest that when you first go to your student-teaching class, locate the point in the course of study/curriculum guide(s) and the textbooks at which the class is working. Scan the prior sections to get sufficient background, then read beyond. Because your teacher might give you the option of teaching the unit or units of your preference, review the guide and the appropriate textbooks with that in mind.

When you begin to prepare for the lessons you will teach, study the relevant sections of the course of study and textbooks. Reflect upon the objectives so that beyond a question of doubt you understand what is meant by each of them. Thereafter, while referring to the textbook, you can begin to set your plans for each one:

- How you will introduce it in such a way as to excite the interest of the students
- What activities you will initiate to make the concepts meaningful in accordance with the conceptual level of the students
- What exercises you will employ to give them experience in using the skills connected with the objectives
- At what point you will begin your assessment of their mastery of the work and your diagnosis of their errors
- What you will do about those errors
- What your part will be, along with your cooperating teacher and college supervisor, in evaluating your unit of work.

As you think through these issues, remind yourself of five basic principles you have probably studied in your courses in education and other disciplines. Those principles are discussed here.

*Be Aware of Different Objectives, Affective as Well as Cognitive.* (See Bloom, 1956; Krathwohl, Bloom, & Masia, 1964.) At any given time a variety of objectives are implicit in the activities of the teacher and the students, not just the explicit one connected with a unit. While we set our goal, let us say, to raise the reading level of the students in certain specified directions (i.e., educational objectives in the *cognitive* domain), we are simultaneously involving the values and feelings of the students (hence, explicit or implicit educational objectives in the *affective* domain).

To illustrate, as young students are learning through newly acquired phonetic skills to read more difficult words in a story about a family, they are having reactions about the family portrayed in the story. It may give them positive feelings because it is like their family or negative ones because theirs (perhaps a single-parent family) seems inferior by comparison. Or, as a result of rapid-paced learning, the able student's self-confidence and satisfaction with school is reinforced while that of a slower child is diminished.

Negative affective outcomes are not inevitable. The sensitive teacher learns to anticipate them and to take measures to prevent or overcome them. For instance, in the case of the slower learner, diagnostic tests enable the teacher to aid that student. In the case of the child from the single-parent family, the teacher can make certain that such a family is not ignored in discussion of the story but is treated in the positive and constructive way it deserves.

*Be Aware That Thinking Ability Changes With Age.*   The thinking ability of humans of different ages, at least prior to adulthood, varies widely. Jean Piaget (Piaget & Inhelder, 1969) identified four major stages of cognitive development, each of which can be broken down into substages. Although the stage theory is still open to question—whether the stages follow strictly in the order given, whether one can be in more than a single stage at a time, whether the movement from one to another can be accelerated, and whether these stages are found in all cultures—there is considerable agreement that individuals' minds tend to follow a general pattern of development.

We briefly describe the stages here to refresh your memory (or to acquaint you with them if they are not familiar to you). We do it particularly to highlight the qualitative differences in thinking at the different stages.

1.  The sensory-motor stage extends from birth to about age 2, when the child starts to acquire language.

2.  The preoperational stage, which runs from about age 2 to 7, includes preschool and the first years in school. During this time the child can focus on only one dimension at a time.

The classic example used to illustrate this point involves showing a child a round ball of clay. Then right in front of the child, the clay is rolled into a long "sausage." The child thinks the sausage is bigger and therefore is made of more clay. He or she cannot coordinate the two dimensions—thickness and length. Because it is longer it is bigger to the child—he or she does not consider the fact that it is thinner.

The meaning for the teacher is that this child should not be expected to be able to work out problems that require simultaneous manipulation of two or more dimensions. When one encounters a child in this age group who is unable to understand (and most are unable) that a mother, at one and the same time, is also someone's daughter (two different dimensions!!), this child is not backward or dull, but simply at the preoperational stage of development.

3.  The stage of concrete operations extends from about age 7 to 11. Although students in this age group are noticeably different from their younger counterparts in their mental abilities, they still have limitations in their thinking when compared with adults. They are rigid and dependent on a concrete form of thinking—thinking that is tied to what they know through their senses or through manipulation. This means that they are unable yet to work out problems that require them to consider systematically a variety of possible solutions to problems. They are not yet capable of thinking in terms of hypotheses.

In teaching children through the age of 11 or 12, working with concrete materials is of exceedingly great value. Symbols, whether words or numbers, get their meaning from the world of concrete objects. One way to reduce the number of vacant stares during lessons and of failing test scores is to give concrete examples. For instance, help the children learn the concept of subtraction by letting them see the result of "taking away" some pebbles or marbles or pennies.

4. The stage of formal operations typically begins at about age 12. It is at this stage (which not all adults achieve or do not achieve for all kinds of tasks) that individuals acquire the ability to conduct the most advanced form of thinking. They can engage in hypothetical thinking; that is, they can consider a variety of solutions to problems, including those that are not available to their senses.

Having general knowledge about cognitive development and being sensitive to the cognitive level of your students will help you plan your lessons. Still another advantage in knowing how we humans develop our learning and thinking abilities is that it can help us, as teachers, accelerate the growth of those abilities in our students. Although there has been considerable controversy about the possibility of "accelerating growth," the best judgment now is that the kind of teaching that encourages active thinking (and not just memorizing and drill) does facilitate that development (Schwebel, Maher, & Fagley, 1990).

*Be Aware of the Importance of Questions in Teaching and Learning.* There are distinctly different kinds of questioning that a teacher can use, and the teacher should choose the type in accordance with the educational objectives to be met. Questions can be thought of as being at different levels in a hierarchy. Students must be able to answer questions at a lower level before they are able to deal with those at the next higher level. The levels are derived from the taxonomy of educational objectives (Bloom, 1956).

At the *knowledge* (or information) *level* we seek to know if the student has possession of essential facts, let us say, whether the student knows what a state legislature is. Next we are interested in the student's *comprehension level*: That is, whether the student can explain in a meaningful way, in his or her own words, what a state legislature is. At the *application level* the student is asked to explain the services that a legislature performs and the products that emanate from it.

The *analysis level* may be assessed by questions that break down material into its component parts and show relationships among the parts, such as questions that get at committee structure, party control, and lobbies. The *synthesis level*— the ability to put it all together—is tapped by asking for a description of the situation in the state if there were no legislature. Finally, at the *evaluation level* students use their own standards and values to critically assess state legislatures, maybe considering such standards as efficiency or speed and such values as fairness to all constituents and the influence of lobbies. Here, the questions are clearly not to get "right" answers but the students' own thinking and reasoning.

As teachers, our aim is to raise the level of questions so that students will have practice in thinking and reasoning at the highest levels, or if you prefer, in the deepest ways. For your purposes during student teaching, it is enough for you to be aware of the differences and to do the following: Use questions that challenge the students.

In virtually all situations you will surely want to tap the *knowledge* and *comprehension levels* of the students (Do they know and do they understand?). The *application level* is important not only because it is further evidence that they understand what they are studying, but also because students are likely to be more interested in class when they see usefulness in what they are learning. In the long run the aim of our education system is to help students develop to the point at which they can field any level of question. In other words, through questions we take the material apart, to understand each part. Then we put it together and have a deeper meaning of it.

To get the deeper meaning of material (e.g., the U.S. Constitution, the process of photosynthesis, or Keats' "Ode to a Grecian Urn") it is essential to *analyze* and subsequently to *synthesize* it. In the illustrations just given it is obvious that these critical approaches are necessary; however, even in dealing with more prosaic problems like why clothing fashions change so often, such intellectual strategies are invaluable. Teachers can give their students the opportunity to gain deeper understanding through the use of questioning (oral and written) at the analytic and synthesis levels.

As you prepare a unit for your student teaching, remember that the evaluative process is essential to life. Students need practice in establishing a set of values (e.g., democracy) and determining how closely the set of ideas (e.g., the Constitution) come to those values. Therefore, if possible, you will want to develop questions at the *evaluation level*. In brief, you will find when you teach that students enjoy the challenge of probing questions provided they are compatible with the approximate stage of their conceptual development.

One other interesting way to think of questioning is to break it down into the following two types: convergent and divergent (Ornstein, 1987). Convergent questions have answers on which most people generally agree, that is, they "converge." These questions can be as simple as "What is the capital of the United States?" or as complex as "What is the derivation of Einstein's theory of relativity?"

Divergent questions, as you would expect, have answers on which people differ or "diverge." Here is one: "Supposing we were choosing a new capital for our nation, what would you choose and why?" As you can see, such questions — and you can introduce comparable ones even at the kindergarten level — force us to think. Many students enjoy the discussions that follow such questions.

Some teachers encourage questioning to go both ways: teacher to students and students to teacher. When students get good experience in having all types of questions directed at them, they themselves can begin to think in terms of questions. Teachers open the door to curiosity and reflection all the more when they encourage students to share those questions with the class. We are sorry to say that studies show that teachers ask students too many questions (e.g., 40-150 in a 40-minute class) and students rarely ask any—about 2 (Sarason, 1990).

Tim shows that it does not have to be that way:

> 4/19: I made a discovery today! Well, it wasn't a real discovery because Pat (university supervisor) has talked about it a lot lately. For me, it was a great step. First, instead of asking a whole slew of little questions, like "How does the blood stream handle oxygen?" I asked, "Supposing you didn't have a heart, what would be missing?" At first they laughed and said "Your life." Then they started thinking and debating. I had them hooked. With this one question we got into more than half the reading assignment. And before class was over one boy asked what smoking did to the heart. I felt good.

Tim's experience gave him confidence. Children and teenagers do not want to be bored any more than college students. They respond to a teacher who respects and encourages their thinking ability—and who is not afraid to have them ask questions.

***Be Aware That What You Teach and How You Teach are Linked to Students' Behavior.*** Curriculum and the maintenance of discipline in the classroom are finely intertwined. The fact that an appropriate, well-executed curriculum can have a great impact on students' in-class behavior is discussed in chapter 8. Knowing that, and with a unit of instruction selected, you are ready to begin the process of planning your lesson. The process is straightforward: my objective; the road to get there; the time available; the dallying we will do *en route*; additional enriching material or activities to introduce if the lesson is completed sooner than I anticipated; additional time that can be added if, as a result of class interest or need, I decide that the lesson should be extended; and finally, the method that I will use to check out, both *en route* and at the end, how well I did in teaching to my destination.

The planning of a lesson is also a logicopsychological process. Your thoughts may be: The students in my class, no matter how homogeneous they seem, are bound to be different in their past experiences, in current state of knowledge, in interests, and inclination to attend to class activities. True, I am not a psychologist and my job is not to "analyze" them, but I will be better able to teach if, as I prepare my lesson plan, I think of particular students.

That way my plan will be directed to the faster as well as the slower students, the quieter as well as the more vocal, the girls as well as the boys, the educationally disadvantaged as well as the advantaged, the children of racial and ethnic minority groups as well as of the majority. My questions, my illustrations—yes, even my physical positions in the classroom when I teach—will be attuned to these differences and will enable me to capture most of the children's attention for most of the time.

We, too, are engaged in a psychological process as we present these ideas to you, a member of a diverse group of student-teacher readers. We are considering the questions and concerns that might arise in your mind, like: How in the world am I going to keep all these ideas in my head while I am teaching? Answer: Do not try to. The suggestions we have given are intended for your use primarily while you are planning lessons. By incorporating these ideas into your plans you will immediately increase the likelihood of a better lesson. In any event, you should not try to juggle dozens of ideas in your head in class. We pass them on to you in the same spirit as a coach advises the players to remember the basics, before they begin a game. For us teachers, the "basics" mean thorough knowledge of the substance of our unit, a solid plan, and a clear link between our plan and the composition of our class.

And another question: How can I be prepared for the unexpected? Answer: No matter how well you plan, the unexpected could arise in any given lesson. And, at least over a long period of time, on the basis of the laws of probability, it is likely to arise. However, you can lower the probability by seeking to anticipate "the unexpected." Consider the different questions students might ask. Answer them now, in advance. If a new one arises and you do not know or are not sure of how to answer it, be straightforward. Explain that you will find the solution by the next day. On the next day you would explain just what steps you took to obtain the answer, for you will be sharing with them the invaluable knowledge about the process of investigating and problem solving. Only then would you give them the solution. An alternative approach to that difficult question would be to make the search for a solution a joint one. Whichever you choose, it need not in any way detract from your status as teacher.

*Be Aware That Students are More Interested and Efficient if They Understand What They are Doing.*   Test out this principle on yourself. Think of how helpful some of your college instructors were when they explained how to go about doing particular assignments. They were even more helpful if they taught you to "step back" and look at your own ways of thinking about particular problems — in other words, how to be your own critic, such as in critiquing your own papers.

This process, as you probably learned, is called *metacognition*. It involves such activities as the following: *awareness* (e.g., awareness that I don't understand what I'm reading and I want to find out why), *monitoring* (e.g., setting a goal in what I'm studying, checking along the way that I'm working toward my goal by asking myself questions), *regulating* (e.g., when monitoring shows that I'm not understanding what I'm reading, I reread, or search for meaning in some sections, or draw on past knowledge to make sense of the text; Haller, Child, & Walberg, 1988).

When we prepare a lesson plan, *we* know what we are about. However, our students may not have the slightest idea what it is all about. So they go through the boring process of rote learning, or of trying to. One of the easiest jobs in

teaching is often neglected, that is, explaining what we are doing. The following
study shows the value of doing that.

The study involved children and teachers in 22 fifth grades in 13 elementary
schools (Book, Duffy, Roehler, Meloth, & Vavrus, 1985). The study focused
on teaching reading. Using a good system of controls, about half of the teachers
(the treatment group) were trained in the "explanation model." The model, which
they were to use in developing their lessons and in teaching reading, included:

> (1) an introduction of the skill to be taught (what, how, and why), (2) an explana-
> tion of the skill which includes the thinking process modeled aloud by the teacher,
> (3) teacher interaction with students during which (a) students are given a chance
> to practice the skill and to explain their thinking of the process, and (b) the teacher
> corrects mistakes and tries to get students to think through the use of the skill on
> their own, (4) practice in using the skill (e.g., on worksheets), and (5) application
> of the skill in connected text (e.g., books). (Book et al., 1985, pp. 30–31)

Besides learning about these components, the treatment group was shown,

> how to task analyze the skills they wish to teach, and how to put that thinking into
> the introduction of their lessons. They were asked to incorporate these components
> into their regular basal text lesson, and then to check their success in communicat-
> ing this task analysis to students by having the students answer the questions "what
> was learned?", "why is it important?" and "how do I do the task?" (Book et al.,
> 1985, p. 32)

The results were very positive. They showed that if teachers are trained to
use *explicit explanation* of what they are teaching, students *are more aware* of
the following: what was taught, how they would use the skill that was taught,
and why it is important. Furthermore, the investigators found that as they made
observations and interviewed the students during the study, these learnings became more pronounced. Students in the control groups showed no such progress.

The further "happy news" from this study is that the results were equally positive for students in the low reading groups. They, too, much more than their counterparts in the control group, were able to articulate what they learned, how they
would use it and why it was important.

As teachers, the more we try to put ourselves "in the shoes" of our students
and try to understand what they are experiencing in our classes, the more likely
we are to follow the example of the treatment group of teachers. We help them
understand what the lessons are all about so that they can monitor and regulate
their part in it.

We have a final point in connection with this section on teaching and the curriculum. Many student and beginning teachers have a tendency to prepare lengthy
lesson plans. That can be a valuable exercise. However, it is no substitute for
a concise plan with which you are so familiar that you hardly need consult it dur-

ing class. Effective teachers proceed through their lessons smoothly, keeping an open eye on student attentiveness and response and shifting emphasis as needed.

## Using the Arts

The arts belong in education and not only in their own right, as courses in the arts. Why? They have special appeal to people of all ages. Besides, they can be helpful in virtually any subject you might teach. Notice the excitement when you tell your students that you are going to present a movie. They will show similar reactions about putting on a play, doing dances, playing music, singing, or painting.

The arts usually involve attributes that attract young people:

1. *Human feelings,* as in the play, "Romeo and Juliet," the movie musical, *West Side Story,* the painting, "Mona Lisa," the song, "Yellow Submarine", and the novel, *Tom Sawyer;*

2. *Activity,* such as painting, sculpting, dancing, singing, performing a role, composing;

3. *Applications,* or seeing theoretical topics made more concrete, as when first and second graders learn arithmetic by "going shopping" in the make-believe store, fourth and fifth graders learn about similarities and differences in ethnic cultures by doing their dances, and high school students learn history through mock conversations between Jefferson and Hamilton, through listening to and comparing the music of northerners and southerners in 1860, and by examining the fiction, drama and poetry produced during the depression of the 1930s.

In the book called *Academic Preparation for College,* the College Board (1983) included the arts along with English, mathematics, science, social studies, and foreign languages. Then, in *Academic Preparation in the Arts,* the College Board (1985) showed how the arts help develop the following basic academic competencies: reading, writing, speaking and listening, mathematics, reasoning and studying, and also such basic skills as observing and computer competency.

We are highlighting the other side of the coin, that is, how the arts can be used to make the teaching of *the other subjects* more interesting, more exciting, even more learnable. It takes only our imagination to make good use of the arts. We can use any of the many art forms.

Role playing has special merit because it requires no equipment and especially because it catches the attention of children, teenagers, and adults. It can be used in virtually any subject, on any topic. For example, you could set up an imaginary conversation between Pasteur and those who ridiculed his germ theory in 19th-century France, or a confrontation between two imaginary friends to show how to resolve an argument.

## Using Technology

Welcomed or not, the era of "high tech" has arrived in America's classrooms. Look in any urban, suburban, or rural school and you will find computers and various other pieces of high-tech equipment. When you started kindergarten, teachers could manage to get by if they had working knowledge of only a few machines—maybe a phonograph, a tape recorder, a ditto machine, a film strip projector, and a movie projector. You will have much more machinery to master—but then you will have many more tools at your disposal.

What thoughts come to your mind when you hear the words "technology in the classroom"? Amy, a high school foreign language student teacher, made these entries in her log:

9/7: On my way to my cooperating school today, my first day, every fear I ever had crossed my mind. Would I get lost on the freeway or on the roads through town to the school? No, I practiced the route on Sunday. Would I get nervous when I walked into the classroom and saw Mrs. G., my cooperating teacher? No, I met her last month. She's nice and she'll help me. Would I put a Spanish verb in a French sentence during my first chance talking to the French 2 class? No, I'll be fine.

But a worry I never considered turned out to be the biggest one. The classroom computers. After all, I spent time and money in college to steer clear of computers. I mean I wrote my papers out in long hand and hired people to type them, etc.

Who expected you'd need to know how to operate computers to teach foreign languages? Well, Mrs. G. loves computers and worse yet, there's a bunch of computer whizzes in our classes. I'll have to admit to them that I don't even know how to turn those machines on. What will they think of me?

9/10: I stayed after school today. Just me, THE MACHINE, and a computer-tutoring program. Getting started was difficult. I'm 10 thumbs when there's mechanical and electronic stuff involved. But, with Mrs. G.'s help, but mostly by myself, I came to terms with this high tech thing. I'm a teacher and I'm proud to be one. I have to be a model, a good model for the kids. I tell them they can learn irregular verbs if they try hard enough, I'll have to do the same with the machine. Besides, I have to face REALITY. We are living in a high tech world, and my time and effort will go further if I use computers in my teaching. Reality can be painful.

11/11: I developed learning materials for my kids on the computer. IBM beware—here I come.

12/18: I went with my dad to pick up my own Christmas present. You'll never guess what Santa is going to be bringing me. Yup. My own computer.

By the end of her student teaching experience, Amy had become a "high-tech nut," a convert from the world of the computer-phobic. Under Mrs. G.'s guidance she learned how a teacher can harness the power of a machine and use it to enhance her students' learning. Ironically, during a farewell dinner that Mrs. G. hosted for Amy, Mrs. G. said to her:

Beware, Amy, computers and other high-tech teaching equipment are seductive. Don't be lured by their gloss. They are tools, just plain tools. And you are the crafts-person. You will find that for many of your teaching tasks the good, old-fashion, low-tech tools, like the chalkboard and the pen and paper, do a better job than 100 computers would.

One other point, please don't fall victim to thinking that new material delivered on a VCR tape or CD can provide a magical cure for a student's learning problem. You, the teacher, help the child solve the problem, perhaps by deciding to use a machine. In other words, don't let the availability of a new machine or a new tape tempt you to wonder, how can I shoe-horn this stuff into my lesson, when the question you want to ask is, what material should my students be taught and what is the most effective way to deliver it.

You know that thoughtful use of audiovisual and other instructional equipment makes teachers more effective, whether they are working with kindergartners or graduate students, or with exceptional children or those in any other classrooms. Developing your skills with instructional equipment is like any other task that you face during student teaching. If you want to maximize your chances of being successful, you need to analyze the situation, and determine what steps you can take to lead you toward your goal. In this area you can begin as follows:

1. Now (or as early as possible as you begin your student teacher assignment) and later, when you have your own classroom, conduct an equipment survey. Identify every TEACHING AID available (from the school, your home, your university, friends' loans) that could help you accomplish your teaching goals. This list should include chalkboards, bulletin boards, tape recorders, special books, phonographs, CD players, radios, slide projectors and filmstrip machines, office machinery (duplicating machine, photocopying machines, laminators), VCRs and cameras, overhead and opaque projectors, and televisions.

When your list is complete, do the following:

a. Place a check mark next to every item you know how to use.

b. Conduct a self-assessment to determine whether you find any of the items or equipment intimidating. Put a double check next to any item so identified.

c. Next to items without checks, put a target date by which you will want to have read the directions for the use of that item, and tried to use it.

d. Next indicate the target date by which you want to identify a resource person who will help you master the items with double checks.

2. Paste a copy of your master list of resources in your appointment book or somewhere else where it will be easily available to you. Each day, after you identify the objectives of the lessons you will be teaching, think about the best ways to get your points across. Consult the list of the resource aids that are at your disposal.

## How Much Individualization?

You are probably wondering why such a question should be asked. After all, individualizing instruction is a keystone in American education. However another keystone complicates matters: Ensuring that students spend a high percentage of time in academic learning activities, rather than in conversational asides, reading comic books, or staring out the window. Unfortunately these two important instructional principles collide. With about 25 children or teenagers in a room, it is difficult to work with one individual or a group of 4 and at the same time monitor the rest of the students (Copeland, 1987).

Some educators have characterized teachers as "decision makers." According to this model, teachers carry out routines watchful for *cues* about how instruction is proceeding. If a cue tells you it is not going as planned, you decide whether the situation is beyond your tolerance. If so, you decide what move to make (Shavelson & Stern, 1981).

For example, you asked a question about Tom Sawyer's behavior with his aunt. After several student comments, boys in the back start their own conversations, laughing loudly. That cue is beyond tolerance, so you interrupt the general discussion and tell the disruptive boys that they may talk in their turn and their comments would be welcome.

Every day, every class period presents challenges like these and you must react almost instantaneously. For example, in the lower grades, one child is crying, another must go to the bathroom, and a third is pushing a fourth. In an eighth-grade class, one is cursing another, a third has her head on the desk, a fourth is shoving a fifth. As Doyle (1986) said, teachers face very complicated sets of cues of different kinds and many of them come at the same time.

When you individualize, you focus your attention in one direction, and not in other directions. As much as you can help those students you are working with, you lose touch with the others. The fact that you cannot monitor the behavior of the others explains why individualized instruction is so difficult, unless a class has few students or the teacher has well-trained aides.

## ASSESSMENT

You have completed your first unit of teaching, and you come now to a salient feature of student teaching or, to be more accurate, of teaching in general. Assessment of progress during the course of the unit. And this is not the easiest or most comfortable process.

For the most part we are bound in retrospect to find some flaws in our lesson plan, our mode of instruction, our interaction with the students, and so forth. For this reason, we tend to put off criticism and self-criticism until tomorrow. Yet when things are fresh, it is of extraordinary value to review the entire process of planning and conducting the class through the unit, recognizing what parts of it went well, what activities, experiments, drills, performances, and the like were and were not effective and with what kinds of students.

You want to consider the interactions with and between students and your handling of the unexpected. Then come your findings from your interim diagnosis of progress, your change in plans resulting from that, and finally your end of-unit evaluation of student progress. How well did your students fare?

Ideally, you should do this type of critique prior to receiving evaluation from your cooperating teacher or college supervisor, so that you have practice at doing this independently. Even if circumstances do not permit that, you will find it to your professional advantage to engage in self-criticism.

Another critical step is to ask yourself about the future: What will you do differently and what the same the next time? To what extent will you change the proportion of whole-class to small-group teaching? Will there be more or less student participation? Will you again use the same reading materials, exercises, workbooks, illustrations, poetry, role playing, experiments, instruments, outside consultants? Will you plan to use the same kinds of questions? Were the questions that were representative of more than one level of questioning appropriate to the cognitive levels of your students?

If you record the critiques, yours and others, in your log or elsewhere, you will be able to evaluate your professional growth as you progress through student teaching and your first year as a regular teacher. You will also have a record of the resources, aids, techniques, methods, questions, and personal styles of your own that worked for you and that you might want to use in the future.


## NEXT YEAR

Lo and behold, your student-teaching experience will be behind you and the new school year will be upon you much more quickly than you anticipated. The summer is a time for preparation. Like a squirrel collecting food for the snow-covered winter months—that is the way you should occupy some of your available hours.

Get acquainted with the neighborhoods in the school district and the student composition that is likely to be represented in your class or classes. With that information and the curriculum guide and textbooks, you will be in a good position to prepare for your work next year.

Build a collection of resources for the units, at least those scheduled for the first part of the school year. Review all of the possible sources of materials: former cooperating teacher and college supervisor, other teachers in the school where you did the student teaching, your student-teacher peers, friends, and acquaintances who teach.

This is a time, too, to collect a set of materials that interest and excite students of the age group you will be teaching. These could take the form of quiz shows, cartoons, anecdotes, games, experiments, and how-to activities (repairing cars or baking). High school students will welcome illustrations and materials that are representative of teen-age culture.

We conclude the chapter by noting that, beginning next year, you will possess the power to plan your own role as a teacher. You will not be dependent upon others to tell you how to teach and manage the class or what materials to use. Advice is different. You will find it useful to receive and you may even seek it out. But you will be free to choose from it what you consider helpful and to incorporate that, as you see fit.

# 8
▼▼▼▼▼▼▼

# Expectations: What You Expect of Your Students

"There is nothing so practical as a good theory." Those words, attributed to psychologist Kurt Lewin, convey the spirit of this chapter. As far as any practitioner is concerned, research of value is that which can be applied in the work setting. Today thousands of investigators around the world are conducting studies that have potential value for teachers. We welcome any useful concept, method, procedure, instrument, or material they develop that enables us to work in the classroom at a higher professional level.

The teacher's life in the classroom is both predictable and unpredictable. Research helps us know what is predictable. Fortunately, enough of it is predictable to enable us to be comfortable and effective in our work. The rest of it, the aspects of teaching that are unexpected, gives this profession both its novelty and its challenge.

Regrettably, research has acquired a reputation that alienates many teachers from it. For some, it is veiled in a mystique as if it involved a unique and superhuman kind of intellectual process. The facts are different. Researchers engage in the same kind of thinking as teachers who seek reliable answers to everyday questions.

This chapter focuses on ideas that can have a powerful effect on your teaching. These ideas are about your expectations. What do you expect of your students in general? Of students who are "special" in some way? Of children of minority-group parents, of poor, maybe homeless parents? What you expect, and the consequences of your expectations are the subjects of this chapter.

## EXPECTANCY AND SELF-FULFILLING PROPHECIES

Many years ago an experienced, older social worker in an institution for children without parents (then called a "home for orphans") said to her young assistants: "It's what the children see in your eyes that counts. It's not so much what you say as how you say it that tells them what you think of them—what you think they can do and they can be. If we really believe they can learn, they will learn." She meant, in her wonderfully insightful way, that children respond to the expectations they sense.

She might have added that our expectations of children also shape our behavior with them, so that if we think they will do well we tend to do those things that help bring it about. Thus, we help to see that the expectation (or prophecy) becomes fulfilled.

That was the wisdom of a deeply sensitive woman, unforgettable to those who experienced it personally, but lacking in the controlled observations essential to convince a profession of its significance. Years later researchers began systematically studying teachers' expectations for children.

In a classic study by Rosenthal and Jacobson (1966), about 20% of the children in 18 elementary school classrooms were randomly selected as experimental subjects. Their teachers were told that these particular children's scores on an IQ "test for intellectual blooming" indicated they "would show unusual intellectual gains during the academic year." In fact, these children differed from others (control subjects) only in that they had been identified to their teachers as "children who would show unusual intellectual gains." And they did! Eight months later all the children were retested, and those in the first and second grades (although not the upper grades) who had been falsely identified as highly promising showed dramatic gains in comparison with the other children.

Hundreds of studies have been conducted since that one, and the results of these have been somewhat mixed. Educators who do not put much stock in the phenomenon have seized at these results to argue against expectancy.

As vocal as the opponents have been, however, there is too much evidence to discount the impact of expectancy. For instance, Rosenthal (1973) reported that 84 of 242 studies conducted showed that the expectancies of teachers (or subjects playing the role) did affect the performance of students (or other subjects playing the role). On the basis of this statistic and other literature, by the mid-1970s it seemed safe to conclude that the self-fulfilling prophecy was at work at least in some classrooms and for some children, and to recommend that teachers be mindful of it.

Since the 1970s, other studies have told us the following: Yes, teacher expectations lead to self-fulfilling prophecy effects, but not to any large extent. Generally speaking, teachers base their expectations on the students' past performance. They expect much from students who have records of good grades, and they expect less from students with low grades. In other words, as one psychologist said in a review of the literature on role expectancies, it seems as if student achievement has stronger effects on teacher expectations, than teacher expectations have on student achievement (Jussim, 1990). We expect future performance to be the same as past achievement. (Of course, past achievement may have been handicapped by inaccurate expectancies, maybe due to stereotypes about gender, race, or ethnic group, but more on that later.)

The same psychologist (Jussim) also said that "even though expectancy effects may be relatively small, this *does not* mean they are unimportant or do not contribute to social problems" (p. 30). Let us be more specific. If the "relatively small" effects were corrected through a change in expectancy, this could amount to a 20% improvement in performance (Rosenthal, 1984). In practical terms—in the lives of the children and the teacher—that is anything but "small" (Rosenthal, 1985)!

One important question has not yet been answered: Supposing that high expectations (i.e., higher than past performance, but judged to be realistic for students) were held not just for 1 year or less, as in many studies, but for many years, what would be the result? In other words, supposing a girl who has been doing "D" work in arithmetic gets the message year after year that she could do at least "B" work?

It is possible that the quality of her work would improve, because a small effect of self-fulfilling prophecy may accumulate over the years and have a sizeable effect on individuals. The negative can happen, too, for example, when a teacher in an early grade indicates in a permanent record, or orally informs the next teacher, that a child is disruptive in class. The child becomes earmarked as a disrupter and teacher after teacher could, in expecting that behavior, act toward the child in such ways as to encourage its fulfillment.

Gender differences must enter our discussion. The effect of negative expectations may explain certain differences in achievement between the sexes. There is evidence that parents perceive boys as being more competent than girls in math and sports. Their perceptions lead girls as a group (certainly not all girls) to value these two less and also to be less interested and involved in them.

It is human to choose activities in which you expect to do well. If your parents give you the impression that math and sports are not what your gender excels in, you are likely to look elsewhere. For girls, that "elsewhere" is English, in which parents expect females to excel (Eccles, Jacobs, & Harold, 1990).

These differences in the socialization of the two sexes can have serious consequences. The self-fulfilling prophecies for girls may lead them to have skills that do not qualify them for the better-rewarded traditionally male occupations (Eccles, 1987). Far fewer women are in the high-paying business world or in math–science positions.

We as teachers have little opportunity to influence parents' stereotypes about gender (or racial, ethnic, religious) differences. But we can make sure that we do not perpetuate them. First, let us see how our expectation can influence our students.

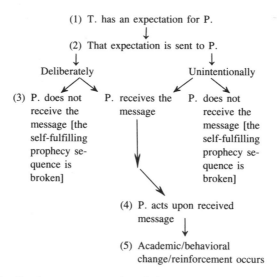

(1)  T.  has an expectation for P.

(2)  That expectation is sent to P.

Deliberately                                    Unintentionally

(3)  P. does not        P.  receives the        P.  does not
     receive the        message                     receive the
     message [the                                    message [the
     self-fulfilling                                 self-fulfilling
     prophecy se-                                    prophecy se-
     quence is                                       quence is
     broken]                                         broken]

(4)  P. acts upon received
     message

(5)  Academic/behavioral
     change/reinforcement occurs

FIG. 8.1.  Teacher expectancy and pupil change. Adapted from Leigh (1977).

In order to depict how a teacher's expectancy can affect a child's behavior or academic performance we have presented the chart in Fig. 8.1. It shows that the process begins when a teacher (T.) develops an expectation for a male pupil (P.). That expectation could be based on a student's past behavior, academic achievement, "reputation" in the school, dress, body build, gender, name, or other variables.

At Step 4 of Fig. 8.1 we see that the student acts on the teacher's message. That could mean he behaves like an angel, assumes a leadership stance with peers, or begins to make rapid growth in reading skills. It is easier to understand how a pupil can change his behavior, or assume leadership at his will, than it is to comprehend how he can "decide to make great progress in reading." Nonetheless, it can happen.

An ingenious study by Ira Goldenberg (1969), then of Yale University, shows how such "unexplainable" growth in reading could be fostered. He compared the amount of time the teachers spent with each reading group, and whether each group was given "prime time" (early-morning time when the teacher and children were fresh) or "least prime time" (before lunch or dismissal) or "neither prime nor least prime time." The results were unequivocal: Unwittingly, the teachers generally spent more and "better" time with the more advanced reading groups. That is, their expectancy was for higher achievement from these children, and the teachers performed in such ways as to have this prophecy fulfilled.

A more recent study of first- and second-grade reading groups in eight schools showed distinct differences in the ways teachers interacted with low versus high reading groups (Grant & Rothenberg, 1986). Children in the higher groups, but not the lower ones, were helped to acquire the skills, values and styles of behavior that gave them advantages in school. Teachers *do not deliberately* deny children in the lower groups these advantages. What teachers, themselves, are taught about slower students and about teaching leads them to treat the two levels very differently.

For example, Grant and Rothenberg, who were interested in the personal relationships between teachers and children in these groups, found that one important indicator of closeness was evidence of chats between teachers and students during lessons. They noted that chats made relationships less formal, more relaxed, and broke down social distance. To illustrate, children in a higher group chatted with the teacher about their homes. The teacher, in turn, talked about national parks and asked if any had been there. The students then shared their experiences. Some of this occurred in the low groups but to a lesser degree. For instance, when a child in a low group wanted to talk about his brother's birthday party, the teacher cut him short saying that they had to finish a story and they would talk about his brother's party at another time, suggesting that his comment was a diversion.

In summary, the teacher's chats with the students contributed to a pleasant, relaxed environment, one that carried over as the group turned its attention to academic work. The investigators also pointed out that these findings were consistent with other studies that show that teachers frequently created a warmer socioemotional atmosphere for brighter students.

The significance of these studies is clear. As a teacher you have considerable influence over the development of your students. That impact comes only partly from your effectiveness in helping them master important skills and knowledge. It comes also from what you as a teacher convey to them about themselves. They look hard at your communications, actively trying to "read" you. And this they do by listening to your words, watching your expressions, and noting your body language. You need, therefore, to be conscious of your communications to them, to be as sure as possible that you are conveying a positive outlook and the expectation of maximum possible development. It is then incumbent upon you to help them fulfill that prophecy through well-planned activity.

## WHAT YOU EXPECT OF STUDENTS
## WITH SPECIAL NEEDS

As you may have gathered from the prior section, what you expect of "special" or "special needs" students is likely to impact heavily on their educational success. Later in this chapter we consider whether we should think of all students as "special." First, we review some background information.

As you know, the term *special needs* applies to individuals at the two poles of the continuum of learning ability, students who are gifted and students who are mentally retarded, students with learning disabilities or behavioral disorders as well as those who have sensory, neurological, or other physical disabilities. A 1975 federal law (The Education of All Handicapped Children Act, PL94-143), implemented in 1977, mandated that a system be introduced into each school district involving the periodic review of each handicapped child for placement in the least restrictive setting. Unless the review weighs heavily against it, mildly and moderately handicapped children are placed in regular classes ("mainstreamed") and the school provides necessary specialized equipment and services on an individual or group basis outside the regular classroom.

In the 1985-1986 school year, 67% of all students who were certified as handicapped were in regular, mainstreamed classes, full or part time (Lipsky & Gartner, 1989). Under the circumstances, it is probable that you will have one or more mainstreamed students in your student-teaching class. If your knowledge of special needs children is limited, you will find some publications helpful. One of these is *The Special Educator's Handbook* (Westling & Koorland, 1988). Some books were written for the purpose of improving the professional's understanding both of the handicapped child and of the child's parents, with the special objective of facilitating effective communication with them. The authors of one such book, *Two-Way Talking with Parents of Special Children* (Chinn, Winn, & Walters, 1978) include a section on the needs of the special child. These authors explained that the handicapped student is first of all a child. His needs are those of the normal child, but their satisfaction is complicated by virtue of his handicap and especially by the ways in which people in his environment react to that condition. We now examine the important needs.

A primary need is for clear, honest communication. These special children do not need to be shielded from the realities of their handicap and its effects upon their lives. And they are harmed rather than helped if a teacher, out of pity, sets lower standards of scholastic performance and social behavior for them than for the rest of the class. A second basic need that has special meaning in the case of the handicapped is that for acceptance. A teacher, of course, can monitor whether or not this is happening in the classroom and intervene if necessary. A third basic need is for freedom to grow.

One of the ironies about the handicapped is that the parents' genuine concern about safety, health, and welfare leads them to inhibit their children's opportunities to, in effect, spread their wings and fly. By "protecting" them they can cripple them psychologically and physically. Teachers also fall victim to such overprotectiveness, so they must reflect on their own feelings and actions as a way of guarding against that.

These three basic needs hardly exhaust the list, whether for handicapped or normal children. However, they are illustrative of the special attention handicapped students require and of the sensitivities that teachers need in order to secure for them a facilitative climate.

Investigators have assessed the outcomes of mainstreaming in experiments in which regular and special classes are compared. Here are some examples of influential thinking and research.

The sensitivities required of teachers were highlighted not long after the important mainstreaming concept was enacted into law. For example, the author of one paper on physical education wrote that teachers should accept the fact that "sooner or later" they will have mildly and moderately handicapped students in their regular classes (Jansma, 1977). The article, devoted to inservice training programs, proposed covering many topics.

Not surprisingly, the topic given major attention is the attitude of teachers who have never had handicapped students in their classes. In the absence of what we would call an open attitude toward the students, teachers will be unable to become self-sufficient in serving handicapped children in their own classes.

For instance, teachers of diabetic children must be open enough to recognize and accept that although there are limitations to be aware of and precautions to follow, diabetics can engage in virtually all kinds of physical activities (Engerbretson, 1977). Teachers must also help other students to understand, for example, that the diabetic student may have to pause during physical activity to eat a sweet.

The mainstreaming of blind and visually impaired children has been found to work under specified conditions (Rogow, 1978). Most of them have already been cited, but for emphasis we repeat that the teacher must be ready to accept them as children or young people who have a handicap and must be acquainted with their special requirements for learning.

It is true that the successful integration of the blind into the regular classroom requires the assistance of specialists and the equipment and instructional materials designed for them. Still, effective mainstreaming of the blind depends most on the classroom teacher's readiness and that of his or her students: Both sets of students, the normal and the handicapped, must be ready to accept each other.

A review of the literature on role taking concludes with a call for further research to provide "educators with ways to increase the sensitivity of children toward the feelings, limitations, and needs of others" (Kitano, Stiehl, & Cole, 1978, p. 71). The authors reported that the relations between the handicapped and the normal were not positive and that the normals were generally unreceptive, especially to retarded children.

Asch (1989), herself a professional who is blind, quoted from a personal communication written by B. Davidson, a handicapped person. She wrote about schooling prior to the federal legislation of 1975:

Socially: We were isolated. Symbolically, and appropriate to the prevailing attitudes, the handicapped and retard classrooms were tucked away in a corner of the school basement. . . . Summing it up, the only contact we had with the normal children was visual. On these occasions I can report my own feelings: Envy. Given the loud, clear message that was daily being delivered to them I feel quite confident that I can also report their feelings: Yuch! (Asch, 1989, p. 190)

"Yuch!" This reaction, we believe, is less common now that fewer students are segregated. Nonetheless, the need to prepare students to feel comfortable with each other is urgent.

There are various ways of preparing students. A good one involves structuring class groups so as to bring the handicapped and the normal into a close working relationship. Another effective procedure that, like the one just mentioned, also arouses great interest in the students, calls for the use of role playing. Role playing, carefully planned and sensitively carried out, can help students in the upper elementary and higher grades appreciate the feelings and limitations of being handicapped.

A teacher's feelings about the handicapped make a vital difference in the classroom climate. Sensing that, one student teacher asked the following question:

I'm troubled by something that surprises me. In some of the classes that I'm student teaching in, a few of the teenagers are mainstreamed. I don't know much about that—but that's not the problem. One boy has trouble walking, uses a crutch and all that. One girl has trouble with her speech—stammering and halting speech. Also there's a big 16-year-old who is mildly retarded. I'm bothered by it, I get distracted. Sometimes I pity them and get upset. I wonder if I'm going to have kids like that in my own classes? I had sort of a problem like this when I came to college. You see, I came from a pretty-much all White town, but after a while I really got used to being with Afro-American, Hispanic, and Asian students. The same thing is now happening with handicapped students.

We framed the following answer: Chances are you *will* have special-needs students. After all, one major objective of the Education of All Handicapped Children Act of 1975 is to see that students are schooled in the "least restrictive" environment. That means they should, if at all possible, have the opportunity to learn in regular classes in the company of their nonhandicapped peers. It also means that teachers have to modify their teaching. For example, your teaching strategies may now call for special emphasis on auditory communication for the sake of visually impaired children, or increased repetition and more simplified explanations for the mildly retarded students.

The physical environment has to be considered, as in the case of having wheelchair accessibility. When it comes to tests and grading, you take into consideration such facts as the poor handwriting of some neurologically impaired students and the need for extra time for students with certain learning disabilities. The needs of any given student are spelled out in their Individualized Education Program, usually referred to by its acronym, IEP. This is prepared for an individual student by a team, including a representative from the school's special education department as well as the classroom teacher and other school personnel. Each school year a student's IEP is revised and a parent conference is held to review the plan.

Having said all that, we have still left your important question unanswered. Because it is so honest, you are already on the road to dealing with your problem. It is not unusual for caring people to be upset in the presence of children or adolescents who have handicapping conditions, even if those individuals are accustomed to their handicaps and are well adapted to life.

One way you can help yourself is by getting to know them as individuals. That way you will find that they don't need and don't want pity. You will also find out what you discovered when you came to college and began to mingle with racially and ethnically different people—that they are different and yet the same. They, too, have insecurities and fears but also strengths, and they too enjoy humor and lightness. They *do* have special needs, and we cater to those needs. Beyond that, we try to interact with them as we do with other students.

In all probability you will be able to do that once you sit and talk with those three students in your classes. If the problem persists and you continue to feel uncomfortable, you might want to discuss your reaction with a member of the team that prepares the IEPs, maybe the special education teacher, the school counselor, or psychologist.

The law calling for placement in the least restrictive environment has been in effect long enough, it seems, to test its effectiveness. So far, the results of evaluation studies are by no means conclusive. Evaluation is essential considering the estimated costs of special education exceed those of regular education by as much as one and one-half to four times.

The job of evaluation is made difficult by the very features that make special education special: Special "curriculum, materials, methods and techniques that are not routinely used in regular education settings" (Kavale, 1990, p. 35). With variations in defining which students are handicapped, differences in the definitions of the handicaps, and differences in curriculum, materials, and so forth, it is not easy to get clear-cut and reliable results.

Problems about defining handicaps are serious. The current system of classifying students and certifying them as handicapped has been called into question. For example, the label of *learning disabled* is one of those considered to be vague and ill-defined. Although some students do have neurological problems, when literally millions were found to be classified as having "minimal neurological dysfunction," the label lost its credibility among some specialists (Coles, 1987).

As a result of questioning the diagnostic classification system, some states are moving away from its use. Instead of classifying students in terms of their disorders or disabilities, they are categorized in terms of need. For example, some students need close supervision and small-group instruction; others need intensive study of language, and so on. This functional system may become more popular in the years ahead.

Despite the definitional problem about *who* is handicapped and *how* to categorize him or her, research results do favor mainstreaming. A meta-analysis of 11 studies examined the following: How well did special education students in mainstream classes compare with those in segregated programs? The overall results suggest that mainstreaming results in:

1. improved performance as measured by achievement in subjects like reading and mathematics;
2. improved attitudinal outcomes such as students' self-concepts, attitudes of mainstream and regular students toward each other, and parents and teachers towards mainstreaming;
3. improved process outcomes, such as interactions among students and between students and teachers (Wang & Baker, 1985-1986). Prior studies had found the academic but not the other outcomes, so this was an important one.

Wang (1989) emphasized the need for more research before concluding that mainstreaming is the answer. While mainstreaming is being evaluated, the fundamental idea of separating any student on any basis is being challenged. There is an inclination among some to oppose the concept of the "least restrictive environment" on the grounds that this involves segregation. Once regarded as progressive, it is now seen by some as an obstacle to integration for those in great need of that. For example, Lipsky and Gartner (1989) argued, "the current failure to provide quality education to all students, and the perpetuation of segregated settings is morally unsound and educationally unnecessary" (p. 285).

Asch (1989) believes that too many disabled are still getting "crumbs." Yet, in her opinion, "the law provides the right guidelines when thoughtfully applied. Although it works far too little of the time, it does work sometimes, and it can work far better" (p. 204).

Thus far we have concentrated on the handicapped. Only in our first paragraph have the gifted been mentioned in connection with special needs students, and then only in passing. That we have neglected them up to this point and that we devote much less space to them is not fortuitous. It is, in truth, a sample of the treatment the gifted have received in the professional literature. The limited research has, however, indicated that there is a definite need to identify children who are gifted in order to challenge them and stimulate their intellectual activity (Schlichter, 1977).

Among the teaching-learning procedures recommended are some that are equally appropriate for many less-than-gifted students. One procedure of that kind, self-directed learning, has been characterized as a "priority for the gifted and talented" (Treffinger, 1975). The author identified some misunderstandings about that kind of learning: It is not random, disorganized, or unstructured, and it does not "just happen." On the contrary, self-directed learning must be cultivated.

Treffinger derived his proposals from research both on the gifted and on programs for stimulating independent thought and learning. He formulated four steps in the process of moving toward self-directed learning: (a) identify goals and objectives; (b) assess the entering behavior of the students; (c) identify and implement instructional procedures; (d) assess the students' performance.

He then provided four stages within each of the four steps. In each stage the student achieves a little more independence. It is helpful for teachers to note that even gifted children need instruction in how to study if they are to assume ever greater responsibility for their own learning.

Many models for the education of the gifted have been proposed. These models attempt to enrich the curricula and introduce teaching strategies suitable for such students. The models are presumably useful whether you are a specialist teacher of the gifted or a regular teacher who has some gifted students in class. Our belief is that the strategies (discussed later) can be very useful to the regular teacher.

The models that have been proposed include such variations from usual procedures as those in content (greater depth and elaboration), in process (such as independent study and research), and in product (such as addressing real-life problems) (Maker, 1982). The models proposed strategies like acceleration, creativity training, and use of higher-order thinking skills.

Do teachers of the gifted use these strategies? Do they use them more than regular teachers and pre-service teachers (like you)? And if they don't use them, why not?

Starko and Schack (1989) designed a study to get answers to those questions. Their subjects were 57 teachers of the gifted, 85 regular classroom teachers, and 176 pre-service teachers. Through a questionnaire, the teachers indicated "how well the identified strategies met the needs of gifted students, how confident teachers felt in using the strategies (teacher efficacy), and how often they actually used the strategies" (p. 119).

The researchers found that as they went from pre-service to regular teacher to teacher of the gifted, the subjects saw a higher need on the part of the students for those strategies, greater teacher confidence in using the strategies, and greater frequency of use. In other words, experience, specialized training and teaching made a difference in their attitudes toward needs and strategies.

We believe that a most useful finding for student and beginning teachers is the following: The researchers found a much closer relationship between teacher efficacy and use of strategies than between their recognition of need and use of strategies. Teachers had to be confident and comfortable, it seems, before they used a new strategy. That is hardly surprising, yet often forgotten.

The researchers recommend the following to those responsible for staff development: There is less need to persuade teachers that these strategies are useful than in giving them simulated and real-life practice in using them. Practice leads to feelings of mastery and confidence and these lead to usage.

## EXPECTATIONS IN A MULTICULTURAL SOCIETY

Many Americans travel abroad to enjoy the "difference." They find pleasure in diversity—different foods, different expressions, different practices. In our multicultural society we are blessed with that diversity right here at home. We can walk through most cities and many a town and find restaurants representing half a dozen or more nations. And they are represented here by more than food. Their cultures and, to some extent, their ways of life are here too.

Such cultural differences can be used by teachers to great advantage. They can liven a class by opening up new and interesting views of life. Before we turn to those positive sides of multiculturalism, let us look at some negatives.

These are not negatives about multiculturalism itself, for we would be hard put to find any. These negatives are problems that arise as a result of stereotyped thinking about people who are different. Such thinking stems from an ethnocentric view of the world—from seeing the world only through the eyes of one's own group. People who think this way usually are not deliberately narrow-minded; they just have not had the opportunity to correct the stereotypes they learned. As a result, they usually expect less than the students' potentials. Here, in Irene's log, is an example of stereotyped thinking.

> 2/21: Today I tried to do some "teaching" in the teacher's room. Quite unexpected. I was all alone having coffee in my free period when Jim [another student teacher] came in. One class he teaches is algebra. We got talking about our classes. He has an odd classification system: "These kids are good in basketball, these others in putting on nail polish and doing their hair and those in working a grill, so I don't expect much from them in algebra." He said it with a straight face and really believes it. He said he has good classes, no problems, because he "knows their nature." He doesn't put any demands on them.
>
> When I started to point out some social reasons for concentrating on sports or appearance, he cut me off. Believe it or not, he blamed it all on evolution! I told him that I teach biology and that evolution has little if anything to do with the work they get into. That's when a couple of teachers came in and changed the subject.

People like Jim can retain such stereotypes so long as they avoid and deny information that challenges their beliefs. That kind of thinking makes it easy for teachers in one sense: If students are not learning, it's their own fault, their ethnic or racial genes. The teacher does not have to challenge him or herself by setting higher expectations and trying every means possible to encourage the students to aspire to and to achieve higher goals.

Ordinarily, as we said earlier, when we travel abroad we enjoy the national and ethnic cultural differences. Whether we find them "quaint" or "colorful," we usually take pleasure in describing them to our friends. "You should have seen them in that town on the sea! You should have seen how they eat (or talk, dance, greet each other, etc.)" Yet, when we "live" with those "different" practices, we are not so comfortable, partly because we do not recognize them as such. Here is an example.

A high school in Stockton, California had a school population composed of about one third each of Hispanics, Blacks, and Asians. Because of racial tensions and the outbreak of fights, the Community Relations Service of the U.S. Department of Justice offered its services to introduce a problem-solving strate gy. That involved a series of meetings with parents, teachers, administrators, and staff. It began with 2 full days of student sessions (Hule, 1989). On the first day, students met only with their own race/ethnic group, on the second, in mixed groups. The effort was well worthwhile. For example, within 1 year, the suspension rate during a quarter dropped from 147 to 47.

The student discussions revealed ignorance about each other's practices. For example, it became apparent that the Asian students felt intimidated by the Black students. How were they intimidated? The Black students, they said, stood in the middle of the hall and talked loudly. The Asian students, having freely shared their concern, now learned a helpful principle about culture: Cultures differ in many ways and one of these is in their style of speech; some differ, for example, in how loudly or softly people speak. Knowing this, students are less likely to be frightened by a loud-spoken person or group, or to attribute shyness or submissiveness to a soft-spoken person or group.

The strategy of the Community Relations Service was to bring the differences—uniqueness—to the surface in the interest of solving problems of group relationships. We can bring them to the surface for this purpose and for other reasons, like making our teaching more interesting. Cultures relate to every subject we teach. They are obviously related to literature and history. Virtually every culture has given something of value to the arts. And members of so many different cultures contributed to knowledge in mathematics and the physical sciences.

We can bring cultures into our classes, either by indicating their contributions to the topic under discussion or by having representatives of cultures make presentations, depict native dress, or share distinct foods, authentic speech, and unique customs. Often our aim in doing this is to bring concepts to life and to add spice to classroom experience. One way to test the potential benefit in doing this is to run through your own experiences as a student. So to speak, rewind the mental videotape of your elementary and secondary school history. See where your teachers might have added cultural examples to enrich and enliven your learning experiences. Could it have made a difference?

In summary, when you walk into the classroom as a teacher, for the most part you carry with you the identity of a single culture. The challenge you face as true professional is to serve students who together may be identified with a dozen cultures. To serve them well means keeping your expectations deservedly high. You cannot know the distinct meanings of the birth of a sibling, the death of an uncle, a smile, a touch—certainly not for all the cultures in our country, but you can become aware of the meaning of differences, as the students in the California high school did.

Racial and ethnic differences in our country are no longer submerged and denied. In reaction to the years of glorifying and imitating the White Anglo-Saxon status type (or really a stereotyped version of it), other groups are now strongly identifying with their past and proudly and publicly displaying their present image of themselves. Probably because of years of oppression, some act in ways that exaggerate their separateness.

Dorothy was a White student teacher assigned to an elementary school in a poor neighborhood. In her second-grade class about 25% of the children were Black. One of them, Thomas, concerned Dorothy because she felt that he was much more capable than he showed in his work and that he lacked self-confidence. Her expectations were higher than his own: Her problem was how to get him to aim higher. Dorothy's excitement about the possibility of helping Thomas is shown in the first of two log entries that were written on two successive days.

1/10: When Thomas came back from the testing (by the school psychologist) Ms. K. was assigning math to be done before the lunch bell. For the first time Thomas did all the problems. He came up to me saying, "Look, I finished just as the bell rang!" I replied, "Thomas I'm so excited for you—you have the problems all done. May I check them?" Thomas: "Yes." I continued to examine his paper. When I found a problem wrong I would ask him to recheck the problem. Thomas would and then bring it back to me. It appeared that the psychologist showing interest in him motivated Thomas to work. I'm very pleased with the math problems Thomas did.

1/11: Still having a tremendous discipline problem. Felt it's due to the lack of stimulating the children's interest plus the fact of someone new in the classroom and they are testing how far they can go. During reading groups Thomas continued hitting other students, causing confusion and disturbance. I asked Thomas to sit at the experience table to finish the work Ms. K. had assigned the class. It appears that the daily English, spelling, and writing assignments do not hold his attention. Thomas continued jumping up out of his seat, hitting other children, and they then started shouting, "Thomas is bothering me."

He got Keith and Horace siding with him, and then when Horace's reading group came back to work with me, Horace refused to do anything. So I moved Keith to a desk by the reading group and he began to do work. I told Horace to read. I did not give him a choice—he read but grumbled. I now had become very upset with Thomas, so I took hold of his arm and told him to sit in his seat. Thomas shook his arm loose and said, "Don't ever grab me again." I replied, "Thomas, I'm wrong for grabbing you, but you must get in your seat and do your work." Thomas did sit down and start working.

Next day in seminar, after being complimented by the other student teachers for the effective way she reacted to Thomas's complaint, Dorothy explained that she was taken aback by his reaction. Because he grabbed and hit other children it seemed so ironic, she said, that that kind of complaint should come from him.

A Black student teacher helped Dorothy and the rest of the group understand what it means to many Black people to be physically restrained or controlled, and how jealously many Black parents restrict the right to use physical means to discipline their children, granting it only to those who they believe do have the children's interest at heart.

Black children are very conscious of that attitude, having been well trained in it. The Black student teachers were the first to point out that despite her ignorance about that cultural fact, Dorothy had respected the child's feelings while insisting that he do as she demanded.

Another illustration of lack of knowledge about or insensitivity to cultural variations was observed by Eleanor, a student teacher.

> 1/28: Mrs. B. wasn't there today and we had a substitute teacher. She and Marshall had problems from the beginning. Marshall was out of his seat and she told him to sit down. As usual Marshall did not respond. She grabbed him by the arm and said, "Now listen here, boy, you get in your seat and don't let me catch you out of it again." Marshall replied by declaring that he is not a boy, he is a person, and she was not his mother or father and he didn't have to do anything that she said. Marshall is Black, and as with many Black males he objects to being called boy.

Eleanor did not report the substitute teacher's response. We would have said, "I will not call you 'boy' again because you don't like it. I'm not your mother or father, but I am your teacher today and I will tell you what to do whenever I have to. Now I tell you that you are to stay in your seat and do your work. If I can help you with it, I'd like to do that."

The words we used are not special. What is important is to convey understanding and respect combined with unwavering firmness about our expectation of the student's behavior. However, these are not easily achieved if we are not in touch with lives that may be very different from our own. Being aware of these differences alerts us to the substantial need for anthropological-sociological input in teacher training and for the need for student teachers to try to appreciate the students' perspectives and how they differ from their own world view.

Jeff's experience as a social studies student teacher shows that an ethnocentric outlook is counterproductive if not destructive. Jeff's cooperating teacher, Mr. Y., had asked the 11th-grade students to write a paper about a significant historical character, indicating the reasons for their choice. He gave Jeff the first opportunity to read the papers and write comments on them, which Mr. Y. then reviewed.

During a free period Mr. Y. praised Jeff for the worthwhile questions he posed in his comments and the positive reinforcement he gave to many students. Then he added that he was surprised by comments on two papers. One Black student, who wrote about Malcolm X, agreed with the latter's argument that Blacks must stand strong "as a nation." Jeff's comment was: "I thought we were *all* Americans!" An Hispanic student chose Cesar Chavez, the head of the Farm Workers

Union of America who organized a consumer boycott against grapes. Jeff wrote, "Couldn't you find a more significant person than Chavez?" Jeff did not yet understand that by attacking role models he was undermining his students' confidence and their self-expectations. Here is Jeff's delayed reaction:

> 3/13: A week ago, when Mr. Y. pointed these things out, I knew immediately that I had blundered. I wished the earth would open up under me. But I grew up in the suburbs as an "all American boy." When I got to college and mixed with other people, I guess I learned about their ideas and values. But I put that knowledge in a separate compartment. I still sort of believe that we're all Americans, who all have the same opportunity but the other part of me knows it's not 100% true. I must reconcile the two different "me's." I owe a lot to Mr. Y.

## EXPECTATIONS OF STUDENTS LIVING IN POVERTY

The poverty of some students confronts student teachers with a form of culture shock. It is one thing to sit on a comfortable chair in the tranquil surroundings of a university library reading about poverty and oppression; it is quite another to come smack up against it and its consequences in real life. One of us experienced this as a student teacher, despite courses in sociology and anthropology in which the problems of poverty were examined. She wrote in her own student-teacher log:

> We were returning [to the Bronx] by bus from an all-day trip to a nature park in Staten Island. The fifth graders were tired but happy after a very enjoyable day of walking the nature trails, visiting the museum, and picnicking and playing outdoors. The children surrounding me on the bus in this happy atmosphere of the day were conversing in a friendly and trusting way. One girl said she hated to think that her cousin was coming to visit for the weekend. I asked her why, whether she didn't like her cousin. She liked her all right, but the cousin, a girl her own age, was coming with her whole family. That meant, she said, "Us children will have to sleep on the floor."
> Very naively I asked what was so terrible about that for a few nights? She looked at me, now a little embarrassed, perhaps at my own innocence, and said, "I can't get myself to fall asleep on the floor because I'm afraid of the big rats." Of course, I had read about poverty and rats and malnutrition and brain damage from lead poisoning in hungry little children who eat the peeling paint off the wall, and more, but I had not connected them with my children, with this girl who I had felt was not much different from me only 10 years before.

One of the authors vividly remembers an experience in an inner-city teaching assignment early in her professional career. She and her first graders completed a unit of study in nutrition. The teacher was giving herself a pat on the back. What a success her lessons had been—a trip to the local supermarket, a "tasting" day of new and exotic fruits, an afternoon of making "Stone Soup" with a variety of vegetables children had brought to school.

On one particular morning the class was reviewing some of the concepts learned. "What vegetable did you have for dinner last night?" Various children responded — french fries, greens, carrots, corn, and so on. Tiffany's response was "tomato soup." How clever — she's really made the connection. For some reason "tomato soup" kept sticking in my mind that day. As the day was coming to a close, I finally remembered why. A day ago Tiffany had said her stove was not working. I took Tiffany aside and asked how her mother had cooked her soup. She hadn't. She had opened the can and Tiffany had cold soup for dinner. Tiffany never returned to school after that. Two weeks later I was notified she had moved and her new school was requesting school records. Tucked into her records, I placed a note to her new teacher to keep an eye on Tiffany's home situation.

At various points during your student teaching experience and next year, when you have your own class, go through your roster and ask yourself about each student, "What are my expectations about him or her?" "Are they realistic and will they promote maximum growth and development?" And think about your behavior toward each individual. Ask whether it conveys your caring, support, and belief in them. Does it lead them to know that you expect them to learn and to grow?

# 9
▼▼▼▼▼▼▼

# Classroom Management: Discipline for a Productive Learning Environment

"Discipline!" The word captures our attention. Everybody who knows anything at all about education today is well aware that keeping order is top priority in many schools.

We take it for granted that "discipline" is very much on the minds of student teachers. What about "old hands" in teaching? Problems of discipline can be so difficult that they are on the minds of experienced teachers as well, as you can see in the following words, reported by Clapp (1989):

> Discipline and classroom management were my biggest fears as I entered teaching. After 19 years of teaching (though I am considered by others to have very good classroom management — my principal always recommends that visitors observe my classroom), each summer before school starts I still have nightmares featuring my class in an out-of-control situation. (p. 32)

This teacher was one of 1,388 respondents to a questionnaire study of 10 educational issues by the education magazine *Instructor* in 1989. Discipline was ranked first of the 10 issues by 69% of the teachers who responded. It ranked ahead of such issues as teacher salaries, teacher preparation, and teacher empowerment.

Take note of another important finding. Most of the responding teachers (almost 80%) were in Grades K-6. They ranked discipline at the top even though they were not teaching teen-agers.

Two positive findings are worth considering. First, the teachers did not blame themselves or the children. They saw discipline problems as the result of larger social issues. For example, 38% attributed class disruption and the other assorted discipline concerns to changes in the American family. One teacher said, "It's hard to punish a child for misbehaving . . . the breakdown of families causes poor self-esteem and results in discipline problems" (p. 32). Another teacher said, "What used to be high educational priorities are no longer such. . . . Hunger, abuse—physical and sexual—neglect, etc. . . . are issues in the suburban public school I teach in" (p. 32). The behavioral problems, these teachers say, are evident in the children but they were caused by social problems over which teachers have no control.

The other positive finding is that teachers try very hard to be more effective in coping with problems of classroom management. Most of them seek help from other teachers. In this survey they also sought help from school administrators, college professors, supervisors or mentor teachers, and support staff. Student teachers got help from their cooperating teachers and their college supervisors. When they were asked which was most valuable of all the resources they used in the area of discipline, almost one third cited Lee Canter's Assertive Discipline program. That program is discussed later in this chapter. First, we turn to the meaning of discipline.

## WHAT IS DISCIPLINE?

The word "discipline" has several meanings. A common one that is often applied to education is the punishing of students for the sake of maintaining order. Less common, but of greater importance, discipline also denotes a positive approach to education: the kind of order that enables a class to achieve its objectives and, by virtue of that, enables students to become competent and more confident.

In general, we speak of a disciplined way of life as one that follows a consistent pattern. The reason people organize life that way is to help them fulfill themselves, to accomplish what they set out for in their professional and personal lives.

The same may be said about a disciplined way of teaching. You have your objectives; you have your plans for meeting them and your built-in policies to bring your students along with you. The "perfect marriage" of teacher and students comes when class members experience you as a person interested in strengthening them. If they recognize you as such, they will accept as appropriate almost any form of classroom management. They will, as a group at least, if not all the individuals, accept as required whatever measures you consider necessary to maintain a disciplined class.

A disciplined class can be more or less structured, more or less permissive. Your crucial objective is to be consistent and keep the kind of order needed for your method of instruction. "Order" is as necessary in a classroom as it is in a family, and in both settings children prefer orderly situations and orderly lives, even if circumstances lead some of them to behave as if they did not. They like it, want it, and need it, as much in a permissive or open classroom as in a traditional one.

Without some order there can be no teaching and very little learning. Consequently, the student teacher's priority is to maintain his or her kind of order. Psychotherapists believe that resistance to therapy must be dealt with before anything else: If the client persists in fending off the therapist, the two engage in a struggle of wills and nothing worthwhile is accomplished. The same struggle can take place in the classroom, and it is the teacher's role to circumvent it. Here is an example taken from Steve's log reporting on the problems of his cooperating teacher, whom he regards as a good teacher.

> 1/15: The children do not listen to the teacher when she is presenting a lesson. They are doing a thousand other things. Some children were playing tic-tac-toe, others were playing cards, some were coloring, while still others were doing homework. She is a good teacher, but none of the children were listening, so they don't even realize that she is a good teacher. While Mrs. S. was giving the language arts lesson, only about 7 or 8 students out of 30 were listening.
>
> What have I learned from this observation? I have learned that I must have the children's complete attention in order to really teach. It doesn't matter if I'm a good teacher if nobody is listening. One of the things that I am going to demand from my students is that their desks be cleared off—as many distractions as possible must be eliminated. That is not to say that I will have their complete attention, but at least it will be a start.

By no stretch of the imagination could Mrs. S. be classified as "a good teacher" on the basis of this observation. Perhaps what Steve was reacting to was a well-organized presentation of valuable language-arts material. That is of no value whatsoever if, as he himself said, "nobody is listening." Facing this kind of situation, a teacher must give up his or her present method and experiment with others until he or she finds one suitable to the children in his or her class.

Under other conditions (say a class of children accustomed to listening from experiences in home and in school) the teacher might have been well received. And it is possible that her current mode of presentation would be usable at a later time. However, if she is to be able to use this method successfully, these children must first be "taught" by a series of experiences that teacher–whole-class presentation lessons are a time to listen, watch, raise a hand for permission to participate, and so on. As Steve came to see, when Mrs. S. finally exploded and scolded "all over the place," it silenced the children temporarily, but "hollering" and scolding usually are not effective as long-run solutions.

When a teacher relies on loud scolding to curb disorder, inevitably disruptions will escalate and the class will not come under control until the teacher again scolds loudly. It is better by far to introduce the ultimate means of control when your voice and demeanor, although firm, have not reached your upper-decibel limit. For your sake and that of your students, condition the children to expect that, after a second warning, for example, there are no more, and that the disturbing children are given immediate punishment.

Bear in mind that you have double responsibility to function this way. First, you owe it to the class to lead (you are the leader) in such a way that they will get a disciplined education, one that perfects and strengthens them. They deserve your help in gaining mastery over the skills and content in the curriculum. Second, the most effective way for children and adolescents to learn good citizenship is by living it, not by reading or hearing lectures about it.

Obviously, maintaining order in the classroom is essential to effective teaching. In the survey of 1,388 teachers reported, 69% saw discipline as the most crucial of 10 issues in teaching. About 50% said the biggest discipline problem was disruptive students, "those who interrupt, are rude, leave their seats, are sarcastic, and who seek attention" (Clapp, 1989, p. 32). Similar concerns about disciplining disruptive children were expressed by teachers in Corcoran, Walker, and White (1988), in their book called *Working in Urban Schools*.

How can you, as a student teacher maintain order and how can you manage that disruptive child? What guidelines can be provided? There are four important principles for successful discipline that will help in any classroom. Note that these principles depend on action you take *outside* of the classroom.

## FOUR PRINCIPLES OF SUCCESSFUL DISCIPLINE

### Functioning as a Teacher

The first important step you can take toward being an effective disciplinarian is to recognize and internalize the fact that you are on the other side of the desk now, and must function as an adult leader. You, who are looking forward shortly to work, self-support, and perhaps marriage, may regard this statement as superfluous if not patronizing. But it needs to be said, considered, discussed, and most important, acted upon. This is so because we all have some of the child in us.

That is good because the child in us enables us to enjoy life more and does not permit us to be bogged down all the time with serious concerns. As a teacher, however, we are the adult given the social responsibility for a portion of the education of children and adolescents; and as a teacher we are the only adult in the classroom, even if some of the youths in the class tower over us. We are not complete adults in class if still in a corner of our brain there lurks the consciousness of being one of them, or the feeling that we would want to be one.

Amy, in telling of her problem with Randy, shows her "shock" that the child followed her instructions. Amy had not yet converted herself into thinking "adult leader," a necessary step for being effective with discipline.

4/25: I have noticed that I have to be firm with some of the children and I definitely have to follow through with what I say. Although I always knew this was true, seeing the children react to my behavior provided evidence of my beliefs.

One incident that happened today occurred when I had a few of the children outside: Three boys wanted to swing on a tire swing, two of the boys were already on, while the third, Randy was twisting the swing so that it would go around in circles. As Randy twisted, the swing became higher and Jason became frightened. I explained to Randy that he would have to let the swing down some because Jason was frightened. Randy became quite upset and started throwing stones. I told him to stop and explained that if he continued he would have to go inside. He did continue, so I told him to go inside, but he refused. Then I told him that if he didn't go in now, he couldn't come outside later. Randy didn't go in. So I let him be, with the understanding that he would not be able to come out later. As we were all preparing to go in, I told Judy [the cooperating teacher] about the incident and my decision. She supported me. She just wanted me to remind her later that Randy was not to go out. Later in the morning I was outside with the children and Randy came out. I reminded him of the situation and he went back in quietly without any comments. He followed my instructions. I was really shocked!

Remember that all the Randys view you differently from the way you view yourself. Although Amy may think of herself as somebody just a few years out of adolescence and as a learner in the classroom, to Randy she is an adult, a teacher. At various points during your student-teaching experience assess how you think the students perceive you. Then check your perceptions by noting how students actually do react to you.

Asserting oneself as a teacher means being strong and effective, but that can often be done in thoughtful and quiet ways. As we said earlier, problems can be avoided by such means as minimizing boredom for students, keeping the class lively, listening attentively to students as they express concerns, and rewarding good behavior, usually by praise. Using CONTROL-C to disentangle the causes of some ongoing discipline problems is also a "quiet" approach.

## Developing Your Own Theory of Management and Discipline

This is the second principle of successful discipline. In your education courses you probably became familiar with several different approaches that would allow you to manage a class effectively. You might want to consider four different discipline models proposed by Balch and Balch (1987).

*Behavior Modification.* Encourage favorable behavior mainly by giving positive reinforcement (like praise) to that kind of behavior. The teacher controls the class by conditioning the students through the use of commands and rewards and, when necessary, punishments. The teacher does not look for the causes of the behavior. This general approach is described by Madsen and Madsen (1974).

*Assertive Discipline.* Assertively communicate disapproval of the behavior and explain what behavior is acceptable and the consequences of misbehavior. Canter and Canter (1976), leading proponents of this method, give special weight to spelling out the class rules. The consequences of breaking a rule, which are given equal prominence to the rules themselves, should be acceptable, even comfortable, for the teacher and respectful of student rights. The third part of the Canter model is composed of the motivational strategies the teacher will employ as positive reinforcement for appropriate behavior.

*Reality Therapy.* With responsible behavior as a prime goal, use class discussions to help students become responsible for their behavior and also find problems that are barriers to their responsible conduct. According to Glasser (1969), the teacher is an enforcer who confronts disruptive students with their misbehavior. He or she shows how the student is irresponsible in violating the rights and disregarding the needs of others. Punishment is not considered to be effective and, for the most part, is limited to removing privileges or isolating the student, but even then not as punishment, rather as an opportunity for the student to consider how others have been injured by the misbehavior.

*Low Profile Classroom Control.* Focus attention on content, avoiding the distraction of calling out to an inattentive student. Instead use students' names to keep them involved in lessons. The point is not to make mountains out of mole hills, but to distinguish between classroom problems that are teacher-made versus those that are student-made. As Gordon (1974) said, the teacher does not seek to control, enforce, or punish, but rather is an enabler, one who listens, supports, and facilitates. The teacher does not exert his or her power over the child or teen-ager.

One author, himself a teacher, finds pluses and minuses in the methods just described. Seeman (1988) claimed that the books we have cited are useful resources but have weaknesses that he sought to correct by adding the following points. We think these are important:

• When does a situation or a problem deserve to be called a "disciplinary problem?" Because teachers differ among themselves, and even within themselves from time to time, this question is not easy to answer. Sometimes teachers transform a non-problem (like a joke a student cracks) into a disciplinary problem. Sometimes, Seeman said, a mishandled difference about a grade or about a student's motivation unnecessarily turns into a discipline problem. In his definition of a discipline problem, note especially what he puts in parentheses:

> a behavior (not merely the expression of a feeling) that disrupts (or is potentially disruptive to) the learning of the rest of the class (not just the learning of the disruptor), or disrupts the role responsibilities of the teacher (not just the personal feelings of the teacher). (Seeman, 1988, p. 42)

• In order to prevent discipline problems, we ask, what are the sources of them and what events precipitate them? In a study he conducted, Seeman found, for example, that some problems originate outside the school, some inside the school (but not in the classroom), and some inside the classroom. Those in the last group could be due to classroom climate, student interactions with each other or teacher–student interactions. There is a big pay-off to teachers who, early in their careers, learn to classify the origins of problems and introduce ways to prevent them.

• Why does one technique work for one teacher yet not for another who is in virtually the same situation? Ms. Doe calls for order and the class is silent; Ms. Roe does the same and you would think no one had heard her. Seeman's study revealed the important concept of congruence: How students react to directions, assignments, and reprimands depends on how believable they evaluate the teacher to be. If they regard the teacher as credible, they respect and obey him or her. If they see the teacher as a "phoney," they do not. "Sincere" and "genuine" are apt terms to describe the way students perceive teachers who command respect.

• Why limit oneself to a reward and punishment system? That could result in ignoring the sources of the problems as well as the feelings of the students. In Seeman's view, classroom discipline should be based on a good relationship between student and teacher as well as on the teacher's power, and not just on the latter.

• Why limit oneself solely to nurturing and empathetic relationships or to the use only of reason? Such limited approaches neglect the value of reward and punishment (hopefully exercised by a respected and respecting teacher). They also tend to be applied to the needs of the individual at a cost to the class as a whole.

An eclectic approach, one that draws on whatever strategies you find useful, seems most desirable. An effective approach must fit with your personal values and personality—you should feel comfortable with it. Besides suiting you, the approach should give your students the feeling that you mean what you say, whether you are talking in caring and supportive or demanding and critical ways.

## Problem Solving

A third important principle for successful discipline is to routinely use a logical problem-solving process, such as the CONTROL-C method described in chapter 2. Even for the experienced teacher, effective management practices and procedures for handling disruptive situations come with careful thought. After reviewing and analyzing the day's events, a teacher is in a better position to handle whatever difficulties might develop tomorrow. The following sections are on "effective problem solving" and "impulsive problem solving and inconsistent behavior."

*Effective Problem Solving.*   The entries here, written by Janet, show how she used her log to actively analyze what was happening in her class and to plan for the days ahead. Although her wrestling with problems was sometimes frantic, Janet battled like a young "pro" determined to master her craft.

> 3/11: Some days are good and some days are just awful. Today was awful. When it comes to a group activity I lose so many of them and I don't think it's me; it seems to be because a couple of children disturb the rest, and when I'm trying to take care of them the others start talking and I can't blame them. When I say some children disturb the others, it's a physical disturbance that has to be dealt with. I guess I have to try and keep things going at a faster pace to try and eliminate any "time" for them to hit. Even though the rest of the day went fine, that small part discourages me.

Janet is engaged in an important problem-solving process: She has already diagnosed the onset of problems as resulting from a couple of children who, by drawing her attention, lead her to neglect the rest of the class. Besides, she has detected a tendency in herself—a common one for student teachers—to magnify the difficult moments. A few days later Janet recognized that the children don't mean it personally when they exhibit "testing" behavior.

> 3/15: Things went better today, I had my head together and things went a lot more smoothly. I still have trouble keeping everyone's attention, but I think it's because I don't use Andrea's techniques; as a result they keep testing me. I don't mind, because I know they don't mean it personally and it's not taken as such. We started a new subject today, the circus. I'm excited and am looking forward to it.

Janet had one of those good days, the kind that make you feel you are gaining mastery. As she put it, "I had my head together." That sounds like a Wimbledon tennis champion talking about the need to concentrate on the game and to have confidence. Having our heads together while teaching means not getting rattled (essential to good problem solving) and remembering that we are teacher/adult in the presence of student/child or adolescent. A month later Janet wrote:

> 4/15: The day was crazy. Talking about it in seminar made it sound worse than it was. It's just an incredible feeling of frustration—having so much I want to accomplish and to have the children do, that I get hung up in "management" problems. It's more than that. It's that I'm getting hung up in my idealism and how things seem to be. I know I'm making progress, but it's so slow; maybe I just need more positive rewards by immediately seeing what I'm trying to accomplish. I don't know. It's hard to be your own teacher when you're constantly in someone else's shadow.
>     Something else bothers me: my supervisor's idealism—I guess it holds for the seminar leaders too. All of you come up with good suggestions, but most of the time it's impossible to implement them to the fullest. I come up with so many ideas and suggestions, activities, etc., but I'm only one person with a classful of active

children so I can't always be with all of them, meeting every need all of the time.

By the next day, especially after the seminar, Janet was again allowing herself to feel overwhelmed by the work. She sensed that she was imaginative like her supervisor and seminar leaders, but she compared herself with them, a beginner with three pros, and she found herself wanting. She did not compare herself with them as they were or could have been as beginners, which might have been more valid and reassuring. At least, however, she was near recognizing that it was not *they* who were setting inordinate demands upon her but she herself, and that those demands were creating some of her problems in managing the class.

4/17: The day want a lot better. Things went smoother and the children were some-what more responsive. I'm trying to get them to pick out "worthwhile" activities by making suggestions. It just takes time, I guess. I also seem to plan more than I can accomplish.

In the 4/15 log entry, Janet wrote that her frustration was due to her wanting to accomplish so much that she got caught up in management problems. But management is part of a disciplined class and the hallmark of a master teacher. Good management calls for setting realizable goals and organizing the day in such a way as to be sure the goals are realized.

Janet, in her 4/17 log entry, showed that she recognized that she defeated herself by trying to "accomplish" too much. She had now gotten a clearer idea of her role as teacher. If she learned nothing more in her student teaching, she learned one of the vital lessons. The classroom is no place for superwomen (or supermen). Real people do much better. They do not demand of themselves or of their students more than humans can accomplish.

Janet developed as a teacher because, as we noted, she regarded her difficulties as problems and she went about working them out in a thoughtful, problem-solving way. On a regular nightly basis she used the CONTROL-C method to define problems, to understand her relationship to them, and to test out different hypotheses. She dealt with her own problems, the kind she called "hang-ups," with courage. Her reward was success as a student teacher.

Kimberly's assignment was in a difficult city middle school. During her first few weeks she felt overwhelmed by the job and did not see herself as an adult — an adult who could be competent. In an interview Kimberly said, "Believe it or not, I was saved by reading material supplied to me by my supervisor." Material like the following suggestions by Balch and Balch (1987) can be useful. Note the emphasis on consistency, good organization, keeping students busy, and also, humor. We consider all of these to be important.

1. Be consistent in your approach.
2. Keep students busy in a constructive way.

3. Be organized and prepared.

4. State a limited number of rules and discuss these with students.

5. Have a sense of humor.

*Impulsive Problem Solving and Inconsistent Behavior*    Joyce, by comparison, was not functioning as a good problem solver. Instead of using her log for systematic problem solving, she simply recorded the day's events.

Because Joyce did not think ahead, when she had difficulties with her class she had to make important decisions on the spot. As a result, she could do little thinking about the causes of the discipline problems she faced and she acted impulsively, trying to gain more control in the class. Typically, she acted first and thought about it only after she had recognized that her actions had not worked. Obviously such an approach tends to be ineffective, as her log entries suggest.

> 1/19: I sat Frankie next to Michael to see what effect Michael would have on Frankie. Michael is a bully and he started punching out Frankie. He defies any type of authority. I kept him after school to talk to him, and he sat there and looked at me as if I were crazy. This has really upset me. I've got to reach him somehow, but nothing seems to work.

> 1/20: Susan was a real problem. But some of the fault lies with me. I changed seating arrangements. Susan sat next to Eva. Major mistake. She talked, talked, talked.

Within 2 days, Joyce had rearranged the seating of two difficult students and in each instance, almost immediately after doing so, realized her mistake. Joyce became very disturbed over her inability to cope with the situation, and no wonder. When she kept Michael, the "bully," after school and he "looked at me as if I were crazy," she became very upset. This fifth grader raised doubts in a young adult about whether her own behavior was "crazy."

Joyce is distressed by the behavior of her class and wants to understand the students better. However, instead of analyzing the situation, defining the problem, and developing a plan of action, Joyce behaved like the proverbial chicken with its head cut off. Her difficulties were not due to a lack of talent, as she began to think they were, or to a lack of concern for the children. Rather, her problems were largely due to what she was not doing outside of the classroom: logical problem solving. Let us look more closely at Joyce's interactions with Susan as reported in her log over a period of 8 days.

> 1/18: Susan is her usual, quiet self. All morning she has spoken to no one. Occasionally she looks toward the rear of the room where I am sitting and looks at me shyly and timidly. Every time she glances at me I get the feeling she wants me to pay some attention to her. But, on approaching her with a smile, and a "Can I help with anything, Susan?" she stares at her desk and shakes her head no.

Math seems to be her most difficult subject. She's constantly looking on Ben's paper for the answers. The sad part is, Ben doesn't know what he's doing.

1/19: During history class, Susan got up from her seat four times to get a Kleenex to blow her nose. Nothing is wrong with that, of course, only that she was trying to see what I was writing. Her attention span is very short. She finds everything to do except pay attention.

1/20: The class was super noisy, so they spent 10 minutes with me after school. Susan was included. She was truly upset. Her eyes watered and she walked out of the classroom and did not say goodbye. [This was the same day Susan's seat had been changed.]

1/21: Before I got seated Susan came to me and said, "Miss W., I'm going to be quiet today. You've got my word."

1/25: Susan came up to me and was asking me a question. I couldn't pay her any immediate attention—but when I looked at her, she was chewing gum. I made her spit it out. I had to report it to Mr. P. because his policy is "a swat for chewing gum." I had to be a witness, and it really hurt my heart. She cried and grabbed my hand. She said nothing the rest of the day—all she did was glance at me and lower her head.

In summary, on 1/18 Joyce was aware that Susan wanted her to "pay some attention to her." However, when Joyce offered her help, Susan shook her head no. On the following day (1/19), Susan again sought Joyce's attention, this time by walking near her. On the next day (1/20), Joyce moved Susan's seat and then realized her error. On 1/21 Susan again seeks out Joyce, promising to "be quiet today." Susan appears to want Joyce's attention and approval. But a few days later (1/25), when Susan finally sought Joyce's direct help, Joyce responded to the gum chewing and not the request for help.

At times Joyce related to Susan in supportive ways. Then when Susan took the initiative to go to her and ask her a question, Joyce could not give her the attention to respond to the question, but could give enough to note that Susan was chewing gum, enough to report it to the cooperating teacher, and enough to serve as witness during the paddling. We can begin to understand why Joyce thought Michael was looking at her as if she were crazy. The inconsistent, contradictory behavior that Joyce engaged in, like the kind she used with Susan, confuses students.

Joyce's assignment was not an easy one. The attitude of the teachers in her school was that discipline was of the utmost importance and that you had to be in strict control every moment of the day. In Joyce's difficult assignment her only solution was to follow the style of discipline in her school; her cooperating teacher gave her no choice.

Joyce did not learn what she might have about the "strict approach" to maintaining order and associated consequences. Further, because she failed to use a logical problem-solving technique like CONTROL-C, she continued to depend on impulsive, on-the-spot decisions. This meant she made unnecessary mistakes. For example, once when students complained that she was assigning too much work, Joyce justified herself by getting an affirmative answer from many children to her question as to whether they were learning. She got a "yes," she said, from all the children except the "troublemakers."

George, like Joyce, also had a difficult student teaching assignment. His was by choice, however. He wanted to teach science in an urban high school. In his words, "The first week was a disaster."

Mr. L. had him work with a slow group of six students. To George's dismay, after listening to his lesson for a few minutes, they just ignored him. They conversed among themselves, or fiddled with a pencil, or just sat there turned off. By the end of the week George was in crisis: "Do I ask for a transfer to a nice well-behaved suburban school? Do I change my career? Or do I follow my fantasy and run away to a sunny beach?"

Although he fumbled during the first week, trying this and trying that, a talk with his supervisor on Friday afternoon helped him "get back on track." She warned him about impulsive and inconsistent behavior and encouraged him to spend the weekend thinking about the situation, critically and logically. He concluded that he had been too idealistic in expecting the teen-agers "to bloom," in the hands of a caring, permissive teacher. And, he decided he could only maintain his sanity and his commitment to urban schools by experimenting with different structured approaches and setting realistic expectations. He remembered what he had studied in class earlier this year and told himself that he needed to follow the "three Mores": More structure in his lessons, more patience, and more realistic expectations. After 3 weeks of reminding himself of the "three Mores," and after several conversations with his supervisor, this is what he said:

> 2/12: I feel that some of the kids see me as being on their side—that I'm really interested in them. They're listening a little more and some of them know I mean it when I say, "Let's get down to business." Most important, they're beginning to see that what we are studying does have something to do with their lives. I've got to keep reminding myself to be patient.

George's experience reflects the principle that a teacher's style of management has to be adapted to the circumstances in the school, and doing that calls for effective problem solving. Children and teenagers who see little if any connection between school and their lives are different in their classroom attitudes and behavior from those who see a close connection.

You as a student teacher, like your classmates, supervisor, and cooperating teacher, were motivated by a career goal to succeed in school. We have to put ourselves in the shoes of George's students to understand their experiences so that we can choose the most appropriate teaching approaches for them.

In recent years, new instructional approaches have been developed for stu-

dents who have missed out on learning essential skills. These approaches were
designed to give students the important knowledge and skills that other children
acquire in the preschool years and in the elementary and secondary school years
(Feuerstein, 1980; Feuerstein & Hoffman, 1990; Haywood & Brooks, 1990).
Depending on your assignment, you may want to use these resources in planning
your lessons.

## Planning: Where Discipline and Curriculum Meet

The fourth important factor in discipline that happens outside the classroom is
planning: planning a day thoroughly, preparing for contingencies, and keeping
in mind the needs and interests of the students.

*Balancing the Curriculum as Problem Prevention.*  Sheryl's logs show
that she is developing into a "pro." Already she plans a balanced program (which
is itself a problem-preventer) and in class reveals a combination of firm control
and stimulation. In her log she described her preparation for a morning of giving
her students opportunities to get the satisfaction of working out problems and
receiving appropriate rewards.

> 1/27: I had the kids by myself the whole day. I had a chart on liquid measurement,
> and I asked them very simple questions and we went from cups into quarts, and
> pints into gallons. Then they did board work and had an exercise in math, which
> for the most part they did very well. I would check their answers with the book
> and check the wrong ones and let them try again. When they got it wrong the se-
> cond time, I would write in the answer and tell them to figure out why it was right.
> When they could explain it to me, I gave them a "100" and many were eager to
> explain why the answers were right. After math, we had health. Our health discus-
> sion was excellent. It was very mature. Everyone participated, and many interest-
> ing questions were raised. There are a lot of things to learn about bacteria, and
> we discussed the topic until 10:20. . . .

Besides content, Sheryl also had thought about what behavioral limits were
tolerable as far as her lessons were concerned. She insisted on the kind of behavior that was necessary for the children to profit from the activities she had
prepared. Also, as the log shows, she had planned the day carefully but was still
able to give the children a choice in the use of time and to reschedule the restroom trip because the situation demanded it.

> 1/27 [continued]: Then we had film strips, and the children were so talkative and
> inattentive that I turned off the machine. I told them they didn't want to watch it,
> so they could watch a blank wall if they didn't want to pay attention. They got quiet
> after 5 minutes, and I told them they could make it up after school. They had been
> working pretty hard, so in the afternoon all I had planned for them was music and

then working on their masks. There was no scheduled recess and I let them vote if they wanted an early recess or get to work on their masks. They voted to work on their masks.

Since they got restless, I took them down to the restroom about 25 minutes early. We took 20 minutes because they cannot behave in the halls and we started all over every time I heard them talk. I plan on doing this every time, no matter how long it takes. I keep insisting that they can talk quietly in class but not in the halls. Of all the kids, mine are by far the worst. In a way, I think they appreciated it because they knew I was tired too and wanted perfection. For the rest of the afternoon, I let them work on their masks and they played records. At 3:00 they began clean-up and had it done in about 8 minutes, which was quite an improvement. I read *Charlotte's Web* and the kids really listened. That was a good day for me.

Sheryl's day was successful because she planned learning activities that involved her students. She got everyone to participate in the health discussion that dealt with topics that interested the children. She firmly required orderliness both in the use of the film strips and in the hallway. One senses in reading her report that the children felt she was setting requirements as much in their interest as in her own. Most children respond favorably to rational authority, that is, to a leader whose demands make sense to them.

Sheryl's next report was positive: Most of her plans worked perfectly; the class was becoming a cohesive group enjoying the exercises, activities, and discussion. However, Sheryl's log entries also contained the inevitable ups and downs. A few days later Sheryl wrote she was "just miserable," because she had yet to find a way to cope with the few disruptive children. She did not have a solution, but she was not baffled by the situation and was actively searching for answers.

Sheryl was a determined problem solver who learned from her own successes and mistakes and from those of her cooperating teacher. She learned to plan activities that appealed to the class as a whole. She developed the self-control necessary to avoid becoming angry and being drawn into bitter battles with students who had serious problems. A regular user of CONTROL-C, Sheryl persisted in trying to solve discipline problems. She never yielded to the easy temptation simply to blame the children. She liked them, struggled to understand them, and sought ways to make school more interesting for them. Here is her final report.

3/18: This will be the last time I write. My class is getting better and they are controlling themselves more. They still are fighting and arguing, but it's more verbal, more reasonable and less physical. Frances and Mindy will have trouble for the rest of their lives. Things frustrate them so easily. Steve is a pain but a smart one and is a leader and salesman.

They are getting their health reports done at last and working on their skits with some success. Mrs. R. told me that their spelling tests have improved, which pleases me. The kids still get away with more with me than with Mrs. R., but when it counts, they are with me. It will be sad leaving.

The choice of content and method (what and how we teach) is important in preventing and correcting discipline problems. In planning specific class material, one can do much to enhance the likelihood of order simply by taking into account the needs and likes of the learners.

Earlier in this chapter when Steve referred to his cooperating teacher as a good teacher, you probably wondered why we included his statement in a chapter on discipline. Most of the children talked, played, and did anything but follow her lesson. You probably thought there must be something wrong with a lesson plan that fails to hold even some of the attention of 75% of the class. You were right.

"Discipline" and "curriculum" are inseparable in some very important respects and noticeably so when most of the class is unruly. Any time such disruptiveness occurs the effective teacher asks, "What is wrong with my objectives or my plans to carry them out?"

In many cases the students have no personal interest in the content being presented. This problem sometimes can be dealt with by combining unappealing subject matter with appealing illustrations. For instance, fractions can be taught using pies, football fields, coins; geography by following the road trips of major-league baseball teams; literature, like Shakespeare's "Romeo and Juliet," by referring to popular music favored by teen-agers. The effects of the choice of content cannot be underestimated, as illustrated by the case presented here.

One of the authors taught a ninth-grade English class for boys in which the behavior of the teen-agers was almost uncontrollable. This was the lowest-rated section in a homogeneously grouped system, and some of the students, having been kept back a year or two during their schooling, were big 15- and 16-year-old adolescents. With the consent of the chairperson of the department, the teacher brought in books that he thought would interest the students — sports, adventure, mystery, mechanics, and science fiction. He encouraged the students to bring in anything they preferred.

Many class periods were devoted to silent reading of a book or magazine of the student's choice. This was followed by discussion about the reading or about a personal experience that the reading brought to mind. Sometimes small groups of three or four would be organized for reading aloud and small-group discussion. When this approach was well established and all students were participating (and most of them eagerly), they were then asked to write a few sentences, then a few paragraphs, and later still a few pages about their readings.

Was this a mysterious, almost miraculous transformation in behavior? Not at all. The students had viewed school as a place where they were forced to go to study topics that did not interest them.

It is easier to compel children to attend school than to compel them to study. Real learning is an active process, and no one can force anybody into it. These ninth-grade English students resisted not because they were mean or recalcitrant but because education had no meaning to them and made no sense. The teacher said, "Look, you have to be in school. I'm not requiring it, but the state does.

As long as you are here you can either waste your time, get into trouble, or make the best possible use of it. I'll help you find whatever you'd like to read—whatever you'll enjoy reading—whatever you'd want to read to learn something for your use—not my use but yours."

When they heard that, not once but repeatedly in words and actions, they came to believe it, and they made better use of the time. Instead of chalk throwing, foot tripping, and outright fistfighting, they were reading, discussing, and writing about repairing cars, baseball, whether the heavyweight champ was as great a fighter as he was supposed to be, how to finish a basement with recycled materials, and some easy ways to estimate the charge for various handyman repair jobs.

As the weeks passed, they took to discussing characters in some stories, and even the way these characters dealt with problems not unlike some of theirs. These students learned, perhaps for the first time in their lives, that reading could be enjoyable and useful and that school could be in their interest and for their benefit.

Contrast that English teacher's perspective with Nicole's, who wrote: "I feel that . . . [the students in her cooperating class] are working for me when we are working on something." We added underlining to emphasize a point of view that is not helpful. Indeed, learners do behave in positive ways to please their parents and other adults whose approval they wish. However, education cannot be sustained on that kind of external motivation alone. Much more important is their sense that school is an agent for their own developing strength as individuals.

Before turning, in the next chapter, to what can be done in the classroom with regard to specific discipline problems and maintaining order, we want again to highlight the four principles discussed here:

internalize the student-teacher-as-a-leader concept,

develop your own internalized theory of management and discipline,

regularly use a systematic problem-solving method, and

thoroughly plan classroom activities.

Think of these four as equivalent to prerequisites to career success. We believe that if a teacher follows these guidelines, he or she is likely to build self-confidence and feel in control.

# 10
▼▼▼▼▼▼▼

# Relating and Coping
# as Classroom Management

During your observations in the classroom you probably noticed the teacher's attention turn from whole class to individuals to whole class, or perhaps whole class to groups to individuals or vice versa. As teachers, we relate to each of these entities: class as a whole, small working groups, individual students.

How we divide our attention among these entities is worth considering. The whole class has our major claim. The welfare of the whole class is our first priority, so that we guard against the demands of some one student distracting us from this prime responsibility. We also have to guard against our own temptation to give so much attention to a student in need that the class gets out of hand. In these respects teaching is a balancing act.

As we examine some of the tough problems that teachers find in relation to individual students, let us keep the class as a whole always in the foreground.

## MEETING INDIVIDUAL AND CLASS NEEDS

This section focuses on behavioral problems of individual students and the approaches teachers can use in resolving the problems. You will note our stress on not losing sight of the needs of the class as a whole.

We begin with Kate, who was pleased that the experienced substitute teacher got involved with the children and was less of a "babysitter" than a previous substitute. Kate was most impressed by the way the substitute teacher interacted with the children. After school Kate discussed discipline with the substitute and gained some new insights.

2/9: As I thought about it later, I decided that I need to learn to be a little firmer with the children. At times I tend to sacrifice the needs of the group for individuals because I am afraid of hurting their feelings. Consequently when a child begins a monologue completely sidetracking us from the group's discussion, I will usually let the child continue his/her story. But, meanwhile, the rest of the class becomes bored and fidgety. As I get to know the children better I am beginning to realize that children's feelings do not bruise that easily. For example, today I asked Glenn to go on an errand for me. Cindy asked to accompany him, but I told Cindy that I only needed one person for this job. Much to my surprise I got a cheerful "OK," and she went back to what she was doing.

Kate had the good experience of being an effective leader for the children. More important was her recognition that concern about the feelings of a particular child should not stand in the way of what is important to the welfare of the class.

Kate was correct about the principle involved, even if her example was a very tame one compared to many reported in the logs. Before we turn to the very difficult ones, let us read how Julie dealt with a student who frequently spoke out in class, this time during the vice-principal's observation visit.

3/15: Mr. R., the vice-principal, came in to observe me this morning. I was surprised that I wasn't more nervous. As a matter of fact I was very calm, I thought. I was in the middle of a lesson on the concept of "more and less." The children were all attending to what was going on—their participation helped to keep them all interested. Mr. R. told me later that he thought I did a fine job, so I was glad it worked out well.

As I was doing my lesson, Crystal began blurting out all kinds of things, including asking me why I wore glasses. This is not unusual for Crystal: Her attention span is not as long as that of some of the other kids. Of course when you're being observed you want everything to run smoothly, but when my patience was wearing thin concerning Crystal's outbursts I stopped momentarily and asked myself, "Are you trying to look good in front of the vice-principal and forgetting Crystal, or are you trying to do a good job of teaching?" I knew instantly that I had to stop Crystal from disturbing the class. I did, and I feel good about it.

The day before the scheduled observation, Julie had discussed Crystal with her cooperating teacher and had planned how she would handle her. Julie, knowing that Crystal was an impulsive child who had not yet internalized the social controls necessary for concentrating on a subject under discussion, provided the control externally. Julie walked close to Crystal and said something like: "Crystal, I want you to listen—to listen very carefully—and I don't want you to talk again until I call on you. Do you understand?" Crystal responded both to Julie's words and to the tone of her voice.

After Julie had called on several of the children to answer questions or to give an example to help illustrate the lesson, she called on Crystal. That step is an important one in the process of helping a child incorporate controls. It rewards the child for the control he or she has exercised, no matter how briefly, and informs the child that with such self-control he or she will still get attention from the teacher and have his or her turn in class.


## THE DEFIANT STUDENT

Steve recognized very early, at least by his third day in class, that the children were undisciplined and that the cooperating teacher's practices contributed to their behavior. For example, Mrs. S. would pass out two worksheets at once, with the result that as she was giving directions on the second, the children were working on the first. She would also inform the children which worksheets would not be collected and graded by her, a strong incentive to resistive children to ignore them.

Steve was not thrown by the situation. In his third day as a student teacher, 10 of the boys were chewing grape gum. "I would ask them to throw it away and they would fake throwing it away. I finally ended up taking a piece of paper and telling them to put it on the paper and then throwing it away myself. The children have no self-discipline."

His statement was not that of a teacher in panic. He knew that the "gum" misbehavior was directed at him, a test of the "new teacher," and he took it in stride. When his first attempt did not work he shifted gears and succeeded in passing the test: He maintained his authority as teacher and enabled the group to do the work of the day. Thereafter, with the same spirit, Steve searched successfully for activities and larger projects that won the active participation of all students some days and most of them on other days.

Steve did not have an easy time with John, who is typical of a type of student who challenges teaching professionalism. Sometimes youngsters arouse the animosity of the teacher, a situation that often leads to a battle for power and an almost total preoccupation with how to subdue the student. Such a reaction, although understandable under provocative circumstances, denies the teacher the chance to understand and resolve the problem. Also, the preoccupation with this struggle gradually erodes the teacher's effectiveness with the class.

If the student teacher gets caught up in such a contest, he or she will have less time and energy to concentrate on the class as a whole. Steve's experiences, reported in his log entries, give examples of what a student teacher must do to avoid getting caught up in such problems.

1/28: Today John was totally obnoxious. It is spelling test day. I gave the children about 10 minutes to study. John just sat there and wrote about five words on a little piece of paper—a cheat sheet. Right before the test I took it away. Then I gave the first spelling word—he spelled it out loud—I ignored it. I, however, reminded the whole class that they must be silent. John shouted out the spelling of the next word. I crushed his paper. Then when we were in line to go to the restroom, he pushed a girl down. Mrs. S. saw it and scolded him harshly. He had been performing for Mrs. S. all week too. He then acted like the scolding was the greatest thing that ever happened to him.

Steve recognized that John's actions were not directed against him personally, for Mrs. S. had trouble with John earlier in the week. For whatever reasons in his personal life, John, at this point in the school year, had a need to get attention, defy adult authority, and attack a female classmate. We may not know what provoked him. Nevertheless, as effective teachers we convey the attitude and behavior of rational authority that says to John the following, but in simplified form:

> John, you have your reasons for doing what you are doing. We know you are not doing it as your preference, because no one chooses to get into trouble and be a failure and a loser. But whatever the unfortunate needs that drive you to it, your behavior is disruptive to others and destructive to you. It is unacceptable and will not be permitted. I will use every means available to me to prevent it, preferably the most humane and least humiliating. While I recognize that ultimately you are not now responsible for what you have become and how you behave, that will not in the least cause me to equivocate. In your interest too, I must act decisively to prevent you from further damaging your self-concept and from further alienating yourself from members of the class.

Steve handled the cheating encounter relatively well. However, when John defied him by spelling aloud the first word he gave on the spelling test, Steve might have said: "I know that you are looking for attention. I cannot allow you to get it in this way because you are disturbing the class." This tells John that the teacher understands him but will not permit him to behave this way.

Steve also could have said, "I know you're trying to get our attention by doing something you know is wrong. But you can't do that—you can't get our attention by doing something that keeps us all from our recess." Another alternate method would lead Steve to discuss John's *behavior* with the class and allow the children to tell him that it was foolish or silly or stupid, as they would, thus having his own peers reject his *behavior* (not him).

Because Steve had handled the incident with John so effectively, in subsequent log entries John's name linked with trouble appeared only once more. Whether the situation at home (or whatever else had instigated his outbreak of rebelliousness) had improved, we do not know. We only know that Steve was infrequently faced with disruptive problems from John or others.

Student teachers often ask about effective measures to cope with the disruptive behavior of one or two students who use too much time and energy of the student teacher, leaving too little for the rest of the class. Studies have shown that fortunately teachers have a great deal of power to influence the behavior of their students.

It is common for teachers to ignore the children who are working steadily, while being occupied and sometimes entirely preoccupied with the pupil who is disruptive; or to ignore that same pupil when he or she is actually beginning to do classwork. Unfortunately, the whole class gets the message: "If you want to be noticed, stop working or, better yet, cause trouble."

The practice of giving attention primarily to the troublesome pupil is self-defeating. In contrast with the habit of noting primarily negative behavior is that of praising positive behavior for the purpose of reinforcing it. Here is a study that shows how teachers can introduce custom-made methods of changing behavior.

The investigators (Madsen, Becker, Thomas, Kosen, & Plager, 1972) sought an effective way for teachers to correct the behavior of first-grade children who were standing when they should have been working. Typically, the teacher directs the offender to sit down and get on with the work. The researchers found that when teachers concentrated on the violations of the children by telling them to sit down (their voices sometimes increasing in intensity) the misbehavior continued, and when they increased the commands to sit down, standing up behaviors actually increased. However, when the teachers turned their attention to praising behavior that was incompatible with standing up (i.e., sitting and working properly), the standing up declined.

A successful approach was this: The teachers "caught the child being good," giving praise, attention, or a smile when a child was seated and at work. When teachers saw a child standing and walking unnecessarily, they ignored the child and instead went to a neighboring child and praised him or her for being seated and working.

The success of this approach may be seen in this finding: In a class of 45 children and 2 teachers, there was a decline of 100 standing-ups per 20 minutes, a substantial difference in the functioning of any class.

Anna tried various techniques in an effort to stop a group of several adolescent girls from talking and/or giggling when she was presenting material. Anna explains:

> 11/4: I reprimanded the girls since Day 1. It didn't work, so Ms. C. suggested our putting some teeth into my discipline. I had them stay after, write lines, clean the chalkboard. Nothing worked. Then I gave a quiz after one lesson. They all failed—but that didn't seem to change them. Then Ms. C. and I re-thought things. I lecture. The girls talk or giggle. I yell at them. The boys think it's great—I'm yelling at the girls, and so on. This week I stopped yelling at them and let them talk. Instead I praised kids that answered my questions. The girls came around. They are definitely listening longer now—last time there were no flare ups.

We become accustomed from our experiences growing up at home and in school to focus primarily on misbehavior. Shifting our gears to a new way of functioning is not easy, but it is worth accomplishing, because we can learn to be more effective teachers (and parents as well).

No one should be left with the impression that this procedure means being "soft" on students who violate rules, disrupt classroom activities, and seek to undermine our authority. On the contrary, the objective of using methods that modify behavior is precisely to eliminate or at least greatly reduce the incidence of such kinds of unacceptable behavior.

## THE INTIMIDATING STUDENT

Ruby had a different and more serious problem than any we have yet examined. About 6 weeks into her student teaching she began to understand that she, as a teacher, was afraid of one of her second graders.

> 2/28: I didn't realize until this morning that my feelings about one child in particular, George, are becoming terrible. George is the one who gets and keeps the class out of hand, and when he isn't there, things go so smoothly. I can do extra things with the class which are a flop when George is there. This morning I found myself hoping that George would be absent. I think that I'm afraid of him.

To begin with, Ruby's classroom assignment was hardly the most conducive to learning. Her cooperating teacher had been given all the "problem children" in the grade. Ruby silently disapproved of some of the cooperating teacher's practices, especially her frequent shouting. The cooperating teacher openly disapproved of Ruby's quiet manner, insisting she must shout at the children. The cooperating teacher was absent frequently, and there was a turnover of substitutes.

These circumstances made life difficult for Ruby; her experiences are no less instructive, however, because even with better conditions, student teachers (and experienced teachers too) find themselves at similar loggerheads with one learner or another.

We analyze the reasons for the development of fear on Ruby's part, an emotion that can immobilize a teacher and make him or her an ineffectual classroom manager. In doing so, we refer to log entries made earlier than the one just cited.

About 7 weeks before the previous entry, Ruby made her first reference to George in the log and made her first series of mistakes.

> 1/11: George is testing me to see how far he can push me. I don't quite know how to handle it. Today he and Matt were having an argument over who Mrs. W. had said could take the ball out. Matt had the ball and George walked up and hit him in his stomach. I separated them and George said, "I'm going to kick his butt after school on the way home." I said, "No, you're not." He said, "Yes, I am too." I said, "Do you want to stay in for recess?" He said, "I'm not staying in nowhere." I didn't really want to make him stay in and I didn't want him to fight with Matt, but because of other encounters that we have had I felt that I should do something. Just as this happened, Mrs. W. came in and told everyone to go outside. I didn't say anything.

Ruby interpreted George's behavior in a personal way—that he was testing her. She was being tested as a teacher but not by design; George was behaving in his characteristic manner. She got enmeshed with George as much as Matt did, responding to George's threats to Matt in an unrealistic way (a teacher obviously cannot police children on their walk home from school). She then threatened punishment (staying in for recess) and did not carry it out.

Ruby, it should be noted, gave him his choice, to cease being belligerent or stay in during recess. When she failed to carry out the punishment, he learned that she wilted under his domination. Nothing so quickly undermines the authority of a teacher than failure to carry out the consequences of unacceptable behavior.

1/20: Today I had my first crisis in the classroom. George started about three little battles in the classroom. After I settled the third one down (between George and Raymond), George hit Raymond with his fist on the side of his face. Raymond was crying and George was threatening to beat him up after school. While this was going on, the class was getting completely out of hand. I had no idea where Mrs. W. was, and all I could think of was to take George up to the office and come back to quiet the rest of the class. Raymond was still crying when I came back down. I quieted the class and tried to talk to Raymond. He wouldn't talk, but the side of his face was swelling pretty badly. I took him to the office.

1/23: I had problems with George today. He was disturbing the class, running about the room, talking and constantly out of his seat. I finally had to take his recess away. He said he wouldn't stay in. I talked to Mrs. W. about it, and she said I couldn't handle George the way I handled other kids. (This was obvious.) Authority turns him off. Mrs. W. suggested that I talk privately with him, discuss what he'd been doing, and let him choose his punishment. I couldn't let him go out after that, so I told him that I wanted to talk to him during recess. He waited without much fuss. We decided that he was talking and that he should stay in. I turned my back to talk with a reading group and he left. When he returned we talked again and decided that he had to give up half his recess tomorrow. I was afraid that it might look to the rest of the class as if I were favoring him, but Mrs. W. said that they didn't pay that much attention and this is the best way to handle George.

1/24: George didn't come this morning and afternoon recess was only 5 minutes long, so I ended up letting him go to recess.

Ruby has now "taught" George that he can control the classroom situation. On 1/23, Ruby took her cooperating teacher's advice and gave him his choice of punishment. She then failed to carry it out both on that day and the following. So, 2 days in a row George's earlier lesson was reinforced—the new teacher (Ruby) does not carry out punishment.

Two weeks later (2/7) Ruby recognized that George was the key to the problems she was having with the few children who were disruptive, but she continued to show her hesitancy about being the adult teacher, the rational authority in the classroom. The next day (2/8) she was "amazed" to find that this child behaves like a child when the authority figure behaves like an authority figure.

2/7: Today was about the same as most days except for an unusual number of problems with George, Chad, Alex, and Stewart. George seems to incite the problems and the others follow. Once this happens it is almost impossible to get things running smoothly. George was really bad today, but I can't tell how far to let him go before stopping him.

2/8: Today was a very short day, but George was disturbing the class again. I decided that I had to stop it early today. I took him by the arm and took him outside of the classroom and talked to him and he agreed to stop. I was amazed. He was completely submissive to being taken out, reasonable and honest in the discussion, and much better behaved in the classroom. The class behaved much better too.

Students like George, who have learned to behave disruptively, do not change as a result of one good experience with a teacher or even after several good experiences. They fluctuate from day to day. Of course, so does the behavior of the teacher who may not always mobilize herself to act as the adult.

About 3 weeks later Ruby realized that fear was at the root of her relationship with George, as she had written in her 2/28 log entry, quoted earlier. He was absent for several days, during which time Ruby reported good and enjoyable hours in the classroom. The first day he returned, the first sentence in her log entry was, "George came back today and everything eventually went back to the usual upset." In Ruby's 3/3 log, the last on George, you see how her cooperating teacher had put George in an exceptional position in the classroom, and how that handicapped Ruby in dealing with him effectively. With her cooperating teacher absent, Ruby asserted herself:

3/3: George was here again, but things went much better. He didn't want me to do my unit and he insisted on running all over the room and talking until the kids couldn't possibly remember anything I said because every sentence was broken by my having to correct him. Finally, I just told him to get into the coatroom until we were finished. He will have to do his unit work at recess on Monday. If the substitute hadn't been there, I wouldn't have been able to do the lesson smoothly for the rest of the class because George would not have let us. She sat near him and watched to make sure that he was doing as I said. George is afraid of only one thing, going to the office, but I'm not even allowed to send him because Mrs. W. thinks that he should be allowed to do more than the other kids are allowed to do.

George needs help, much more than Ruby can provide. Only an investigation of his personal life and of his health and school histories, could give us clearer notions about his school behavior. The student teacher has neither the time nor the competencies to accomplish that. If student teachers are to survive (and develop as teachers), they must be able to cope with the Georges they encounter.

That means they must overcome fear when it arises; they must be the adult to the child.

At several points when Ruby had more pleasant exchanges with George, largely through her own solicitousness, she thought she had won him over. Those were acts of trying to placate someone who was feared, a kind of behavior that is just as ineffectual in the classroom as anywhere else. George's behavior must be dealt with firmly, decisively, and rationally. Such action requires careful and systematic thought, the kind associated with systematic problem-solving methods like CONTROL-C.

## Using CONTROL-C With the Intimidating Student

If Ruby had used CONTROL-C in helping her plan her work with George it would have very likely led to the following:

1. Private talks with George to explain that while nonparticipation is acceptable providing it does not disrupt the class, Ruby would like to help him to participate, to become stronger, to learn more, to be successful. Ruby conveys her interest in knowing how she could help him.

2. Firmness about disruptive acts without exception: Firmness, not vindictiveness, firmness preferably through methods that end the disruption and at the same time bring him back into class activities (e.g., "No, George, you may not run in this room. You are disturbing us. Return to your seat. I want you to do the work we are all doing. And even if you don't work, you must sit at your desk").

3. Some special tasks to use George's energy and to give him a sense of accomplishment, such as handing out some materials (but not after an act of aggression so that misbehavior gets rewarded and not, out of fear, to placate him).

4. A reminder to Ruby that George is a child and a victim of some unhappy experiences. We do not need to delve into his history, although knowing it will help us understand him better.

5. A reminder to Ruby that sometimes a teacher's "fear" is really a fear of letting loose anger against a student who has made classroom life hellish. Children are not hurt by the anger of a teacher who is trying to be effective. They will generally respect such an expression of feeling and learn from it. Furthermore, a teacher who expresses anger and finds it accepted can free herself from restraints to respond spontaneously to the quickly changing scene in the classroom.

6. A reminder to Ruby that in many classrooms under present circumstances there is at least one student, and sometimes many more who, for reasons not of their own making, get minimal help in school, if any. As a teacher you do everything possible to understand and be supportive to such youngsters while still protecting the class from disruptive behavior.

7. A reminder to Ruby that in 10 weeks or so she can hardly accomplish what regular teachers are unable to do with some children like George in a year.

8. A reminder to Ruby to reinforce George (and others like him) when he is engaged in school work or other appropriate behavior.

9. A reminder to Ruby that seating arrangements have some profound effects upon the activities and behavior of the children. One of us studied the impact of various seating arrangements on behavior, attention span, and teacher's attitude. We found, for example, that assignment to the first row (closest to the teacher) had the best status and gave the students the most teacher-attention (Schwebel & Cherlin, 1972). Comparable results would very likely be obtained in a study of seating in less traditionally arranged classrooms.

With regard to this last point, seating arrangements, there is no point in juggling them unless the teacher knows the learners and has a clear purpose. One student teacher in a middle school lost all benefit from seat reassignments by doing it on almost a daily basis and as a form of punishment. "Since you two talk all the time, I'm separating you." The student teacher was not dismayed when she found that those two talked during class no matter where they were placed: She continued to move them and others, but to no avail. Optimally, seating assignments can be made for positive reasons, such as to get together students who can help each other and who work well together.

## SEXUAL ISSUES

The developing self-confidence and comfort of the student teacher are of paramount importance when it comes to classroom management. Problems in class in regard to sex shake the confidence and comfort levels even of experienced teachers.

Chances are most student teachers receive little instruction, if any, in coping with sex-related problems, such as the kinds of difficulties Sheryl and Carla faced. Sheryl wrote the following in her log.

2/15: I really had a teaching problem. Frances wrote a note that said "Steve in Meg's pussy," and Steve got hold of it and brought it to me. I really wasn't sure what to do. I took Frances outside and asked her if she wrote it and she said she wrote some and Steve wrote some. Steve denied it (I only asked him if he wrote it), and then I spoke to Frances again. She admitted writing it. I asked her what she thought I should do. She said that she should apologize, which she did to Steve very nicely. She was crying and I told her I knew her mother would be upset and that I was disappointed. I told her to rip it up, which she did. I know harsher punishment would not have helped and it would have ruined anything that I had going with her.

The best that can be said about this report is that Sheryl did not evade the situation. Although she thought that she had spared Frances, she was unaware of the fact that she had greatly magnified this little note and aroused considerable guilt about sex. Yet she had not even asked Frances why she wrote it. Compare Sheryl's behavior about this sex matter with her actions the following day.

> 2/16: Many of the boys were clowning around, and I ended up putting four names on the board to stay in for afternoon recess. Steve immediately erased it and I chose to ignore his doing that. However, when it was time to go out, Mrs. R. reminded him. He put on another fit and said, crying, he was going to be bad for the rest of the time I'd be here and punishing him like this would not do any good. I ended up letting him write something 50 times and hand it in the next day.

The boys clowned. Steve erased the names Sheryl put on the board, he put on a fit and threatened to be bad for days. For all of that, Sheryl had him write "something" 50 times. Surely by any standards of what disrupts a class Steve far outstripped Frances. By any standards of what kind of behavior must be discouraged, Steve's was more self-destructive than Frances'. Why then did Sheryl react as she did?

Carla's experience helps us answer that question. Carla's cooperating teacher, Sylvia, informed the class that there was going to be a "good" and a "bad" list on the board. Carla, she told them, was in charge of who went on which list. Those on the bad list would not get one of the freshly baked Valentine cookies. Carla described what happened:

> 2/11: The children would run up to me and ask me to put them on the good smile list. I don't know if I like labeling kids good and bad, and I don't want to be seen just as the disciplinarian—somebody who can dispense rewards and punishment—and that's all.
>
> In circle, Kelly wouldn't put a book away after consistently being told to, so Sylvia put him on the bad list (I didn't want to put anyone on bad—they were either good, or weren't on at all). Then Josh pinched me hard and he went on the bad side. Later I crossed them both off, but Sylvia said they had to stay on bad. So they got no cookie—and did they every cry! Sylvia said there was no excuse for Josh's pinching me, and I guess I agree, but Kelly with the book? Well, I guess he'd never do what we say if our "threats" (no cookie) don't come true.
>
> Later Josh jumped on me and started lifting up my shirt and pressing at my breasts (and I know he meant to—it wasn't that he just happened to touch there—because of the way he looked at me as he did it). I read an article on "Sex in the Classroom" and how to discuss it, but it didn't go into a situation like that. I looked at Josh meaningfully (I hope) and moved his hands. I didn't know what else to do.

We would agree with Carla that Sylvia's lists were hardly suited to aid Carla or any student teacher. We have no knowledge about the part the lists played in Josh's behavior. We do know, however, that Carla did not raise the slightest question about Josh's first attack upon her.

Does it not seem surprising that seemingly without provocation he should pinch her? (She did not say where she was pinched.) Would not any student teacher be perplexed and interested in seeking an explanation? But the first aggression was so overshadowed by the sexual aspect of the second one that she seemed oblivious to the cause of the first. Yet, the first was much more mysterious than the second, which was "provoked" by Josh being put on the "bad list."

Quite understandably, Carla was startled and frightened by Josh's behavior. Her description suggests some of her bewilderment. We do not know how he jumped on her or how he looked at her (e.g., was it in anger or did she see sexual passion) or what her facial expression was like when she looked "meaningfully" at him. Did she show anger or humiliation or embarrassment?

These questions are not meant to belittle Carla's responses to a difficult interaction. They are meant to indicate the special problem we adults have over sexual acts. Carla halted the behavior and thereafter made no issue of it. We are left without knowing whether the pinch was "sexual," even whether Carla's perception of the pressure on her breasts was sexual, whether these were Josh's nonsexual reactions to a frustrating mother substitute, or whether other factors were at work. We do learn from Carla's next log entry that Josh is socially backward for his age and "acts out" rather than "talks out" his anger.

2/12: Josh and Tammy and Megan all wanted to be the engineer and Josh was pushing and biting the two girls because he wanted to sit in the front chair. Sylvia put two other chairs there and said now we'll have three engineers. (Would I have thought of that? I think so.) I just wish that Josh could verbalize instead of constantly hitting and pushing and kicking and then crying when he gets hit back. I keep telling him to "tell me" or "tell them," but he runs over and hits.

Josh acts out his emotions. He pushed and bit because he was angry. Probably his touching Carla was also motivated by anger (rather than sex impulse), and part of helping such a child is in letting him or her know that he or she may not express emotions physically that way, with teacher or students. The child must, in fact, never be rewarded for such action as Josh was by Sylvia, the cooperating teacher, who provided extra chairs so that he and the two girls could all be engineers. Coming as that action did immediately after "pushing and biting," she simply reinforced inappropriate behavior.

In connection with sexual problems, we recommend the following:

1. Avoid impulsive reactions to sexual talk. What each of us has learned about acceptable references to sex varies from individual to individual, family to family, and culture to culture. No one set of rules about sex talk by students is proper or correct. What is acceptable to you, may be frowned upon in some communities; whereas what you disapprove of or are even shocked by, may be acceptable in the district to which you are assigned. Furthermore, the code of acceptable

speech that you learned in elementary and high school may have changed drastically in the intervening years.

Needless to say, we are not arguing for a do-as-you-may policy in regard to the use of sexual expressions. However, we are arguing against a teacher reacting impulsively with self-righteousness or outrage. To guard against that kind of response we advise you to curb any tendency to act based on your emotional reaction alone, and instead to be thoughtful about coping with the use of sex language that disrupts the class or upsets you.

2. In this area, as in others, preparation is a key to effective classroom management. Talk to your cooperating teacher and to fellow teachers to learn what their practices, preferences, and rules are. Ask them about what problems have come up this year and in past ones. Think about how you would handle different situations that might arise.

3. When a student uses sex language that disrupts the class, treat the behavior as you would any other. You will want to stop the disturbance, which is sometimes best achieved by ignoring the provocation. You will, in any event, want to pursue two steps in dealing with a student who makes regular use of sex language that deviates from the mores of the school. The first step is to consider the reasons for the behavior. For example, does this student come from a family very different in culture and/or social class from the rest? Or, alternatively, has this student learned that sex language gives him or her attention and relationships not otherwise attainable with his or her repertoire of social skills?

The second step is to develop a plan of action. If it turns out that the student is employing home-bred vocabulary, a discussion with him or her (and with the parents) is in order, not to express disapproval of the family's language but to explain the difference between language usage at home and at school. In the more likely event that the student uses sex expressions to gain attention (sometimes by provoking the teacher), your plan might include giving him or her attention for positive behavior.

The subject of sex became more public and prominent during the past several decades. Complex social forces led to more open discussion of the topic and to the infusion of highly sexualized content in films and popular music. Naturally, school atmosphere and class discussions were bound to be affected by these societal changes and by the fact that children were getting a good deal of exposure to sexual issues at young ages. Then, during the 1980s, with the rise in the incidence of AIDS (Acquired Immune Deficiency Syndrome), the nature and prevention of this disease became subjects for discussion in many high schools, and in some, condoms were distributed.

As you know, there are no easy answers to the enormous social and health problems related to adolescent sexuality. Teachers can only do their best to help students, in age-appropriate ways, to understand and cope with the effects of living in a sexually charged society.

## THE STUDENT WHO STEALS

Discovering that students are stealing is upsetting. One student teacher, Celia, told about an incident that we mention only to alert others to the need for care about safeguarding valuables and avoiding temptation for children and adolescents. Celia said,

> 6/2: I got to school late and parked my car in the last faculty spot, adjacent to the student lot. I had more than I could carry in the car and left my tape recorder and papers on the front seat. I came out between first and second periods, but the tape recorder was gone.

Celia was student teaching in a suburban high school. Sandra, whose log appears here, was assigned to an elementary school:

> 3/23: An unfortunate incident: While we were out on a nature walk, someone took money from my pocketbook in the coat area of our room. There is one fifth-grade boy in another class who has a record of doing this. I reported it to the school the next day because it wasn't discovered until I got home.

Thefts of this kind occur for a variety of reasons. Some are obvious ones like wanting money for its own use. Others are indirect ones, like getting back at the authority for what has been perceived to be an injustice, an abuse, a grievance of some kind, committed by the victim or by another school person or by a parent.

A student teacher should take preventive and self-protective measures. If you are victimized and the guilty youth has been identified, it is wise to avoid indignation. Instead, react like the rational authority who disapproves of the behavior, applies appropriate punishment, and if possible gets the individual to face up to the reasons for the offense.

One of us had an experience that was different from Sandra's in that another pupil's property was taken. In general, the reasons for such thefts are somewhat different from those perpetrated against the teacher. Although the child or adolescent can be motivated by the overpowering desire to have the money or the property taken, it can also be instigated by envy of another student's success, beauty, popularity, relative wealth, athletic skills, and so on.

In the experience just referred to, one of us was the teacher of a seventh-grade class in which Ralph was seen going through the bookbag of another boy, Lewis. The teacher was not surprised by this behavior because Ralph, who was husky for his age, acted the part of bully-boy with the smaller boys after school and surreptitiously tried to provoke other pupils in class. Following is an approximate replay of the interaction between the teacher and Ralph at the end of the class period after the other pupils had been dismissed for lunch.

TEACHER:   Ralph, is there something you want to tell me?

RALPH:        What about? I don't know what you're talking about.

TEACHER:      About what you did in class this period.

RALPH:        I don't know what you're talking about. I worked on the reports.

TEACHER       [looking intently but not angrily]: You don't know what I'm talk-
              ing about?

RALPH         [shifting uncomfortably in his seat]: Well . . . no . . . I don't.

TEACHER:      Let's just sit here until you remember what you did this period,
              apart from some work. Something you did that you should never
              do.

RALPH         [after a moment's pause]: What's the big deal? I didn't take
              anything.

TEACHER:      You didn't take anything?

RALPH:        No.

TEACHER:      Well, just to be sure, let's get Lewis in on this. We'll have him
              examine his bag right here in front of us.

RALPH:        No! Don't call him. I'll give it back.

TEACHER:      Mmmmm . . .

RALPH:        I just took a Scout badge. I'll give it back. [He gets up to leave.]

TEACHER:      Hold on, Ralph. What are you going to say to Lewis?

RALPH         [looking puzzled and angry]: I don't know.

TEACHER:      If you go to Lewis this way you'll just cause even more trouble
              for yourself. I'll give you a few more minutes of my time to
              help you prepare.

RALPH         [angrily]: What do you want me to say—I stole your Scout
              badge? Here it is?

TEACHER:      I offered to help and you got angry. Is that what you do when
              people try to help you?

RALPH:        Nobody helps me. I don't need it.

TEACHER:      Don't need it?

RALPH         [after a long pause]: I'll say I'm sorry. I'll say I won't do it again.

TEACHER:      Yes, Ralph, and that's a good thing to say.

RALPH         [at peace for the first time]: Can I go now?

TEACHER:      When will you see Lewis?

RALPH:        In the cafeteria.

TEACHER:      All right. You may go now. But I want to see you again after
              you've spoken with Lewis.

The teacher's aim here is clear: to handle the situation in the most constructive
way possible. This means Lewis' property will be returned and, if possible, Ralph

will also learn from the encounter. A change in his behavior is the hoped-for goal. The teacher did not make him defensive, did not get aroused by his initial belligerence, and did not get angry when he denied that he had engaged in any untoward behavior. The teacher, through an understanding approach that involved following his feelings very closely, sought only to have Ralph remedy his behavior. The teacher knew that a heavy punitive approach would do much less for Ralph than one that elicited his thought and behavioral change.

## STUDENTS WITH LOW SELF-ESTEEM

Many students with low self-esteem often go unnoticed because they are not troublemakers. After student teachers manage to deal with the aggressive students, they often become aware of the passive withdrawn ones. A student teacher asked for advice from colleagues in his seminar, "He never raises his hand, talks almost in a whisper so that I can't hear him, and has no friends. Except in geography, he barely earns passing grades. What can I do, especially to get him to learn more?" This is the advice he got:

This student has a many-faceted problem and you, as his teacher, have to understand and treat it accordingly. First apply a systematic problem-solving procedure like CONTROL-C. Through the use of CONTROL-C you would develop your list of options. They might include:

1. In geography some possibilities are: (a) You can use the student's strength to build his self-confidence through positive reinforcement. You can call on him to answer questions and praise his responses immediately after they are given. (b) You can have him make a special report to the class on some phase of geography. If he should speak too softly when delivering his report (or at any other time), you could say, "I like your comments very much and I want to be sure everyone in the class can hear them. Could you speak up, please?" Then praise him for even the smallest increase in volume.

2. Dramatics offers possibilities: (a) Although he is afraid to speak up under ordinary circumstances, he may be able to do this behind a puppet stage or as an actor with a small part in a class play. (b) Choral reading or singing can benefit this student as well as the whole class. It can be followed by having small groups and then individuals alternate in reading or singing.

3. Peers can be helpful: (a) You could enlist an outgoing student to befriend him and include him in some playground games or other activity. (b) You could arrange to have him do peer teaching in geography or be taught by another student in the other subjects.

With imagination and CONTROL-C you can delineate many possibilities. Because there is no one correct way to help this boy, you should experiment until you find one or several that work well.

Remember that student teachers (or regular teachers for that matter) are not miracle workers. Work toward your goal with patience, but do not expect to transform a highly withdrawn student into a highly gregarious one, not in 3 months, not in a year.

A somewhat similar question and request for advice came from a student teacher in industrial arts: "This term almost everything is going fine. Not my fifth period class, however, perhaps because the students are in the lower track and several have very low self-esteem. In such a situation shouldn't the student teacher try to help the students improve their self-view?"

This question stimulated extensive discussion. Following is a summary of the conclusions: Most educators would agree that a quality education fosters the broadest possible growth in individuals. So, as you suggest, it makes sense for student teachers (and teachers) to informally assess their students' self-concept and its development over time, just as they do more systematically with academic achievement.

A person's self-concept plays a crucial role in at least three areas that can affect classroom performance. (a) Behavior: a student who does not see him or herself as able is not likely to act competently. Instead he or she will function in ways consistent with his or her self-view. (b) Expectations: a person who views him or herself as a poor student expects to fail exams. Thus, he or she is less motivated to prepare and more likely to fail, reaffirming his or her self-view. (c) Interpretation of performance: if a student has trouble mastering a technique, and his or her self-concept is low, he or she will likely blame him or herself and perhaps give up trying.

Adolescence, of course, is a time when students go through profound personal changes and inevitably struggle with their self-concept. Help they might receive in bolstering their self-views would be especially useful. In your situation, a first step toward providing such help is for you, under your cooperating teacher's supervision, to informally assess the students' self-views to determine the accuracy of your observations. If, on the basis of the information so collected, you determine that self-esteem is a problem, next steps you might take could include the following:

1. Teach the students to evaluate their performance realistically. This takes time.
2. Try to identify the basic-skill deficiencies that may be presently contributing to their low self-esteem. Find or develop training materials to help them overcome the deficits.
3. Teach the students to set realistic goals. Some individuals with low self-views make excessively high demands of themselves. Setting attainable goals that they must work hard to achieve is more suitable to the building of a positive self-view.
4. Praise is a great tonic. Give it to students when they deserve it; teach them to praise each other and to compliment themselves for work which merits

it. Praise is unlike money in that our supplies are unlimited. Teach the students that they can benefit others and themselves by spending it freely.

Having said all this, however, we must add a caveat. Remember that self-concept is a relatively stable factor that develops over a period of years. Progress in bringing about planned improvement may be slow; yet the actions of striving for it can transform the classroom atmosphere and make your work more satisfying.

## THE DISRUPTIVE STUDENT

The disruptive students often leave the student teacher frustrated. However, the experience of working with them can be instructive, and in some instances, and to some extent, the students can be helped.

In an earlier log entry Julie had referred to Lucas as "the kid who's had me climbing the walls."

> 3/3: Lucas was back to some of his tricks today—banging his feet on the floor during show-and-tell. When asked to step he replied, "I don't care—I don't want to see anyone's show-and-tell. . . . I don't have a show-and-tell anyway."
> On the other days I had answered angrily and tried to outshout him. I knew that didn't work and I'd better try something else. I tried to handle his statement in the best way, a considerate way. I explained that show-and-tell was a time to listen and that the class members have something they want to share with us. It is important that we are polite and listen together. I also invited him to bring in something for show-and-tell. I reminded him that show-and-tell objects can be lots of things—an interesting rock you find on the way to school, pine cones—things that he may be able to find.

A few days later Julie had the kind of poignant experience in her relationship with Lucas that represents some of the rewards in the difficult profession of teaching. Julie shows too that she is a realist and does not expect that a few constructive interactions with a child can counteract all that is destructive. She also demonstrates how positive a force a student teacher can be whether or not that experience elicits a permanent change in the child's outlook, feeling, and behavior.

> 3/8: Today Lucas again was disruptive (singing, stomping his feet, pounding his hands) during show-and-tell. When I asked him to stop, he continued saying, "I don't want to listen." I got to the point where I just tried ignoring his behavior, knowing that attention was only reinforcing his behavior. But he persisted.
> At library time I stayed in the classroom with Lucas (he had not returned his library book and said he didn't want to go to the library anyway). I asked him why he thought I had kept him from the library today, and he knew exactly why. We

began just to talk, and he was very open. I didn't want to lecture him. I wanted
to try and get through to why he is so unhappy. At one point I just wanted to cry
for him. He asked me why he had no friends, and I explained that whenever anyone tries to be his friend he hits, bites, or kicks them and people don't like that.
I told him that he had to be nicer to others and they'd be nicer to him. He then
asked, "How can I like other people when I don't even like myself?"

What a horrible thing for a 6-year-old to be going through. No amount of discipline is going to solve Lucas's problem. He seems crushed, feels he can't do anything right. He has no self-esteem at all. I could only encourage him and point out
all that he has to offer all of us. At the end of our talk he seemed more convinced
of his worth, but our one little bull session alone can't change him. As we walked
down the hall to the library from the class, he reached over and took my hand to
walk with him.

At that point I felt something very special. He had confided in me and that made
me happy. And he showed me how much he needed encouragement and how I had
tried to give it to him. I don't want Lucas to be a puppet—doing everything I ask
him to do without any comment. I just want him to be a happy little boy for once
in his life (I have never seen Lucas laugh).

3/9: Today I made a special point to talk to Lucas individually. I feel that he needs
the extra attention desperately. He had a show-and-tell today. As much as I have
mixed feelings about this activity, I was glad to see him get involved. His show-
and-tell was a poem he had copied for his mom. . . . He did a neat job, and I made
sure that I praised his good work.

Lucas, as Julie now understood, had not sprouted angel's wings! He was a
troubled boy, and she knew she would be pressed to contend with him in ways
that would protect the class from disruption and him from behaviors that alienated him from the class. Now at least she understood him better and also was not
setting impossible goals for herself.

Like Julie, Jane, too, comes to realize that she has been expecting too much
too soon. In her log she explains that after much thought and soul-searching she
came to realize that, to date, she has done little "actual teaching" in her cooperating school. She continues.

2/25: All I have done is just discipline these kids. But every time I think I am getting somewhere and have a few rules set up, they fall apart when Miss F. tries them.
I like her and I think she has some fantastic ideas about teaching, but she has not
helped these kids form any self-control at all. I don't know how to do it either, and
sometimes I feel down about it, but now I'm getting the feeling that I need time.
This year, next year, I don't know when, but I'll help the kids in my class.

Dorothy had a different problem. After 1 week of student teaching she had
that desperate feeling that is so common to the student teacher: They do not take
me seriously. It's the sensation that leads the young teacher to yearn for Friday
afternoon and to dread Monday morning. For the stout-hearted student teacher

that feeling is also a challenge. Dorothy was stout-hearted. At a critical time she did not collapse, even under the turmoil she experienced.

1/14: The substitute was unable to come, so I had to take complete control of our class. I had discovered that the children did not take what I said to them seriously, because all I had been doing was threatening and not carrying things out. I kept telling April, Horace, and Thomas to stop running around the room and making jokes during my explanation of their arithmetic assignment. Was I going to be beaten by this? I decided I would not.

As soon as I got the rest of the class settled down and doing their math (accomplished this by telling them at 1:15 I would collect their papers), I took April, Horace, and Thomas out in the hall. I discussed with them how they were disturbing the class, plus I gave them an opportunity to explain their behavior. Well, all they could do was giggle and make smart remarks. Therefore, I proceeded to take them to the principal's office.

When we got there I became sick all over—the only thing I could picture was him calling their parents and the beatings they would get at home. All of a sudden I felt sorry for them and wanted to cry and tell the principal to forget it. But it was too late, and thank God he only made them stand in the corner outside his office. I'm really afraid that if he had mentioned calling their parents, I would have asked him not to. Someday I'll have to face such a situation—and how am I going to handle it? I really don't think I can answer until I'm in the actual situation, but I must get my logic together so I can support however I react.

1/15: Continued having problems with Horace, Thomas, and Martin. Therefore I kept them in the room while the rest of the class went to a film. I wanted the punishment to be constructive, so I had them help straighten up the room, then made them sit in their seats for approximately 5 minutes. Then we four went to the film.

## ABUSED STUDENTS

Abuse can be sexual, physical, emotional, or mental in character or a combination of these. Neglect includes failure of parents to properly feed, house, clothe, or supervise their child. Current law in your locality may require teachers to report any *suspected* case of neglect or child abuse to appropriate authorities.

Teachers are in a unique position in students' lives. They are often the only adult outside the immediate family to whom a student can turn for help. Teachers have an enormous responsibility in this area—to be alert to students in need.

The physical signs of youngsters in need of help may be obvious: burns, bruises, cuts, inadequate clothing during cold winter months. The behavioral signs, such as listlessness, fearfulness, aggressiveness, and emotional instability, however, may be symptoms of problems other than abuse and neglect, so that one must be cautious about coming to premature conclusions. In any event, if you have suspicions, share them with your cooperating teacher who, in turn, would in all likelihood discuss them with the school nurse, principal, or social worker.

Teachers who become familiar with community resources and maintain good relationships with parents can be helpful in many ways. As a student teacher it would be wise for you to find out as much as possible about the resources available in your school's community: services of food pantries for the hungry, sources of free clothing, settlement houses that might provide after school tutoring or supervised activities for latchkey children, or emergency help with utilities, housing shelters for a battered mother and her child, or the homeless.

Often a student is unable to concentrate in school because of overwhelming problems at home. Although a student teacher cannot change a student's life, it may be possible at times to ease some of the burden. Most parents will welcome any offer to help them with their child's well being. Some are too afraid or ashamed to ask.

## EXPECTING THE UNEXPECTED

Expect the unexpected because it will happen. By expecting it you will not be surprised and will be better able to cope.

Some of the behaviors and events that we consider to be "the unexpected" are: fights, tobacco, drug and alcohol use, weapon discovery, health emergencies such as epileptic seizures, the appearance of strangers in class, and problems at parent conferences between divorced spouses.

We all know that we are supposed to "keep our cool" when faced with such events, and the question we ask is how to do that. The best way is through preparation and rehearsal. Preparation means:

- Knowing your students
- Knowing the resources in the school such as someone you could count on in an emergency, like a teacher, vice-principal, counselor, custodian, your most reliable student
- Thinking of yourself as the authority figure in charge of any situation, cooling down the atmosphere and feeling good that you were able to take control of the situation
- Imagining each of the "unexpecteds" given here, following through until you have resolved them and rehearsing again and again the steps you took to work them out.

Here is advice from experienced educators on handling common "unexpecteds" (Westling & Koorland, 1988).

Fights: Firmly order the students to stop and separate them. If they do not respond to your order, send for help and repeat the order. When they stop fighting, get all students back to work. At this point you want them involved, no matter in what. Later, in an atmosphere of calm, discuss the fight with each of the two students separately and apply class and/or school rules and punishment. Finally, talk with them about how such fights could be avoided in the future.

Stealing: If you know who was the thief, find a time to discuss the action privately. If the theft is admitted and the item returned, the punishment should depend on whether this was the first offense. If the student does not confess, although you have no doubt he or she is guilty, explain that you are disturbed both by the act and the denial. If the behavior is part of a persistent pattern, inform the guidance counselor or school psychologist. No matter how frustrated you may be, if you have no clues, do not punish the entire class.

Foul language: Inquire whether there is a school or class rule about this. In your own class in the future, if there are no school rules, you may wish to make your own and announce them firmly.

Sexual activity: This may be heterosexual, homosexual, or autoerotic. It is wise simply to halt the activity as unobtrusively as possible. You explain, if need be, that this is not the time or place for it. It is wise not to moralize and certainly not to draw more attention to it.

Health problems and physical accidents: Deal with the immediate situation, for example, a seizure, a faint, a vomiting student, and then call for the school nurse or another person assigned to handle such problems. Don't move the student; don't administer drugs of any kind. Prepare a written report of the incident, perhaps on a standard school form. Someone, perhaps you, will be expected to inform the parent.

With mental rehearsals and experience you will learn to take the unexpected in stride. That does not mean you will ever find it a favorite part of being a teacher.

## GROWTH IN COPING

Few of the logs we collected or the interviews we conducted had 100% happy endings a la Hollywood films of the 1950s. What they reported were the mixture of successes and failures of real life. Many student teachers showed enormous growth during their few months of student teaching. Among their other accomplishments, the successful student teachers had become more effective in maintaining a disciplined class.

They learned that they themselves were ready to make the transition from student to teacher and that teachers cannot help students by pretending to be their peers or by avoiding the use of the authority assigned to them. They discovered that being a classroom leader is not the same as being a martinet. They realized that freedom in an orderly system that has its own "rules" is different from the anarchy of a *laisséz-faire* (do-as-you-choose) classroom. And they also came to understand that in a mere few months, some filled with despair, they had learned very much but that it was only what it was intended to be, that is, only a beginning, with years of opportunity for growth ahead.

A study of the logs shows that student teachers began at different levels with regard to their ability to manage a class and ended at different levels too. And that is just what you would expect. But among those who encountered and successfully overcame the toughest discipline problems, there was one common element: They all employed a systematic problem-solving thought process in working things through. In other words, while most of them did not have access to a prepackaged problem-solving plan like CONTROL-C, they did, on their own, develop and follow procedures much like CONTROL-C.

This meant that these successful student teachers took whatever information they could piece together about the problem they faced in order to develop one or more solution strategies. Because they had logs, they could look back and see what thoughts they had had since Day 1. Without their logs they could not have detected the changes that took place in their thinking. And they would have had difficulty remembering clearly what their earlier reactions were (just as one cannot detect children's growth when one lives with them on a day-to-day basis).

The most successful student teachers worked persistently at specifying the problems they were facing and struggled to understand them. To accomplish this, most talked their thoughts and ideas over with their fellow professionals (in and out of seminar) and with friends.

By the end of the year, successful student teachers had begun to come to terms with the real life of the teacher. Some students, they realized, came to school unhappy, angry, and belligerent. They had learned to contend with those emotions and especially the behavior that they stimulated.

Malvina was well into the term as a student teacher in the sixth grade of a New York City school, still working only with individuals and small groups. She saw first hand how classroom management problems are compounded when a student suffers from chronically uncontrollable anger outbursts. And by the end of her assignment, she had learned how to effectively cope with this.

3/6: During the math lesson (which followed the morning reading period), Richard started banging and whistling. Mr. B. spoke to him privately by going up to his desk. The disturbances continued, but Mr. B. ignored him. The noise was beginning to have its effects on the rest of the class. I hesitated, but finally decided it wasn't worth it to the rest of the class to let the commotion go on. I asked him to stop; he now put away the mirror that Mr. B. told him to stop playing with. The disturbances continued. I asked him if he wanted to come to the back of the room so I could babysit for him. He was unwilling to come and I wasn't going to physically force him. The noise still continued. I took my chair and my work and sat next to him. I kept him calm enough so he did not upset the whole class (and I felt that was crucial).

Student teachers who have gone to disciplined schools and then to college are upset at first when a boy like Richard (age 13 and above average in height and weight) bangs on his desk and whistles with no evident provocation, and furthermore continues after his teacher tells him to stop. Two months later, Malvina, who had been stunned by his behavior earlier in the term, handled it in stride. That means she kept him from further disruptive outbursts. By the end of that same week she had an experience with him that gave her hope, very tentative, but hope nevertheless.

> 5/10: I had my first good experience with Richard today. The kids were allowed to make Mother's Day cards. Richard wanted some help in writing something. I had him respond to "What does your mother do for you?" He mentioned close to ten things. I listed them in a nice poetic arrangement. He just sort of looked at me in the end and said distinctly and with feeling, "Thank you, Miss R." Mr. B. saw and heard him do it and nodded to me. He apparently felt as I did. I had really "reached" Richard for a moment—and that's a hard thing to do.

Malvina had indeed reached Richard. Her success, momentary though it might have been, shows how much in the way of understanding, attention, and support some students in our schools need. This can be done only on an individual basis, and to do that teachers typically require more assistance and smaller classes than they get. However, as in Richard's case, attention such as Malvina gave can help, even if it is not enough to reverse the damage and present distress. In any event, Malvina's hopes were set back a few days later.

> 5/14: During a morning lesson time, Mr. B. indicated he had to step out for a moment. I continued with the lesson. All of a sudden a chair is turned over and Richard starts shouting. I had seen Richard go off like this once or twice before. He climbed to a chair, to a desk and kept challenging and baiting Harold to fight him. Harold, normally very patient with Richard, wouldn't put up with it any longer and started to fight. The rest of the class grew rather quiet and inactive. I moved to the back of the room and attempted to separate the boys by placing myself between them. Harold came (with my urging and pulling, if I remember correctly) to the front of the room. Richard kept baiting him and he began to fight. I called to the boys in the class and asked for some help. I had them hold Harold back. I also had worked hard to calm Richard, telling him it couldn't be settled by fighting in school and that I didn't want to be hurt. I took Richard out of the room.

By this point in the term Malvina has become almost expert at handling these crises, even to the extent of getting the help of the other students. Following the principle that there can be no learning in a class devastated by conflict, she took action to quell the fight and to win a degree of tranquility. Malvina began to look for a pattern to understand Richard's behavior and she found one.

> 5/21: I noticed something rather interesting about Richard. At the end of the trip today he began to "go off." I have the feeling that when things begin to go too well,

Richard finds something to "go off" for. During our trip today Mr. B. and I were able to give him more attention—instead of making him happier, he acts up. And it's been true when things get good in the classroom too. This also fits with his answer to the psychologist's form when he said he usually expects bad or unhappy things to happen. How do you deal with a problem like this?

Some people are so accustomed to "things going wrong" that not only do they expect it but also they make it happen. They help bring it about so that the world behaves in the only way they know. They are not happy in that state, but they are at least accustomed to it. A teacher's task working with Richard (and those like him) is to try to help him learn and grow, to become accustomed to things going well. Malvina tried to do that, but she had no illusion about the obstacles both within Richard himself and in the circumstances in the school.

If we are to be effective classroom managers we benefit by taking both a broad and a narrow view of the situation we face. We ask ourselves what, if anything, we are doing to create or maintain discipline problems and, in any event, what we might do to curb them. At the same time we are aware that some disruptive behavior has been stirred up elsewhere, perhaps by conditions at home or by those in school but not in our classroom. In this case, too, a logical problem-solving technique like CONTROL-C will help us develop techniques useful in managing the classroom.

# IV

▼▼▼▼▼▼▼▼▼

# Today and Tomorrow

# 11

▼▼▼▼▼▼▼

# The Student Teacher
# as a Person

In actuality, the individual student teacher and his or her values, experiences, knowledge, and personality, are not separable from his or her orientation toward discipline or his or her relationships with the students, cooperating teacher, and the supervisor. Only for the sake of emphasis do we have a chapter of this kind.

Although some examples from the logs and interviews that we give in this chapter are similar to those quoted earlier, the focus is different. It is on the *person* behind the student teacher, and about the human emotions he or she experiences.

We concentrate on 10 kinds of experiences and associated emotions that are common to student teachers and were apparent in logs and interviews. Each of them relates to the heart of student teaching and each of them, if addressed effectively, has the potential for promoting personal growth. The topics are:

1. controlled exhaustion;
2. being criticized;
3. discovering that teacher peers are people;
4. overcoming self-doubt;
5. coping with stress;
6. coping with ethical issues;
7. becoming socialized;
8. appreciating the college supervisor's support;
9. devotion to the students; and
10. devotion from the students.

## CONTROLLED EXHAUSTION

Many student teachers find the student-teaching experience an exhausting one. In part this is so because they put their whole self into it. Beyond that, the tension from being under observation by a college supervisor and cooperating teacher and in conflict with some children is itself fatiguing. This condition is sometimes compounded by overt and covert differences about important matters, most significant of which is whether the student teacher will be permitted to teach in a way that fits his or her personal style. Then sometimes the student teacher has further university requirements to meet. There are health problems that get exacerbated by tension; and there is one's personal life. "How can I leave the worries and pressures of my class behind," the student teacher wonders, "so that I can enjoy tonight's get-together with my friends?" Here is Joyce, halfway through her student teaching:

> 2/11: Boy, it's Friday. TGIF. Change of pace for a weekend. Teaching can really get you down. I haven't developed the ability to leave school at school. Maybe it's because I'm always so busy planning for tomorrow.
>
> In my opinion, teaching this quarter has made me aware of the stamina I'm going to need if I get a regular position. Like, I'm almost totally exhausted after 5 or 6 weeks. What will I be like after 5 or 6 months! Beats me.

At points the time pressures can become so great that even medical appointments are put in second place. Ruby tells about that:

> 2/18: I had a lot of trouble controlling the class, perhaps because it was Friday or perhaps it was just because I hadn't been here on Thursday. . . . I went back to do my bulletin board and it took me from 3:00 to 7:15, which meant that I had to cancel my doctor's appointment. I'll have to get my iron shot Saturday.

Some fatigue is due to inexperience in performing a task that is in itself tiring. Gary, doing student teaching in English in high school explained:

> 3/11: This week, at last, I got the chance to read the students' papers. I wrote comments and put grades on them (lightly in pencil). Great, but I feel I've been through the meat-grinder. Four classes turned their papers in on the same day (it's the end of the marking period). How much of this can you stand? Or do you get used to it?

But, as demanding as student teaching is, most individuals muster the energy and the hours necessary to emerge from it stronger as teachers and people than at the beginning. Awareness of the limited time frame is one positive factor. Even more important is the conviction that this road leads to a lifetime profession.

If exhaustion is sapping your strength, take steps to adjust. Set aside time each day for relaxation, pleasure, reading, a jog around the block, a favorite television show, or playing the piano. Frequently, the emotional demands of student teaching, not just the long hours, bring about that exhausted feeling. Putting your life into balance, with time set aside for pleasurable activities will help you combat that feeling of exhaustion, both now and in the future. Some of the suggestions in the section on "coping with stress" later in this chapter will also be helpful to you in contending with exhaustion.

## BEING CRITICIZED

Criticism is an essential ingredient in the development of professionals. Artists, actors, and athletes depend on it to enhance their growth in their respective fields. We as teachers need it too.

Teachers regularly use imaginative ways to translate their classrooms into effective learning environments; that is, classrooms that are physically and psychologically conducive to learning. When their innovations are effective, they excite and generate great interest. However, in the process of innovation, one cannot expect that every new idea will work as planned. Mistakes are inevitable. Criticism and self-criticism, as long as these are constructive, will help the teacher develop professionally.

As for student teachers, criticism may be forthcoming for a number of reasons and most of all because a method used was simply not effective. Sometimes a method is not used effectively because it has been learned from a professor's lecture and then applied to an inappropriate situation. In other instances, the method may have failed because it was not part of the experience of the cooperating teacher and his or her pupils. Sometimes, as a result of the strangeness of a method, criticism may come from quite an unexpected quarter, as Laura discovered on her fourth day in school:

> 1/29: Today was a good day with one exception. One of the girls told me that a boy said I was a stupid teacher. That really hurt! I couldn't figure out why he would have said it. I hadn't reprimanded him or anything like that. The only thing I could think of was that I had done some things differently from Mrs. W., so that maybe that's why he thought I was stupid. It was a blow to my ego, but I suppose it won't be the only time it will happen.

Hearing about criticism from one's students is infrequent. Most criticism will come from cooperating teachers, for the very purpose of student teaching is to have practical experience accompanied by vigorous and constructive critiques. For some student teachers, however, the criticisms are difficult to cope with, even when the student recognizes them to be valid. But time, a growing comfort in the classroom, and confidence in oneself usually work to the advantage of student teachers. Criticism becomes increasingly easier to accept and to use.

Occasionally, however, a difference in a temperament or teaching style leads to the kind of ongoing, difficult-to-deal-with criticism that Lynn was subjected to:

> 3/5: Today was another bad day. Mrs. S. thought I took too long doing the math
> paper with the children. She felt the children would grow to dislike math if the papers
> were drawn out too long. I must be in a sensitive mood because I really feel low.
> I mean, her criticisms really got to me. I'm beginning to doubt whether I'll ever
> make a teacher and in fact if I want to be one. If I had to teach this way in a regular
> teaching position I don't think I could last.

Mrs. S. criticized Lynn for the same faults day after day. Why? Mrs. S.'s
way of teaching worked. By that we mean that what she did (i.e., employed a
crisp, thoroughly controlled form of drill), she did effectively. She believed that
it was in the students' interest for Lynn to use this same mode of instruction.
However, Lynn resisted, preferring an approach she had used during an earlier
school field experience.

Lynn's log alerted the college supervisor to this problem, and a conference
with Mrs. S. and Lynn softened the cooperating teacher's stance and Lynn's strong
reaction to criticism. Lynn then tried Mrs. S.'s method and found that she could
work with it, a discovery that gave her more confidence in the classroom, and
also increased her repertoire of teaching skills.

The skills you develop during student teaching are often very different from
those you acquired in the college classroom. In college you were responsible for
more abstract learning, writing papers that demonstrated your understanding of
concepts and developing a broad base of knowledge. But when you step in front
of 28 students you need other skills: personal presence, the ability to hold the
youngsters' attention, flexibility in planning, and "eyes in the back of your head."

Your cooperating teacher is there to help you. Still, these are such new experiences that you may have difficulty rapidly incorporating the necessary skills into
your repertoire of behaviors. You may feel angered, frustrated, and uncomfortable.

At times like that, remember: Usually your cooperating teacher's criticism is
meant to help you. If his or her criticism is getting you down, use CONTROL-C
and consider discussing the problem with your supervisor.

Maureena's comments during her interview show that she finally recognized
the benefit of her cooperating teacher's criticism: "All term long Jan criticized
my teaching. Day, after day. I didn't keep the kids interest (hey, they are high-
schoolers and almost adults), I didn't stick to my schedule every period (hey,
I finished all the units on time), etc. But listening to her and working hard paid
off. When I got my written evaluation and letter of reference, I was mucho pleased.
They were very positive."

## DISCOVERING THAT TEACHER PEERS ARE PEOPLE

You may recall an experience years ago when, by chance, you encountered a
teacher of yours in a supermarket or mall. You may have been surprised to see
her engaged in so prosaic an activity as shopping. One of the rarely discussed

benefits of the student-teaching experience is the opportunity it provides to shatter myths. Teachers are people. They are very human.

The humanness of teachers leads them at times to be less than saintly in their personal behavior. You will find when you spend a free period in the faculty lounge that teachers do not often discuss Schopenhauer's philosophy or Greek tragedies or even the newest educational practices. More likely they will be found discussing recipes, their children, football games, vacations, their families, dates, and yes, school gossip.

Some student teachers come to their first teaching experience with "stars in their eyes," expecting their teacher peers to be like the idealized version of one or two exceptional ones in their own past. What disenchantment to witness teachers expose their feet of clay, as Amy did in an unhappy experience.

> 3/1: The time I spent in the teacher's lounge today disillusioned me. All I heard was *malicious* gossip. I wonder what they said about me when I walked out!
>
> One day during one of my free periods, I was on the phone for about 5 minutes with my roommate. I had been in the midst of some personal problems, and was in a foul mood; however, I managed to keep my voice slightly above a whisper when she asked me how school was going. The next thing I knew was that the principal called my supervisor and told him how negative my attitude was. I was later informed that one of the teachers who had a reputation for eavesdropping at every chance had heard my conversation and repeated it. This is one example of how the teachers in this school constantly work against one another. It is true that what I said was not complimentary; however, the important thing, as far as I am concerned, was that my attitude did not conflict with my teaching, which was my sole reason for being in the school.

Eavesdropping is a popular activity even if it is unsporting, and teachers, being human, engage in it too. Perhaps the behavior of the informer in Amy's case could be attributed to an excessive and mindless loyalty to the school; or, to be charitable, even to a more admirable motive: concern about Amy's dissatisfaction and a desire to have her obtain more assistance. Regardless of the eavesdropper's motive, the lesson is the same. You need to use the same good sense in using the phone and in sharing thoughts about your school experience in the teacher's room as you would in the staff room in any other organization. Specifically, as Amy painfully learned, it is hardly the place to talk in uncomplimentary terms about one's employer.

Another example of the demystification of the teaching profession was reported by Ira, who had attended a faculty meeting. There is no better way to convince anyone that the process of school governance, far from being romantic, is often a bore and a drudge even as it is essential.

> 3/22: What a day of enlightenment; I attended a "Teachers' Meeting" today after school. It is absolutely amazing how people can and do blow such little things completely out of proportion. I never before heard such argumentation and heated dis-

cussions over such petty items. To hear some of the conversation you would never guess that these were all educated people talking.

Ira, as we see, had his "enlightenment." Over time he will come to appreciate the importance of meetings in helping all teachers have an opportunity to contribute to policymaking in their school building. Although an effective chairperson can facilitate movement and avoid the merry-go-round effect during faculty meetings, he or she cannot and must not unilaterally circumvent discussion of agenda items relevant to the teachers, even if some do not see them as important.

Teachers can of course be excellent in their field without active participation in teachers' meetings or, for that matter, socially in the teachers' room. You make your own choices. Whether you choose to isolate yourself or not, you ought to do it with your eyes open, recognizing, on the one hand, that teachers are indeed human and behave like humans and, on the other, that the welfare of your professional group depends on its organizational strength.


## OVERCOMING SELF-DOUBT

One of the toughest obstacles to overcome in teaching, as in almost every human endeavor, is self-doubt. It does not necessarily announce itself or make itself known in obvious ways. It comes on wearing different cloaks. For Elaine, who had been having a relatively good time of it as a student teacher, it first took the form of insecurity about the future.

> 3/25: Besides not feeling well, I really didn't want to go to school today. I am worried about my plans for next year, about finishing courses this year, and I am preoccupied with other things. Since I am teaching, I feel kind of left out of college life. I feel like I've already graduated and am in a world of my own. I guess I'm getting kind of scared about the insecurities of the future and it is affecting my interest in teaching.

Elaine had been excessively demanding of herself. Does that kind of drive make one an exceptional teacher? The answer is an equivocal *no*. People in the condition of constantly demanding more of themselves rarely find any lasting satisfaction in their accomplishments. They whip themselves so unmercifully that, even apart from any concern we might have about their personal contentment, they are so stressed that they are subject to cracking under the strain of any new tension and having, as a result, nothing to offer for a period of time.

Elaine was so stressed that her confidence and self-esteem showed signs of erosion in the presence of a substitute. Note that these losses were not caused by any identifiable behavior on the part of the substitute; rather, by Elaine's conclusion that under a set of new circumstances, the hospitalization of her cooperating teacher and the arrival (March 31) of a substitute, she had to prove herself all over again.

> 3/30: Today did not go well at all—I didn't get "good vibes" from the kids nor did I feel much was accomplished. I am so frustrated by the fact the kids are dependent on adult direction; also, the room, the way it looks is not making me too happy. I wonder if I am being "lazy" and not doing enough. Today I found out Mrs. R. had gone into the hospital and I had the full responsibility for the kids—it was all on me. I am glad today is over.

> 3/31: Today was no better. I feel as if the substitute was looking at me very curiously and saying to herself: She doesn't know what she is doing—I would do it this way. I "won" Mrs. R.'s respect, and now it's as if I have to prove myself all over again. I think I'm afraid to assert myself today with her. I don't know my limit or how far I should go. I'm beginning to wish everything was over.

> 4/1: I have the same doubts today as I did Tuesday and Wednesday. I had the confidence that what I was doing was right, but now I'm beginning to wonder. Having to win approval of the substitute is really putting pressure on me. I seem so uncreative and unimaginative compared to her. I don't know. I feel as if I'm doing a terrible job with the class. I don't think I'm enjoying my experience as much as before. I sense I can do it, but I feel her critical eyes all over me all the time—I'm glad the day is over!

On 3/30 Elaine learns that her cooperating teacher has gone to the hospital. She is alone with the children, and there is no substitute teacher. She feels "lazy," as if, when there is no one present whose approval she has to win, she does not have to expend energy. She is also concerned with "the looks" of things. Ironically she, who seems so dependent on how other adults react to her, is frustrated that "the kids are dependent on adult direction."

By 3/31, her self-doubts have reached the point at which she is projecting them on the substitute, that is, she acts as if she knows, without being told, that the substitute has a poor opinion of her. (Chances are the substitute had never been in a class with a student teacher, and she herself had to adapt to a new situation.) Elaine tells us that she had had to win the respect of the cooperating teacher and feels she has to start all over and do it again with the substitute. Why does she have this attitude?

On 4/1, her confidence ebbs as she compares herself with the substitute. Instead of benefiting by this opportunity to observe still another person's work as a teacher, Elaine used her observations to put herself down—nothing short of that. Instead of seeing teachers as colleagues from whom she can learn, she sees them as threatening "big people," as if she has to perform to win mommy and daddy's love. She feels "critical eyes all over me all the time." With her supervisor she even raised the possibility of quitting.

Fortunately for Elaine and for everyone concerned, she had a capable and sensitive supervisor. On the margin of her 3/31 log entry the supervisor wrote,

"Elaine, we need to *talk*!" At the end of her 4/2 log entry she noted:

> Elaine, bring this week's logs and let's get together. I've observed you and I know
> several things about you: (1) You have fine qualities. (2) You are doing many good
> things. (3) You are sensitive. (4) You are willing to try. The question is why don't
> *you* know this? In my own opinion, you have the potential of becoming an *excep-*
> *tionally* good teacher, not just average, and I guess I'm wondering how we are see-
> ing this at such opposite extremes.

Having a mini-crisis of self-doubt, as Elaine's was, is part of life. It should
not be the cause for withdrawing from teaching unless, at the end of the student
teaching and after very careful analysis, a person decides the field is not for her
or him. Instead the individual should do what Elaine did, with help from her supervisor. First, she examined her logs. Through that process, she discovered that
she was faced not with the problem of becoming a teacher, but the problem of
becoming an adult. She saw that she was dependent on "THE APPROVAL" of
her cooperating teacher, which we hasten to add is different from wanting healthy
approval for her work (in the form of positive criticisms of your teachings and
a good grade).

Through conversations with her supervisor and others, Elaine saw that she
constantly struggled with an urgent sense of anxiety that if she—her classroom
or her teaching—did not look right to people, they would consider her a complete failure. Having seen this, Elaine learned to "catch herself" when she was
having irrational thoughts that made her tense. When she felt others were criticizing
her teaching—doubting her ability—she reminded herself of what was fact: She
had been assured already that her work was much more than passable. In time,
she had fewer irrational thoughts and better handled those she had.

After this crisis, Elaine completed her student teaching with relative ease and,
after having a successful job interview, took a full-time teaching position in the
town in which her soon-to-be-husband lived.

One student teacher who had an extremely difficult time withdrew from teaching
(Skolnick, 1986). As she explained in an amusing article, "Why I'm Sorry I Don't
Teach English," she was nervous and insecure when she started teaching English
to ninth-grade nonreaders. She explained that during her month of teaching she
was a failure: She was easily flustered and had trouble disciplining the students
effectively and holding their attention. Although she said she is sorry she is not
teaching, by her own report, she (and students) is better off that she works for
a publisher.

Self-doubt is like any of the other problems student teachers encounter, and
can be effectively dealt with in the same manner. If self-doubt begins to concern
you, address it squarely. Use CONTROL-C or another logical problem-solving
plan to delineate the issues, to outline alternatives, and to develop a solution.

One of the best ways of countering self-doubt is by being open to good feelings. If you are open to them, you probably will experience some very positive

feelings that will permeate your life. Brenda and Danette wrote about theirs. Danette's joy as a teacher is apparent in the following log entry.

> 1/28: Today went very well. The activities planned were great, and [the students and I] thoroughly enjoyed ourselves. My only disappointment is that the days go by so fast. I only wish there were more of them.

Here are excerpts from two of Brenda's logs that show her professional development and its effect on her personal life.

> 1/28: I feel more confident than yesterday: the children responded more to me when I took over the morning routine, more than yesterday. For the first time I worked individually with a child while everyone else played. Also I observed Kelly today. I'd like to help him deal with his bad temper.
>
> I'm starting to think about the meaning of being a teacher, and how I must think of myself as a teacher. It's really a nice feeling being loved, having the children hang on to you and hug you, but I must begin to think of what they are learning. Aren't they learning dependence by hanging on to me? What am I trying to teach them?
>
> I feel that I must gain more confidence in myself (and I feel confident I will) in order to be more effective not only as a teacher, but as a person.
>
> 2/13: I found that some confidence I am gaining here is spreading into a lot of my relationships outside of the classroom. I had been feeling stagnant, like I wasn't changing anymore, but now I feel more change and more confidence in dealing with both my Sunday school class and with certain close friends of mine, particularly ones I found it hard to talk to. I feel more able to talk now. I feel less afraid.

Student teaching is often a professional stepping stone and a transition point as one moves forward into adulthood. No longer solely a student, the student teacher is on the front line, sharing responsibility for directing the education of others. This responsibility requires new skills and ways of thinking about oneself. As these develop, you will enjoy your professional work in new, confident ways.

## COPING WITH STRESS

Just about everybody in a school system—principals, supervisors, teachers, and students—experiences stress. So it would be surprising if student teachers did not.

We have become keenly aware in recent years that life is filled with stress. "Life events" like death in a family, divorce, sickness, and unemployment create stress, but so too do some positive events like marriage, a promotion, and a vacation trip. Furthermore, life's daily "hassles" such as commuting (to work or to school or college) or shopping can be stressful.

Psychologists have come to understand that individuals cannot live a stress-free life. We can, however, learn to cope with stress in effective and constructive ways rather than living with tension and headaches or, worse yet, resorting to drugs as an escape.

Before we review good coping techniques, let us look at some findings about stress in student teaching. Forty-four secondary-school student teachers, some graduate, some undergraduate, in their last week of student teaching, filled in a questionnaire designed to gather information that might enable faculty to reduce the stress of student teachers (Davis, 1990). The respondents were asked questions about when they felt most stress during student teaching, how intense it was, what factors contributed to the stress, which of the factors they considered the major cause of their stress, and what preventive measures might be taken.

Forty-three of the 44 said they experienced stress during student teaching. They used words like the following to describe how they felt: "pressured," "anxious," "overwhelmed," "tense," and "overburdened." Given a choice as to when they felt most stressed (beginning, middle, end, throughout), "beginning" was chosen most, but "throughout" was chosen almost as often.

We have examined many of the reasons for stress at the beginning: new experience, new role, leaving college, entering the work world, unfamiliar setting, unfamiliar people (teachers, students), ambiguity about the role, and ambiguity about how one is evaluated, and so forth.

Now we examine reasons why the student teachers felt stress throughout their student teaching assignment. We can find these in the factors that Davis' respondents said contributed to their stress: time pressure (not enough time to plan lessons, construct tests, mark papers, etc.); classroom situation (problems in maintaining control, dealing with unmotivated students, etc.); cooperating teacher (the expectations and demands of that teacher, sometimes combined with a lack of direction or a personality clash with the cooperating teacher).

Davis' study had some "silver linings." First, although the student teachers felt stress both at the beginning and throughout student teaching, most said they did not experience it day after day after day. They did not have to endure weeks of unbroken tension because, apparently, feelings of stress would come and then be gone for a time.

Then, the study revealed another silver lining in connection with the intensity of the stress: On a scale that ranged from "slight" to "intolerable," on the average the student teachers chose "moderate." Occasional, moderate stress can be managed, especially if you learn how to reduce its intensity and prevent the occurrence of some of it.

Three useful ways to deal with stress (Lazarus & Folkman, 1984) are:

1. Prevent it. Some of this is possible, for example, by being prepared for each class, by learning all you can about classroom management, by having a thorough understanding of what the cooperating teacher expects of you, by ar-

riving in school on time, by not carrying another job during the student teaching term, and so forth.

2. Modify the stressors. Some of this is possible, too. For example, by arranging a conference with your cooperating teacher if uncertainty about his or her demands are stressful; by modifying your classroom behavior so that if ongoing conversations by two students are irritating you, you got them actively involved in your lessons or change their seat assignments; and so forth.

3. Modify your reactions. Modifying your reactions to stressors is possible and it is good for your mental health. For example, in your life as a student, final exams often may be a stressor. You cannot avoid this stressor and you cannot modify the exams, but you can modify your emotional reactions to them. In doing so—let us say by studying enough to avoid panic and anxious feelings, you experience less stress and probably perform better.

Another way to modify your reactions is to make sure you "keep things in perspective." As to student teaching, you can remind yourself that although student teaching is important, it is not the end all and be all of your life. Or, as some students say, "there is life after student teaching." Here is how you can do that. Let us say that a few students are particularly troublesome one day, or more troublesome than usual. Or the cooperating teacher seems to ignore you or is irritable one day. It is good to be able to appreciate that their own life's circumstances probably account for their behavior and not allow it to depress you. Another way to modify your reactions is by maintaining a balanced life. Do that by seeing that you incorporate relaxation and pleasure into your life during this period.

## COPING WITH ETHICAL ISSUES

Ethical issues belong in a chapter on the student teacher as a person because they touch upon our individual values. They cover a wide spectrum of behavior on the part of both teachers and students. We discuss only a few ethical issues to illustrate the questions they raise and some coping (as well as preventive) measures. Finally, we introduce you to an educator's code of ethics. As a student teacher you may not have to make difficult decisions that involve complex ethical issues. You may, however, witness your cooperating teacher involved in that kind of decision making, perhaps in connection with cheating on exams or homework or in deciding how to punish a student. And you may even, like Karen, have strong differences over school policy.

> 1/6: I have a difficult question, I think an ethical one, and it's about a situation that really annoys me. Sally had her head down on her desk during today's history lesson. After I assigned the class seatwork and everyone had begun working I approached her and asked what was wrong. She hesitated a bit and finally said something like, "It's that time of the month."

She really looked terribly uncomfortable, so I suggested she go to the nurse and get an aspirin. She returned in 10 minutes to tell me that the nurse couldn't do anything for her, that school nurses were not permitted to dispense unauthorized medication. I had aspirin in my purse and was about to give her one when my cooperating teacher stopped me (she had been out of the room earlier when I had sent Sally to the nurse), saying it was against the rules. I really felt it was an awkward situation. Why should Sally have to suffer? Why shouldn't I have given her the aspirin?

We can empathize with Karen's frustration. At the same time we can appreciate the importance of regulations. Many rules that have been established by the school and school board are for the protection both of students and teachers. (The occasional student could be allergic to aspirin or develop a serious disorder from ingesting it.) Because the dispensing of medication of any kind brings to bear all sorts of legal questions, it is best to advise students like Sally to bring their own medication to school on those days they feel they might need some.

Karen's annoyance is understandable. She knew that the aspirin in all probability would have relieved Sally's discomfort and she found it hard to accept a regulation that disallowed it. She is not alone in having that feeling. There is another side: If you were to provide assistance in the form of medication for this type of pain, at what point would you stop? Earache? Toothache? Digestive problem? Broken toe?

If you want the particulars of the relevant laws in your state, discuss the issue of medication with your school nurse. The deeper issue is the ethical one, namely, the right thing to do in a situation like that with Sally and like that raised by Larry in the following:

3/26: By chance I overheard several students in the hall talking about book reports which were due today. One said, "I was too busy so I handed in an old book report of my brother's." These are the questions that ran through my mind: What should I do? Tell my cooperating teacher, talk to the student directly, or ignore the whole thing?

No matter how tempting it may be to "ignore the whole thing," that would be unwise. It would certainly not be helpful to the student. To act professionally and ethically, you want to cope with the problem in a constructive, nonpunitive way. Your aim would be to teach, not to make the student suffer.

As a student teacher, you will want to share the information with your cooperating teacher. He or she will have to decide how to deal with the problem. For your sake in the future—every teacher is confronted with some form of cheating, usually with many more varieties than we like—and because your cooperating teacher might ask for your thoughts, you should consider the following approach: First, to quickly dispel whatever anger you may have toward the student, because its presence can be counterproductive to your own clear thinking. Second, to ask the student why he or she cheated and what he or she thinks the consequences were (e.g., that he or she was really cheating him or herself). Third, to ask the student how he or she proposes to resolve the problem he or she made for him or herself. Finally, to tell the student what your intentions are. Your intentions would probably depend on the student's responses to your prior questions and could range from no penalty (if he or she was genuinely sorry and promptly submitted his or her own book report) to failure.

This approach is first and foremost an educational one. Its purposes are to have a student learn from the experience and to prevent recurrences. That orientation, a preventive one, has been recommended by researchers (Bushway & Nash, 1977) who reviewed past studies on cheating. Their review revealed the following:

1. Cheaters and noncheaters differ in some personal and behavioral characteristics, including cheaters (a) being lower in school achievement, (b) being closer to others in their class, and (c) being more tense and anxious;
2. Situational factors are important, including (a) the moral climate of the school, (b) the likelihood that students could be successful at attempts to cheat, and (c) the teaching style of the teacher (e.g., assignments and tests that are too difficult, or use of the curve in grading);
3. There are many different reasons for cheating, including pressure to get high grades for college admission.

These researchers found cheating in the classroom was widespread. They urged researchers to turn their attention to "strategies that prevent or reduce cheating." That is also good advice to a beginning teacher who is helped by knowing the following: What types of behavior students classify as cheating. How serious students consider each particular type of cheating. How often they practice those types. How students' responses about cheating compare with responses of administrators and teachers. Research provides some answers to these questions. McLaughlin and Ross (1989) administered questionnaires about cheating to 130 middle-class high school students in Memphis, Tennessee and 10 administrators and teachers.

The vast majority (90% or more) of the students classified both copying during an exam and looking at notes during an exam as cheating. Faculty/administrators and students showed considerable agreement about what constituted cheating, although faculty classified more behaviors as cheating and regarded more of them to be serious. For example, all faculty, but only 69% of the students, classified "allowing someone to copy homework" as cheating. Also, faculty considered "allowing another student to copy on a test" to be more serious a violation than students did.

In summary, the findings showed that the students knew what behaviors were unacceptable, even if they considered them to be less serious than administrators and faculty. Yet, students reported that they cheated frequently. Some admitted to copying homework, even taking turns in doing that.

During your student teaching you will be guided by school rules and your cooperating teacher. You will have opportunity to think about your own values. When you have your own classroom you may decide to take action to discourage cheating early in the school year, when there is less pressure to cheat. You also will want to carefully monitor tests and conduct open discussions on the subject of moral behavior in school and outside.

In connection with thinking about ethical issues and discussing them with colleagues you may find helpful the National Education Association's "Code of Ethics of the Education Profession." Approved in 1975, the Code appears in the annual *NEA Handbook*. See Table 11.1 for a copy of the Code.

TABLE 11.1
Code of Ethics of the Education Profession

**Preamble**

The educator, believing in the worth and dignity of each human being, recognizes the supreme importance of the pursuit of truth, devotion to excellence, and the nurture of democratic principles. Essential to these goals is the protection of freedom to learn and to teach and the guarantee of equal educational opportunity for all. The educator accepts the responsibility to adhere to the highest ethical standards.

The educator recognizes the magnitude of the responsibility inherent in the teaching process. The desire for the respect and confidence of one's colleagues, of students, of parents, and of the members of the community provides the incentive to attain and maintain the highest possible degree of ethical conduct. The *Code of Ethics of the Education Profession* indicates the aspiration of all educators and provides standards by which to judge conduct.

The remedies specified by the NEA and/or its affiliates for the violation of any provision of this *Code* shall be exclusive and no such provision shall be enforceable in any form other than one specifically designated by the NEA or its affiliates.

**Principle I**

*Commitment to the Student*

The educator strives to help each student realize his or her potential as a worthy and effective member of society. The educator therefore works to stimulate the spirit of inquiry, the acquisition of knowledge and understanding, and the thoughtful formulation of worthy goals.

In fulfillment of the obligation to the student, the educator —

1. Shall not unreasonably restrain the student from independent action in the pursuit of learning.

2. Shall not unreasonably deny the student access to varying points of view.

3. Shall not deliberately suppress or distort subject matter relevant to the student's progress.

4. Shall make reasonable effort to protect the student from conditions harmful to learning or to health and safety.

5. Shall not intentionally expose the student to embarrassment or disparagement.

6. Shall not on the basis of race, color, creed, sex, national origin, marital status, political or religious beliefs, family, social, or cultural background, or sexual orientation, unfairly —

a. Exclude any student from participation in any program

b. Deny benefits to any student

c. Grant any advantage to any student.

7. Shall not use professional relationships with students for private advantage.

8. Shall not disclose information about students obtained in the course of professional service, unless disclosure serves a compelling professional purpose or is required by law.

*(Continued)*

TABLE 11.1
(*Continued*)

**Principle II**

*Commitment to the Profession*

The education profession is vested by the public with a trust and responsibility requiring the highest ideals of professional service.

In the belief that the quality of the services of the education profession directly influences the nation and its citizens, the educator shall exert every effort to raise professional standards, to promote a climate that encourages the exercise of professional judgment, to achieve conditions which attract persons worthy of the trust to careers in education, and to assist in preventing the practice of the profession by unqualified persons.

In fulfillment of the obligation to the profession, the educator—

1. Shall not in an application for a professional position deliberately make a false statement or fail to disclose a material fact related to competency and qualifications.

2. Shall not misrepresent his/her professional qualifications.

3. Shall not assist any entry into the profession of a person known to be unqualified in respect to character, education, or other relevant attribute.

4. Shall not knowingly make a false statement concerning the qualifications of a candidate for a professional position.

5. Shall not assist a noneducator in the unauthorized practice of teaching.

6. Shall not disclose information about colleagues obtained in the course of professional service unless disclosure serves a compelling professional purpose or is required by law.

7. Shall not knowingly make false or malicious statements about a colleague.

8. Shall not accept any gratuity, gift, or favor that might impair or appear to influence professional decisions or action.

**—Adopted by the 1975 Representative Assembly**

The Preamble of the Code "indicates the aspirations of all educators and provides standards by which to judge conduct." Principle I, on "Commitment to the Student," presents standards of behavior in the educator's relations with students. Principle II, on "Commitment to the Profession," presents standards of behavior of educators in relation to their profession. Both of these are helpful to student teachers: the first, in classifying their obligations to the students; the second, in socializing them into the profession of teaching.

## BECOMING SOCIALIZED

After years as a student, how during the student-teaching experience do you make that step to the other side of the desk? An interesting study by Friebus (1977) sought to identify those individuals through whom the culture of the school and the role of the professional teacher are communicated to the student teacher.

Friebus interviewed 19 student teachers six times each. To ensure representativeness he selected student teachers who had assignments that varied on several relevant dimensions (grade level, school neighborhood, supervisory arrangements, etc.). In analyzing the data he looked particularly for information in areas that had proved useful in studies of other professional groups, three of which are defined below along with his findings.

*Coaching.* Friebus found a surprisingly large number of individuals who served as coach. He defined a *coach* as somebody who "guides and advises the trainee, provides . . . encounters with new activities, and challenges to old identities" (p. 264). These included, in order of importance: the cooperating teacher, college supervisor, other teachers in the school, self (the student teacher), professors, pupils, principals, friends, relatives, and student-teacher peers. These people did the coaching by providing ideas, information about teaching, encouragement, performance evaluation, and certain expectations.

That the cooperating teacher should top the list, followed by the supervisor and other teachers at the site, is not unexpected. The high score for "self" is surprising, however, and it suggests that student teachers are using their own observational skills and sensitivity to learn "how things work" and to generate advice for themselves. How does this work? Friebus provided this interchange between an interviewer (I) and a student teacher respondent (R):

I:   Did the mid-term review give you a sense of progress?

R:   Didn't need it. My progress came from within myself, was evaluating myself.

I:   Who is your main indicator of progress?

R:   Me, you can tell me I'm excellent but if I don't have the feeling within myself it doesn't mean anything.

I:   If you had problems or a question about what you were doing, who was your main source of information?

R:   First and foremost it was me.

*Legitimacy.* The behavior of others confirms the student teacher's growing feeling of being a professional. The behaviors include obedience by pupils in response to the student teacher's directions, an invitation from a teacher to join her for lunch, a comment by a parent acknowledging the difference a student teacher had made for his child, and so on.

Friebus found the pupils and cooperating teacher were by far the greatest reported sources of instances of legitimation. That the students top the list is a fascinating example of human interaction, for it means that while student teachers are devoting so much of their energy to helping their pupils develop academically, the pupils, in turn, are helping the student teacher develop professionally and feel like an adult leader in the classroom.

*Peer Involvement.* Friebus found that contacts student teachers have with their fellow student teachers serve two important functions. First, individuals can compare notes and see how their situation stands in relation to others. Through this process they assess whether they are teaching a fair share of lessons, whether they are overworked or underworked, and so forth. A second function served by peer involvement is support and comfort; that is, having much in common, peers are ideal people with whom to share the varied feelings and inevitable dilemmas student teachers encounter. Out of the sharing can come some profitable exchanges and useful ideas.

Very likely, you, too, will be socialized through your interactions with *your* coaches, peers and students. And among your coaches, one of the leading ones will be *you*.

## APPRECIATING THE COLLEGE SUPERVISOR'S SUPPORT

Repeatedly, the experiences of our student teachers point to the crucial role of the college supervisor and the cooperating teacher. Children can be expected to behave like children, and teenagers like teenagers and when 20 or 30 of them are together, there are bound to be problems, even just the problems of people living and working together. For the student teacher, the major purpose of the apprenticeship experience is to learn to take these problems in stride, in order to deal effectively with them.

If you have your cooperating teacher and college supervisor on your side and have their advice and especially their support, your chances of having a valuable, even if difficult, teaching experience is increased many times over. However, in those instances when the cooperating teacher is hostile toward the student teacher and competitive with him or her, and especially when these attitudes are covert and masked by occasional acts of false solicitousness, then the student teacher can have his or her confidence and self-esteem shaken to the core. Kate had such a cooperating teacher.

> 1/27: I went home Friday feeling quite discouraged. After 3 days of student teaching I still felt like a stranger with my cooperating teacher and even with the kids. After listening to everyone's glowing accounts of their experience in Thursday's curriculum class and reflecting on my own experience, I was really depressed. I thought about it all weekend and tried to explain my feelings to my friends. But I couldn't seem to verbalize exactly what the problem was. I had been so realistic over vacation, but I guess I was picturing things like they were at the end of my field experience, a wonderful relationship with the teacher. Probably I was expecting too much too soon. Also I was used to kids who craved extra attention. Now faced with kids coming from a totally different background who are much cooler in their reaction to strangers, and a cooperating teacher who seems aloof, I have to modify my expectations. All these things were running through my head.

After 2 months of frustration—of no support from her cooperating teacher, despite ever increasing effort on her part—her confidence was undermined to the point that she wrote:

3/29: I am beginning to experience this feeling of anxiety creeping over me. As I make the valiant effort to finish my proposal for my course in School and Community, my mind keeps wandering. I feel very confused. I keep thinking I should throw my proposal down and concentrate on tomorrow morning, but then I realize that the kind of situations I need to prepare myself for just can't be planned. My lessons are ready to go, the materials are set, but. . . .

I don't think I would be so scared except that I feel the issue of taking total control, rather than seeming like a logical, natural step, is beginning to feel like an insurmountable hurdle. Maybe the problem is that I am still unclear.

Maybe I am looking for a simple solution when there is none. I'm afraid to show doubt in myself because then everyone else will doubt me. But at the same time the doubt is beginning to overpower me. Where is all my self-confidence? I know, it's sitting on three and a half years' worth of papers, test grades . . . and somehow I haven't managed to translate it into the real world.

How can a person try so hard and not even come close to achieving a desired goal? Maybe it's the wrong goal? Maybe the answer is that I care too much and I'm getting sick of "maybe's."

The story has a happy ending. Her supervisor helped Kate to recognize what Kate had surmised, that her cooperating teacher had been a destructive force, a person rare among cooperating teachers, who seemed intent upon giving Kate nothing but negative feedback or, at best, no comments whatsoever. Kate completed her 10-week period and went on to another student-teaching experience in a middle school during which she herself became finally convinced that she had the makings of a superb teacher. The second school offered her a position, which she accepted.

Ideally, the student teacher and cooperating teacher form a working team, directing their efforts toward common goals. When this does not happen, when the student teacher does not get the support he or she needs, the best resource he or she has is the college supervisor. Although supervisors typically will be ready to listen at any time and particularly as soon as the lack of support begins to become a problem, it is likely that they can be most helpful after the student teacher has begun to apply the first steps of the CONTROL-C technique to the situation.

## DEVOTION TO THE STUDENTS

Like Kate, Dorothy had a gift for teaching. This was apparent to her supervisor early in the term, although her cooperating teacher never recognized it. Despite the obstacles she encountered, through dogged persistence, through imaginative plans, and through the honest expression of her feelings, as in the passage below, Dorothy had a great measure of success with her class.

1/20: This morning the class was misbehaving and I lost control of myself. Tears started rolling out, and I said to the class, "I don't understand you kids. I go home every night and work on new and interesting things for you to do and I receive no response or respect from you. All you can do is disturb the class. Do you realize I do these things only because I care about you and what will happen to you in the future if you don't learn?" No discipline problems the rest of the day. But I do realize I need to control my emotions, and it is something I will have to work at.

Again and again Dorothy found renewed strength and inspiration from the children themselves. The next log entry conveys the kind of devotion to students that becomes apparent to them and elicits their warm and positive response.

3/3: It's the usual Friday. The children are tired and restless. Very excited about the weekend, questioning me about leaving. Timmy kept saying in reading group that they were going to spring a surprise on me, and Larry would say, "Be quiet, Timmy." The school counselor came in a talked to me today, and I told her that it had been a hard quarter plus a period of shattered dreams and idealism; that I found out that many things the university teaches you cannot be used; also, that I feel the structure of schools increases discipline problems and that every time I punished a child I thought: We are punishing him for many things he cannot help, things forced upon him by the school and home environment. It ran through my mind, and every night I go to sleep thinking of this. But as my father and I discussed, I have to teach the child the appropriate behavior set up for him by this society or he will have many difficulties adjusting later.

Plus in a self-contained classroom with 31 children you have to do what I call *The Ugly Sacrifice* of a child or two for the other 29 or 30. You can't permit two or three to spoil the chance for the other 29 to learn. Isn't it sad that this is what is happening every day in many schools?

Institutions that educate teachers help them develop conceptions of what schools should be like. Sometimes student teachers and beginning teachers who have fine aspirations have not had the experience in the "school of hard knocks" to appreciate the power of the principle of inertia. The status quo is not easily changed, and those who learn that fact of life and understand the reasons for it are more likely to work for realistic modest goals. Dorothy learned that fact of life and, although saddened, was strengthened by it. Nonetheless, even under these less-than-ideal circumstances, over the course of three months, her devotion to her students paid off by making a difference in many of their lives.

## DEVOTION BY THE STUDENTS

Unlike Kate, Dorothy did not suffer from continuing doubts about herself, no matter how discouraging a day or week she encountered. She felt early that in her situation the cooperating teacher was more enemy than ally, and that about the only kind of criticism that she could depend upon getting was the kind that put her down. But she would not allow that relationship to be defeating.

Dorothy felt reinforced by the support she received from both the supervisor and her colleagues in the student-teaching seminar. For one thing, her class-mates agreed that her cooperating teacher was being grossly unfair and unhelpful. For another, when she heard how her fellow student teachers received extra support from their cooperating teachers, she was reassured that most teachers actually are helpful to newcomers and that her unfortunate experience should not dispel her expectation that she would in the future find herself working with kindly people.

Near the end of her teaching, Dorothy used her log to define for herself the role that her cooperating teacher had played and to put her experience in perspective. This prepared her to appreciate her last two days and to take full and clear note of the children and of their feelings toward her. Like every other teacher—of kindergarten, 6th grade, 11th grade, or university—who gives the students the feeling that he or she genuinely cares and works unstintingly, Dorothy got the evidence that they cared, that they appreciated, that she *had* been important to them.

> 3/9: I must admit I had fun with the class today, because for the first time I stopped worrying about pleasing Ms. K. We had our usual reading in the morning, but in the afternoon we did choral reading and had the boat race with the children scream-ing. I read stories to them, then we had gym together. It was great. The class even talked about how much they enjoyed it!

> 3/10: What a day! The children brought me earrings, pins, a rabbit, and a lamp plus a letter that meant a lot to me . . .
>
> Sometimes I feel Ms. K. was truly trying to *stifle* my progress! She definitely had me feeling like a failure on and off through the entire quarter, but thanks to a great deal of thought I gave it Wednesday and Thursday, and encouragement from my supervisor, I have come to realize I am capable of being a very human teacher. Reconsideration of myself plus positive responses from the children and my super-visor helped.
>
> Ms. K. laughed when she saw several of the children crying over me leaving. I feel sad that these children had to suffer this hurt, but I feel good about it too because I realize I have radiated some warmth toward these children which I feel is very necessary in a healthy human development. Geraldine said to me, "I want to tell you before you leave that you are the best teacher I have ever had." Another little girl said she was going to kidnap me. Then Lisa said I was better than the teacher she had before she came to this school. I realize now that instead of listen-ing to Ms. K. so much I should have listened to the children's responses to me all quarter, because I did know they enjoyed me, but instead I worried about Ms. K. and my evaluation.
>
> I'll miss the children, but I feel like a thousand pounds have been taken off my shoulders.

Such are the dramas in the life of the student teacher. They are moving and they are yours to appreciate. Those who choose teaching, knowing it is an occu-pation of decision making and intense human interactions, are likely to have rela-tively "good endings" to their own dramas.

# 12
▼▼▼▼▼▼▼

# From Student Teacher
# to Teacher

About 90 years ago Sigmund Freud said that the mark of adulthood was the achievement of satisfaction through work, sex, and family. Although Freud's ideas have fallen from the preeminent position they held in years past, few would question the accuracy of his statement about adulthood. With regard to work, no one, certainly not student teachers, would deny that having a career is one of the highest priorities in life. That, after all, is the ultimate goal toward which you and your classmates have been striving.

True, there will be days during the student teaching period when you would like to toss the ringing alarm clock out the window and go back to sleep. However, most days you will find student teaching a challenge, as well as a route to a secure position and way of life. Moreover, you will enjoy the satisfactions, so important in life, of being identified with an organization (e.g., a school), of being part of a group of co-workers (e.g., faculty and staff), of utilizing a body of knowledge about students (e.g., stages of cognitive development) and, of having a discipline (e.g., language or science) and developed skills (e.g., to teach students to read, to converse in French, to solve physics problems).

Looking forward to next year, your wish is probably like others in your position: to feel successful in the classroom. As a recent study shows, that feeling is important in separating those who stay on and make teaching their career and those who leave after one or more years.

The investigator, an experienced teacher (Yee, 1990), queried current and former teachers to find out what led most to remain in the field and some to leave it. She found that satisfaction with teaching as a career is associated with:

- Workplace conditions and context such as
    Positive support from administrators and peers,
    Positive community and parent attitudes toward the school, and
    Adequate budgetary support
- Extrinsic benefits such as favorable
    Pay and job security,
    Promotion opportunities, and
    Schedule and vacations
- Intrinsic benefits such as
    Seeing oneself successful as a teacher,
    Viewing students as the chief source of intrinsic reward, and
    Feeling a sense of professional growth.

All three categories are important. The first one (workplace conditions) helps make the third (intrinsic benefits) attainable, and the second one (extrinsic benefits) can surely make life more pleasant. Still, there is no formula that can predict who will remain in teaching and who will not.

Some teachers, Yee found, stay on for the extrinsic benefits (e.g., summer vacation) even when they are not getting satisfaction from the intrinsic ones, the work itself. That condition is not unique to education; you may have already encountered lawyers, nurses, accountants, and others who are unhappy with their work but stay on for the extrinsic benefits. That we share this condition with other professions does not make it any more satisfactory, either for the unhappy teacher or the unfortunate students.

Yee also examined the effects on teachers of frustration with their lack of classroom success. She concluded that some who fail but do not leave the profession physically "withdraw emotionally and psychologically, effectively retiring on the job" (p. 120).

We believe that the careers of many teachers who are dissatisfied or frustrated did not have to turn out in that unhappy way. Perhaps they might have had more favorable career outcomes if their circumstances had been different during the early, crucial stages of their teaching. This chapter is designed to help you move forward as successfully as possible into the next step in your career—to assist you in effectively making the transition from student teacher to teacher.

You deserve success. You have worked for many years to reach this point in your education and to establish yourself as a teacher. Now is the time to find the kind of teaching position you want. It is also the time to lay the groundwork for success and satisfaction in the classroom.

## ESCAPE FROM FREEDOM

When Erich Fromm used the title *Escape from Freedom* (1976) for one of his books, he captured the essence of a problem that plagues many of us. We want the satisfactions of adulthood yet at the same time we have much anxiety about them. (The anxiety is sometimes at such a low level of consciousness that we have only a vague sense of it.) What we are experiencing is a throwback to an earlier time in our life when we wanted at one and the same time to imitate the behavior of an older brother or sister or a neighbor's child but did not want to give up being mom's or dad's little boy or girl. We wanted to stay overnight at a friend's house (or later go out on a first date), but how much "safer" it was to stay at home!

Elements of the insecure or frightened child lead us to "do and not do" at the same time, to go after a job opening and yet to drag our feet, to take the initiative in arranging for an interview and yet to manage to leave doubts in the principal's mind about our single-minded interest in being a teacher in his school. If we are not careful, these elements can lead to self-sabotage, making us a day late in submitting an application or a half hour late for our appointment about a position. They induce us to "forget" to contact the faculty member we met in the teachers' room in our student-teaching school, the one who said he knew of an upcoming position in a nearby school district.

## STARTING THE JOB HUNT

Having such anxieties and ambivalent feelings do not make you abnormal, nor do they ordinarily require professional treatment. However, you should guard against any self-destructive behavior they may cause by being vigilant during your job search. Ask yourself, have I established a plan or am I going about it without direction?

Are you following your plan faithfully or so haphazardly as to raise your suspicions about conflicting motives (e.g., to want to find a job and to not want to find a job)? How effectively is the plan operating? Are you getting responses to your applications? Requests for your college placement credentials? Appointments for interviews? If the answer is negative to any of the questions, consider using CONTROL-C and the corrective measures that flow from its use. There is no profit in pursuing a plan that is not producing opportunities.

If you are getting repeated turndowns, one possibility is that the competition is very great. Another is that your letter and resume do not do you justice, or your letters of reference are not helpful or that in your interview you convey a defeated attitude. A discussion with your college placement officer is in order at such times.

If your field of teaching is especially oversupplied, another plan can involve trying for a different teaching level, such as 7th-grade instead of 12th, or nursery school instead of kindergarten; or a different setting, such as a training program in industry or an adult program for senior citizens. Or you may want to consider job possibilities in other geographic areas.

Studies about how people "land a job" over the years have consistently shown that friends and acquaintances are among the very top sources of leads. It pays to "talk up" your job hunt, to let it be widely known, to encourage others to give you tips about openings and to follow them vigorously. A personal contact usually means that you are more than just another candidate to those who make the appointment. It means that in circumstances when you are among a group of equally qualified finalists, you have an edge.

Of course you will have an edge if you do your student teaching in one of the school districts that gets most of their new teachers from their pool of student teachers (Kolze, 1988). One school superintendent described the ambitious program used by his district to recruit student teachers and to give them rich experiences. He and his staff do this not only to prepare many excellent teachers but also to choose people whose demonstrated performance shows them to be first-rate prospects. The quality of this program is further shown by two end-of-student-teaching activities:

1. The assistant superintendent for personnel conducts a seminar on "How to Get a Job." This includes tips on the job hunt, writing resumes and cover letters, preparing for interviews, and checking on qualifications for state certification.
2. The assistant superintendent holds individual sessions with student teachers to discuss ways to make them more marketable and on additional courses that might be helpful to them.

Most colleges and universities have an active placement bureau that serves its students at little or no charge. Although you may feel too overwhelmed in the midst of a busy senior year to be faced with the task of registering in that bureau, the effort will be well worth your time. This office will send records out for you, no matter how many positions you apply for. As a result, you will not have the burden of asking professors or others to write letters of recommendation a dozen times.

Further, you will be building a file at the placement office good for lifetime use. You will need only to keep it up to date, to have it available and fresh should you apply for another position 1, 3, or 10 years from now. That is all the more reason to give your best thinking to the material you develop for the placement office to be included in your file.

As you draft whatever written material they suggest, bear in mind that your chances of success can be greatly increased if you are able to take the perspective of "the other" person, that is, of the potential employer, the recipient of your placement credentials. Put yourself in the employer's position. If you were he or she, what kind of statement would most impress you?

Determined job hunters will review newspaper advertisements systematically. They will have ready to mail a resume and a prepared letter of interest, both concise and to the point, but striking and well-written so that they will stand out from those of other candidates.

They will also acquaint themselves with the resources available to offer them help in their search. Among those resources is the nearest branch of the state employment service that offers placement services for professional people. Consider registering there, especially in the event that you might want to seek a professional position other than teaching, or at least other than teaching in a public school.

## YOUR RESUME

To be prepared to present yourself persuasively to prospective employers, you will need a personal resume. Learning to compose a strong and appropriate resume at this point will help not only in getting your first job but later ones as well. A resume should be written so that the potential employer scanning it knows almost instantly the highlights of your background. In Table 12.1 we present the kinds of information that should be included and a recommended format with explanatory footnotes. Modify both of these (content and form) to your personal taste and especially to highlight your particular strengths.

Your resume should be brief and to the point. However, it should also be long enough to allow you to effectively present yourself. If your experience cannot be subsumed under the given headings, add others. For example, if any of your writings have been published, by all means include them under a "Publications" heading. Similarly, if you have been active in a noneducational institution (e.g., in a "Y" or 4-H Club) or have engaged in some public service (e.g., a campaign to encourage citizens to vote), include such items under an appropriate heading. The resume is, after all, a vehicle to present yourself well and give the recipient a clear notion of what you are capable of doing; everything relevant should be included.

Keep in mind that personnel in two school districts know you better than any others. They knew you even before you started your job hunt. The first is the one that you attended. True, they have not observed you teach. On the other hand, they do have knowledge about your character and personality and of course, about the kind of student you were. Together, these add up to a lot of important information about a potential teacher. It is very much to your advantage if your former teachers pass the word on to hiring principals they know that you are a dependable and conscientious person, or that students will like you as a teacher.

The other district is the one in which you do your student teaching. They have seen you as a teacher. They do not have to depend on letters of recommendation or your grade in student teaching to make a judgment about your teaching ability; they have much more reliable evidence: what their own eyes and ears have given them. The school district may not want to lose you. Let them know as early as possible if you plan to apply for openings they have or will have.

Table 12.2 illustrates the use of the format shown in Table 12.1. Briefly and clearly it presents a comprehensive picture of the individual.

TABLE 12.1
Recommended Resume Format

## RESUME

**NAME**
Address
Telephone[1]

**OBJECTIVE**[2]

**EDUCATION**
Degree
Academic Program[3]
Name of College/University, Year Degree Conferred
Extra-Curricular Activities[4]
Recognitions, Awards, Honors[5]

Diploma[6]
Program[3]
Name of High School, Year Diploma Awarded
Extra-Cirricular Activities[4]
Recognitions, Awards, Honors[5]

**CERTIFICATION**

**EXPERIENCE**
Dates of Experience: Position of Job Title[7]
Brief Description of Duties and Responsibilities
Employer
Address

RECREATIONAL ACTIVITIES[8]

MEMBERSHIP IN PROFESSIONAL ORGANIZATIONS

REFERENCES[9]

[1]If you have another telephone at which you can receive a call or message, identify the two, for example (home) and (work).

[2]Your objective is the position you wish to obtain, such as middle-school teacher of mathematics.

[3]List major and minor fields plus other areas of concentration (e.g., major in early-childhood education, minor in children's literature).

[4]Cite activity and number of years involved, highlighting those that could make you a more attractive candidate for a given position.

[5]Honor societies, class offices, or awards for scholarship, leadership, athletics, or other activities.

[6]Cite fields of major study (e.g., 4 years of history), and relevant electives (e.g., 3 years of music).

[7]Start with the most recent employment and continue to the earliest. Include all types, because diverse experience, even unskilled, is valuable to one's personal and career development and is appreciated as such by employers. Also include unpaid community work such as hospital volunteer.

[8]Include these only if relevant to the position you are seeking. For example, if you apply for a position in English and you write poetry or, if you apply in science and you are an amateur astronomer.

[9]The current practice is to state the following at this point in your resume, "Available on Request." However, we recommend that you identify your references in your resume. This will help your resume stand out from others.

Give three to five names, preferably persons like your cooperating teacher and supervisor, who can speak authoritatively about your promise as a teacher, and no more than one of three, or two of five, who can report on you as a worker on related jobs (e.g., camp counselor), or related experience (e.g., assistant Scoutmaster). Such diversity shows the range of your assets.

If you already requested references from these persons for your college placement office folio, you do not need their permission, although you will want to give them a copy of your resume and alert them to your search. Following the list of names you will want to note: I am registered with the [Blank] College Placement Bureau. At your request I will have a set of credentials including (confidential) letters of recommendation forwarded directly to you.

Note that the word "confidential" is enclosed in parenthesis. Whether you include the word depends upon your decision about waiving your right to see copies of the letters in your placement folio. If you waive that right, indicate that the letters are confidential. There are obvious advantages and disadvantages to waiving that right.

TABLE 12.2
Using the Recommended Resume Format

## RESUME

**CHRIS SMITH**
123 Main Street
Anytown, Any State 00000
(800) 767-1212
(800) 337-4830 (Message)

**OBJECTIVE**
**English teacher, high school**

**EDUCATION**
Bachelor of Arts
English major, History minor
State University, 1993
State City, Any State 00000
Extra-Curricular Activities: Reporter and Feature Writer
University Student Newspaper; Basketball Team; Nature Club
Silver Bell Honor Society

Academic Diploma
College Preparatory Program
(4 years each of English, Social Studies, Science)
Washington High School, 1989
Springfield, Any State 00000
Drama Club, 1985–1989; Basketball Team 1986–1989
English Award, Outstanding Senior

**CERTIFICATION**
Completing all requirements to teach English in secondary school

**EXPERIENCE**
Student Teacher: English in 9th and 10th grades,
January-May, 1993, Jeff High School; Anytown, Any State 00000
Camp Counselor: 10–12-year-old, Summers, 1990–1992,
Community Day Camp, Springfield, Any State 00000

**RECREATIONAL ACTIVITIES**
Writing poetry, nature hiking, playing basketball, reading mysteries

(*Continued*)

TABLE 12.2
(*Continued*)

MEMBERSHIP IN PROFESSIONAL ORGANIZATIONS
Student Member, Any State Education Association

REFERENCES*

Kelly Baskin, Ed. D., Associate Professor of Education
State University
State City, Any State 00000

Leslie Simon, Ph. D., Professor of English
State University
State City, Any State 00000

Jan Robbins
Chair of English Department
Washington High School, 1989
Springfield, Any State 00000

Toby Bristol
Director, Community Day Camp
Springfield, Any State 00000

*I am registered with the State University Placement Bureau. At your request I will have a set
of credentials, including confidential letters of recommendation, forwarded directly to you.

## THE INTERVIEW

One day you will receive a phone call or letter informing you that you are a candidate for a position and inviting you to come for an interview. It is a thrilling moment: The hiring official was already impressed enough to make you a candidate.

*Preparation for the Interview.*   The personal interview is crucial. It is your opportunity to exceed whatever assessment has already been made of you—that is, to show that you are at least as good as your resume and your placement credentials indicate and as good as your college supervisor and cooperating teacher have rated you. In short, the interview provides you with an opportunity to show that you are an excellent choice for the vacant position.

We have frequently been asked about preparation in anticipation of the interview. Our answer is deceptively simple: Prepare yourself to be yourself. By this we mean that a person relaxed and spontaneous is typically in her or his most self-confident, prepossessing, interesting, and even attractive state. And a person's chances are enhanced if these qualities are apparent to the interviewer.

There is still another important area of preparation. Any interviewer worth his or her salt is going to want to learn several things about you. Why do you want to be a teacher? Why did you choose the level (or the field) that you are in? What makes you think you can be a good teacher? What are your strengths and weaknesses? What do you expect will be your greatest problem the first year on the job? What kind of school would you like to teach in, with what kinds of children? Are there questions about the position or about the school that you would like to ask me? Questions like these are both fair and appropriate. Expect questions like these and spend some time developing and organizing your thoughts about how you might answer them.

Another way to help prepare for a job interview is by using role play. With your student-teacher colleagues, or with friends or relatives, you can simulate the real-life experience. Ask your role-playing partner to be, in turn, a male interviewer, a female one, tough, gentle, talkative, passive, directive in questioning style (e.g., How many credits in sociology did you take?) versus open-ended (e.g., Tell me about yourself). After some experience as the applicant/candidate for a teaching job, trade off with your partner and play the role of employer-interviewer, an experience that gives you the opportunity of seeing the selection process with that functionary's perspective.

You will also find it helpful to discuss the interview and the job hunt with your college supervisor. Do that, also, with those who have been through it most recently, last year's seniors.

*The Interview Itself.*   At last your interview day has come. Be on time! Dress as teachers do in that school district, preferably erring if at all on the conservative side. Be prepared to seek information about the job that is not readily available elsewhere.

As a general rule, if you are relatively comfortable during the interview, your relaxed state will help the interviewer. Consciously or otherwise this will tend to elevate the rating given you.

There are various ways to relax yourself prior to the interview. One of them, a simple exercise that you can use unobtrusively while sitting in the waiting room, calls first for you to breathe in deeply through your nose, exhale slowly through your mouth. Then, after a few inhalations, and while continuing the breathing, think about relaxing the top of your head, inside your head, your eyes, your face, neck, and so on, downward until you reach your toes.

This is an exercise in relaxation worth using at other times as well. However, you may prefer simply to relax by unobtrusively rubbing your palms together and reminding yourself of the years of training you have had.

During the interview, be yourself. Answer the questions posed straightforwardly. Share your strengths. Show your enthusiasm, energy, and determination. Do not hesitate, when appropriate, to ask questions. You may want to know about the school's history, about the neighborhood it serves, about plans for next year, and so forth.

Another important factor to consider during job interviews is the kind of non-verbal messages you send. In one study (Amalfitano & Kalt, 1977), photographs of a male and a female (supposedly job seekers) were shown to 44 interviewers at an employment agency who were then asked to rate them. In some pictures the "job seekers" were looking straight ahead; in others they were looking down. Although the only difference between the photographs was where the subject was looking, those "applicants" making "eye contact" (by looking straight ahead) were more likely to be "hired," and were rated as being significantly more alert, assertive, dependable, confident, and responsible. They were also seen as having more incentive.

Other researchers (Young & Beier, 1977) have found that head movement and smiling are also important nonverbal communication factors during job interviews, although not as powerful as eye contact. What is especially important about their experiment is that these researchers randomly chose half their subjects to display eye contact, smiling, and head movement, and half to minimize it. Those told to display it, whether it was their personal style or not, were rated as more "deserving of the job" than their counterparts in the other group.

When you return home from an interview, make notes about its beginning, middle, and end and formulate an appraisal of how it went. Whether you left the interview with a good or bad feeling, assess the interview and your role in it. Use CONTROL-C to plan future interviews, especially if you left this one with a sense of disappointment.

If you have two successive experiences that left you feeling that "things did not click," it is vital that you take action. For although a first one might off-handedly be attributed to an outside factor—the personality or values of the employing interviewer (e.g., does not want a male teacher in the primary grade)—a succession of interviews that leave you with negative feelings raises questions about your part in those interviews.

We are not at all suggesting that repeated failure at obtaining a position is due to your inadequacy. Not at all, especially not if the job market happens to have many more qualified persons than positions. Our view is only that a critical appraisal of your interviews will help you learn more about yourself, develop further as a professional, and prepare for future interviews at this or later stages in your career.

The conclusions we draw from specialists in the field of employment counseling and from educational administrators about interviews are the following:

1. Consider in advance what is likely to occur during the course of your job interview.
2. Think about the questions that are likely to be asked. Prepare responses that you can give comfortably, taking into account both your own beliefs and the realities of the position.
3. Work at developing self-confidence about the impending interview. Use

any methods that help you relax and give you a positive outlook.

4. Decide what you wish to convey about yourself as a person and a prospective teacher.

5. Find appropriate ways to communicate that, drawing on your experiences in college and at work, highlighting your activities with children and/or adolescents, and your special academic, artistic, and athletic interests.

6. Be yourself during the interview.

7. Attend to your nonverbal communication. Look at the interviewer, engage in eye contact, and find occasions to smile.

8. Check whether you are communicating effectively by observing the nonverbal behavior of the interviewer. Is he or she attentive or distracted, responsive or bored? Modify your behavior as needed.

9. With the questions you ask, work at knowing the interviewer and the school system he or she represents.

10. At the conclusion of each interview, review the flow of it from beginning to end, taking note of the affect as well as the content. Use CONTROL-C.

## THE REJECTION LETTER

Unhappily you may receive one or more letters notifying you that you were not selected for a position. When it happens, remind yourself that you are not alone, and do not put yourself down for it. Instead, use it as an occasion to mobilize yourself to further activity in the job hunt.

Nancy wrote about a not uncommon series of events. You too may find the quest for a job is interwoven into the rest of your life activities. For example you may find yourself in competition for a position with a friend or classmate. You may wonder if your philosophy of education will be acceptable in the school where the position is open.

1/10: Today I called the principal at the other junior high. There's a possibility that I may have a "real" job next quarter. I'm going to the junior high on Monday to observe, talk to the two English teachers, and be interviewed. I'm uptight about it. I really want this job, but I've never gone for an interview before.

1/11: Problem: One of the girls I teach with also wants the job. That's fine. But the principal told me about it first. That's not the right thing to do. Lynn was hurt, and I feel bad about it. If I get the job she'll be bitter. Worse yet, we're good friends. We've both said that we wouldn't let it mess up our friendship, but one of us will probably be hurt. Of course, maybe neither of us will get the job. That would hurt, too. She hasn't filled out her application yet. I'm going to tell her that I have an interview on Monday. I think it's important to be honest with her. She'll be full of questions that I won't want to answer. I sure wish there were two jobs open in March!!

1/15: Today I had my interview. They are very traditional at this school. I'm afraid that they're afraid. They don't want a liberal. They asked me about grammar and how valuable I thought Romeo and Juliet was for ninth-grade students. What can I say? As far as grammar goes, I said that I thought it was a tool to be used in communication. I felt better after I talked to the two English teachers. They are conservative, but not so subject-oriented that they lose their humanity. I think they are doing some good, human things.

1/26: I didn't get the teaching position. Neither did Lynn. He hired a woman with 3 years experience. I feel sort of bitter and I have no right to. No one owes me anything.

After writing this entry, Nancy became bitter and depressed. Within a couple of weeks, however, she had worked through her disappointment and was ready to enjoy her final term at college. Soon after writing the next log entry she returned to the business of planning next steps in her career, and found a good position.

2/15: What can I say? Looking back at my logs I see a definite change in attitude and I know the cause. I wanted that job and I didn't get it. I felt bitter. Then I got depressed. What was I going to do after graduation? What about the future? Know what I decided? Nothing. But it doesn't bother me anymore. I'm going to enjoy the spring.

## THE ACCEPTANCE LETTER

One day the mail carrier delivers the letter you have been waiting for. You have been selected, and after your acceptance and some necessary formalities you will be officially appointed. Assuming that you are a June graduate, you will be fortunate to get that letter in the spring. But it may come in June or late in the summer because some teachers resign or take leave at that late date for such reasons as another job, a spouse's transfer to another area, pregnancy, illness, or a late retirement decision.

Whenever you get your letter, enjoy! After your celebration you can turn to the challenging task of preparing to teach.

## GETTING CERTIFIED

Once you have successfully completed your state's academic requirements for certification as a teacher, you should submit a formal application to your state's department of education. Your college supervisor or other personnel can advise you about the process. Typically, one official is designated as the institution's certification officer and serves as liaison with the appropriate person in the state department of education.

Candidates in more than two-thirds of the states must pass the National Teacher Examination (NTE) before being certified. The NTE is composed of parts, two of which are generally required of all candidates, the general knowledge and the professional knowledge tests. A third part is a specialty area test covering topics that range from art education and biology to physical education and social studies.

The Educational Testing Service (ETS), which designed the NTE more than 50 years ago, will introduce a new version in 1992 and expects to have it replace the old one within 5 years.

There is good reason for change. For many years, teachers and educators have been asking the following question: "How can a single paper-and-pencil test acknowledge these phases [of a person's development: subject specialty, pedagogy, and student teaching], be multiculturally sensitive, and assess the real-life classroom experiences of prospective teachers?" (Merina, 1991, p. 3).

The new test will be administered in three stages. The first, taken early in a student's career, will enable candidates to have plenty of time to get additional instruction, if that should be necessary. The test at that stage is on basic skills (reading, writing and mathematics). The tests will be by appointment, candidates will use computers for the reading and math tests, and compose essays for the writing test.

The Stage 2 tests evaluate subject matter knowledge and general teaching knowledge. These multiple choice and computer interactive tests will be taken after graduation or shortly before.

The Stage 3 assessment occurs after candidates have supervised teaching experience. It includes evaluations of classroom teaching and interviews with the candidates.

If the thought of some or all of these tests is stressful, remember that after 16 or more years of school and college, you are "test-wise." You know what information to obtain about an exam you are scheduled to take, and you know what and how to study. Prepare. Also remember that your institution undoubtedly took into account the kinds of assessments required for certification in planning your program.

## PREPARING FOR THE JOB

When you walk into your own classroom the experience will be very different from that of walking into your student-teaching assignment. On the one hand, you will now know better the feeling of being the teacher, preparing, presenting, and evaluating a lesson, witnessing conflict of one kind or another and having to deal with it, being evaluated and evaluating yourself. On the other hand something you never before experienced will happen. You will enter a class that is going to be *your* class. There will be no cooperating teacher who has the ultimate responsibility, and no university supervisor to consult. And their absence may arouse two different feelings in you: satisfaction commingled with mild anxiety.

The new experience confronting you has the inevitable and unavoidable components of all growth-potential challenges. It places new responsibility upon you as it encourages you to put to work your knowledge, your creative ideas, your feelings, and your adulthood. You will hardly have to start "from scratch," because you will be given a syllabus to follow so that, if anything, you may complain that there are too many constraints. Yet, no syllabus replaces a teacher—his or her style of conducting the class, his or her personality as he or she relates to the students, and his or her style of leadership.

Susi wrote this letter to her college supervisor not many days after she took over a class of her own. The letter validates the joy she was experiencing.

9/10: I've been a real live teacher for one week, and I've been bursting to write you since day one. I can't begin to tell you how appreciative I am to you for reminding me all semester that when I'm in my classroom things can be different. All summer that tempting challenge to try new things has been in the back of my mind, and now I'm having a fantastic time exploring the myriads of educative processes.

I have two classes, a morning kindergarten and an afternoon nursery session for 4-year-olds. The kindergarten consists of 32 energetic children, including one girl who speaks absolutely no English and a boy "genius" of 3 who reads but isn't quite toilet-trained. My first "gutsy" venture happened on our first day when, after reading *The Gingerbread Boy*, I got the class to help make our own 2-foot-long gingerbread boy. It's an idea I adapted from a text I had. The children were delighted, and by the time we trooped past the principal's office to the kitchen the enthusiasm hit its peak. Of course, our gingerbread boy ran away and hid from us for the next 3 days while we followed his notes and discovered our school building in the process. At the end of the week we finished him off for a snack (we found him in the library).

I am learning slowly the delicate blend of freedom and control that is essential to a happy productive classroom. I am disappointed that the school insists on a formalized workbook program in reading and math. It amazes me that people are still convinced children learn best circling and X-ing workbook frames. I had hoped I could have worked some total programs myself. As it is, with time constraints, I am forced to supplement as best I can with more active learning experiences.

Susi found delight in having her own classes and in experimenting with some of her ideas. Also, she was engaged very early in practicing the principle of teaching that is, as we have said, one of the truly preeminent ones. As she put it in her graceful prose, "I am learning slowly the delicate blend of freedom and control that is essential to a happy productive classroom."

Put Susi's words on two 3-by-5 cards. Keep one at home to read when you are preparing for the next day and another in your desk drawer to use as a reminder during the day. Do it whether you teach kindergarten, 12th grade, or at the college level.

Susi found both the freedom that comes from leading her own class and also the constraints of a school-imposed workbook program. Rather than being devas-

stated by it or using energy wastefully by railing against it or going about moodi-
ly in silent anger, she went about her business of finding time and ways to incorporate the more active learning experiences that she valued.

Soon after you sign your teaching contract you will be given the school district's curriculum guide or course of study for your class or courses. If you are
fortunate and still have a number of weeks before the term begins, study the syllabus and, within the limits set by it, develop your lesson plans for at least several weeks into the term. Is that being overprepared? We think not. If the new teacher
does what he or she can in advance, he or she will have more time in the fall
to deal with what could not be entirely prepared for—like the "unexpecteds"—
and to enjoy the "non-work" parts of his or her life.

As you prepare your lessons remember the attention span of your students.
We think you will do yourself a great service if you will also bear in mind the
obvious fact that enjoyment will make the world of difference in your students'
attitude and attention. In all probability you can attest to the validity of that statement on the basis of your own recollections of college courses.

Considering the age, education, and cultural backgrounds of your students ask
yourself what modes of instruction and what student activities would make a topic
most interesting. Susi chose one procedure to add excitement to learning. There
are others, and you are probably familiar with some of them: role playing; so-
ciodrama; creative dramatics; small-group discussions; spelling bees; "Jeopardy"-
style quiz matches; walking "field trips" around the school block or bus field trips
some distance from school; growing plants; using or writing computer programs;
keeping animals; cooking foods; crafting models; making maps; studying
*Newsweek*, the *Wall Street Journal*, or the local newspaper; carrying out various
experiments; sculpting; painting; interviewing guest "consultants" from the neighborhood; and so on.

You can take several other steps in preparation for the new position. First,
following our advice in chapter 2, become acquainted with the school building,
and the neighborhood. Also, learn about the best form of transportation from
where you will be residing to school, the route to take if you drive, the parking
arrangements, your schedule, the school calendar, the teacher organizations, the
school secretary, the librarian, the nurse, and the custodian. You will find it helpful
to get the names of other teachers at your grade level or in your department and
especially other new teachers with whom you will want to get acquainted early
in the term.

## THE FIRST DAY AS TEACHER

You know quite a bit about that initial day before you even walk into your classroom for the first time. You know, for instance, that both you and the children
will be excited and a bit uncertain about what the year will hold. You know that

right from the start you want to present yourself as the adult leader who will insist on maintaining a sane working environment. You know, too, that the students, fresh from a summer's vacation, will be bubbly with news to share with friends.

How then will you show them that you will be a fair adult leader who will be working in their interest?

The first day of class is important. You will start conveying to your students your expectations of them. You do this by word and deed and attitude. If you are positive in your reaction to a student's questions, other students will take note and you will encourage questions in the classroom. If you are positive to student initiatives, you will be encouraging them too. If you are negative to private conversations during a class-wide discussion, you will be discouraging that behavior. You will more likely discourage it constructively if you explain, like a rational authority, that such sideline discussions "disturb the rest of us and, furthermore, we want you to participate with the rest of us."

If you think much of the chatter in the classroom the first day is a carry-over of the long summer vacation, you might choose to organize small-group or whole-class discussions (or other activities) focusing on the vacation for two purposes: To get it "out of their systems" and to mine the very rich material of the vacation months. Whatever your method, you will want to convey to the class from the outset that you require cooperation on the part of all students.

Humor is a great human resource. It can serve many useful purposes, including the function of anxiety reduction. Perhaps you have noticed that tension rises when a speaker and an audience first encounter each other and that it speedily dissipates if the speaker begins with a relevant joke or humorous story. Both speaker and audience feel a great sense of relief at that point.

Humor will reduce your own anxiety and the students' and it will make class more interesting and appealing. Moreover, it pairs well with the firm class control that is a keystone to effective teaching and necessary for students to have fulfilling and effective learning experiences. It deserves to be built into your lesson plans. Patty felt that way, as she said in a retrospective report at the end of the term:

5/30: It was almost impossible to exist in my classrooms without a sense of humor. This is probably true in every classroom. Laughter is a great remedy too. Even days when I entered the classroom in not the best of moods, something would happen to lift me.

On the first day and by his or her own actions, a teacher can begin to condition a class to interject humor. By being alert to cartoons, humorous news items, appropriate anecdotes, you can leaven the serious business of learning (serious business in itself can feel enjoyable, of course) with the lightness of humor. If you do that, your students will acquire the habit. One of the authors tells this joke to his college class during the first minutes of the first day of class each term:

> Here we are. The vacation is over. Reminds me of a story a neighbor told me about what happened in her house a few years back.
>
> It was the first day of school and she heard her son's alarm clock ring, but after a few minutes he still wasn't down for breakfast.
>
> So what could she do? She went upstairs, knocked on the door and said, "Johnny, Johnny, get up. It's after seven! You'll be late for school."
>
> "Ok," he grunted. But as soon as his mother left the room he rolled over to snooze some more.
>
> A few minutes later the mother walked back upstairs, pounded a little harder on the door, walked in and said with more authority, "Johnny, you *must* get up right now. Breakfast is on the table."
>
> "I'll be right down," Johnny said assuredly. But as soon as his mother left the room he pulled the covers over his head.
>
> Five minutes later—still no Johnny and breakfast was getting cold. The mother trooped back upstairs, walked in the room and this time pulled the covers back and said, "Johnny, get up right this second. You are going to be late for school if you don't hurry."
>
> "I don't want to go to school," Johnny moaned.
>
> The mother replied: "But you have to go to school, Johnny. You are the principal."

Besides well-worn jokes, like this one, other forms of humor can help you establish a serious, yet comfortable, working atmosphere in your classroom from the first day on. For example, many concepts you teach can be illuminated by examples that are themselves comical and that makes learning a more lively and involving process for students. Further, humorous role playing can be used (e.g., Columbus coming ashore in America and finding a Wendy's; or Shakespeare completing a manuscript and not being able to find a photocopy machine or the zip code of his publisher).

The classroom situation itself gives rise to humor, although the kind that degrades or humiliates anyone should be strictly discouraged with the reasons for that clearly spelled out: "We don't do things in our class to hurt anyone. We can learn, and enjoy ourselves too, without that."

Another activity helpful to you on the first day is to begin to make mental notes about the students in your classes. To help you to direct your attention to individuals, begin to classify them in several functional categories:

1. The spontaneously active students who enjoy school and participate eagerly. They are as important as any others but need no special attention at this time, except the opportunity to be active in the learning opportunities that you arrange.

2. The interested but marginally active students. They are not high priority at this time; however, just as soon as possible you want to encourage them to participate before the first group of "activists" take over in a discussion.

3. The passive, withdrawn students who seem "out of it." Because such children and adolescents feel more like observers than participants, they will need your attention early. That could take the form of a warm hello, a friendly glance in their direction, a question to encourage involvement, or assistance in a project or assignment.

4. The turned-off students who seem, at first, to be passive but are not so at all. They are quiet because they have no wish to be in school, no interest in class activities and are quietly angry in an environment which they experience as alien and hostile. You can begin the process of trying to identify them so that, as the weeks progress, you can try to encourage them to tell you frankly how they feel.

5. The disruptive students who come to school on the first day of class with learned patterns of behavior that could soon alienate their classmates and school personnel. Although their attitude is not personally directed at you, you must deal with it from the opening bell. Along with a warm offer to these students to join the class goes the unequivocal insistence that disruptive behavior will be dealt with instantly and at its first appearance.

6. The informal class leader, a student who has great influence over the class. The student may be in that position because of past achievement, physical presence, personal charisma, or other reasons. Regardless, this influence, which can be used for good or bad purposes, should be valued by the teacher and brought into service to the class. For example, such a person can be a force in the classroom by virtue of his or her service as a model of good class citizenship for other students.

To make positive use of the student and at the same time to make the class experience productive for him or her, you will need to see the student as very much other than a threat to your leadership. If you begin to react defensively, remind yourself that you are the responsible authority and that your job is to use all resources to make the class a valuable experience. The informal leader can serve you and the class.

7. Students with some physical or mental disabilities, some of whom were formerly assigned to "special education" classes but who now are "mainstreamed" (i.e., assigned to regular classes). Such students will fit into the categories already described. The only special attention they might require is any that their disability might call for (e.g., placement in front of the room because of a visual or aural handicap, additional time for writing because of a motor handicap, and of course sensitivity to the psychology of special needs students; i.e., of people who are "different" in some obvious way and whose special difference sometimes gives rise to internal and external vulnerabilities, including the tendency of some students to tease the handicapped).

If you do not receive it, you should request information and advice on each special needs student from the principal, counselor, psychologist, school nurse, or other person assigned the responsibility of overseeing the welfare of those students.

## THE EVENINGS OF THE FIRST WEEKS

At the end of each day during your first weeks it will be helpful to review and evaluate your experience. In what ways did you meet the objectives you had set? In what ways not? What will you do about objectives you did not meet? Should they be a part of tomorrow's objectives?

Also, ask questions at another level. Review the day's events and ask: What made me feel very good? Can I build more of that in my plans for tomorrow, later in the week, the next week? What about the events of the day that made me feel bad? Was it in my relationship with the students? Which ones? What do I feel about them? Why do I feel that way? What can I do tomorrow so that when that day ends I will not have these bad feelings?

Engaging in this complex thought process will probably seem like a great chore when you come home tired and want to relax and go to bed. And there is, after all, a whole year to solve problems. However, experience has shown that if you struggle with your problems during the first days and weeks, the next ones will be easier.

Questions presented here should be on your personal agenda every day after school until you feel at ease, self-confident, and in control. Then you can consider them weekly. By that time you will in all probability have made assessment an integral part of your professional way of life, an ingrained habit that separates the real professionals from the generally mediocre teachers.

Of course, as you think about each day's events, you might want to use CONTROL-C. Also, if the situation calls for it, make use of the good services of a colleague or a friend to obtain another perspective, especially if you have been unable to work out a problem.

## THE REAL WORLD

In the world you enter when you start your first teaching job, you will not find perfection and you will be disappointed if you expect it. It is wise to set high standards, but not to expect that which cannot be achieved in an imperfect world. Yes, the real world has beauty, abundance, health, and compassion, but it also has unhappiness, ugliness, poverty, physical and mental illness, and brutality. Most students in your classes will not have entirely escaped at least some of the awful experiences in the second set of conditions. They may not be free of those experiences when they come to class and, therefore, they may not be able to achieve what they might have under other circumstances.

If you take a position in a school where student performance falls below — perhaps considerably below — the national achievement norms, you must learn to live with that situation if you are to develop your effectiveness. If you set realistic goals you will enable your students to get maximum benefit from your teaching and, in this way, help them raise their level of performance. Under these circumstances you will find satisfaction in witnessing a fifth-grade child attain the fourth-grade level in a given subject when that child entered your class performing at the 2.5 grade level.

We teachers are in a position not greatly different from physicians. They too serve people who for a variety of reasons are not up to national "norms" (in their case physically). They succeed in sustaining life in patients like that but usually at a less than optimal level of health.

The medical profession has its roots in a great humanistic tradition. So does ours. The medical profession strives for ways to overcome health deficiencies from past neglect. The educational profession strives for ways to reverse the disadvantages in the past (and sometimes the present) of our students.

Our nation will be immeasurably stronger when it decides to institute major programs to prevent health deficiencies and economic and educational disadvantages. We hope that time will come soon.

Whatever challenge you face in your classroom remember that ours is a profession of worth. We serve humankind when we teach twenty or two hundred students a year. We can do that best when our eyes are wide open to the realities of the world and the school in which we work, and when we are open to ourselves.

# References

Amalfitano, J., & Kalt, N. (1977). Effects of eye contact on the evaluation of job applicants. *Journal of Employment Counseling, 14*, 46–48.

Asch, A. (1989). Has the law made a difference? In D. K. Lipsky & A. Gartner (Eds.), *Beyond separate education: Quality education for all* (pp. 181–205). Baltimore: Brookes.

Balch, P. M., & Balch, P. E. (1987). *Cooperating teacher: A practice approach for the supervision of student teachers.* Lanham, MD: University Press of America.

Bloom, B. S. (1956). *Taxonomy of educational objectives.* New York: McKay.

Book, C. L., Duffy, G. G., Roehler, L. R., Meloth, M. S., & Vavrus, L. G. (1985). A study of the relationship between teacher explanation and student metacognitive awareness during reading instruction. *Communication Education, 34*, 29–36.

Bradley, R., & Teeter, T. (1977). Perceptions of control over social outcomes and student behavior. *Psychology in the Schools, 14*, 230–235.

Bushway, A., & Nash, W. (1977). School cheating behavior. *Review of Educational Research, 42*, 623–632.

Canter, L., & Canter, M. (1976). *Assertive discipline: A take-charge approach for today's educator.* Seal Beach, CA: Canter.

Chess S., & Thomas, A., (1987). *Know your child.* New York: Basic Books.

Chinn, P. C., Winn, J., & Walters, R. H. (1978). *Two-way talking with parents of special children.* St. Louis: C. V. Mosby.

Clapp, B. (1989). The discipline challenge. *Instructor, 99*, 32–34.

Cohen, M. W., Mirels, H. L., & Schwebel, A. I. (1972). Dimensions of elementary school student teacher concerns. *The Journal of Experimental Education, 41*, 6–11.

Coles, G. (1987). *The learning mystique: A critical look at "learning disabilities."* New York: Pantheon.

College Board. (1983). *Academic preparation for college.* New York: Author.

College Board. (1985). *Academic preparation in the arts.* New York: Author.

Copeland, W. D. (1978). Processes mediating the relationship between cooperating teacher behavior and student-teacher classroom performance. *Journal of Educational Psychology, 70*, 95–100.

Copeland, W. D. (1987). Classroom management and student teachers' cognitive abilities: A relationship. *American Educational Research Journal, 24*, 219–236.

Corcoran, T. B., Walker, L. J., & White, J. L. (1988). *Working in urban schools.* Washington, DC: Institute for Educational Leadership.

Davis, J. B. (1990). Stress among secondary school student teachers: Factors which contribute to it and ways of reducing it. *The High School Journal, 73*, 240–244.

Doyle, W. (1986). Classroom organization and management. In M. C. Whittrock (Ed.), *Handbook of research on teaching* (3rd ed., pp. 392–431). New York: Macmillan.

Eccles, J. S. (1987). Gender roles and women's achievement-related decisions. *Psychology of Women Quarterly, 11*, 135–172.

Eccles, J. S., Jacobs, J. E., & Harold, R. D. (1990). Gender role stereotypes, expectancy effects, and parents' socialization of gender differences. *Journal of Social Issues, 46*, 183–201.

Engerbretson, D. L. (1977). Diabetic in physical education, recreation, and athletics. *Journal of Physical Education and Recreation, 48*, 18–21.

Fant, H. E., Hill, C., Lee, A. E., & Landes, R. (1985). Evaluating student teachers: The national scene. *Teacher Educator, 21*(2), 2–8.

Feuerstein, R. (1980). *Instrumental enrichment. An intervention program for cognitive modifiability.* Baltimore: University Park Press.

Feuerstein, R., & Hoffman, M. (1990). Mediating cognitive processes to the retarded performer—Rationale, goals, and nature of intervention. In M. Schwebel, C. M. Maher, & N. S. Fagley (Eds.), *Promoting cognitive growth over the life span* (pp. 115–136). Hillsdale, NJ: Lawrence Erlbaum Associates.

Friebus, R. J. (1977). Agents of socialization involved in student teaching. *Journal of Educational Research, 70*, 263–268.

Fromm, E. (1976). *Escape from freedom.* New York: Holt, Rinehart & Winston.

Fuller, F. F. (1969). Concerns of teachers: A developmental conceptualization. *American Education Research Journal, 6*, 207–226.

Glasser, W. (1969). *Schools without failure.* New York: Harper.

Goldenberg, I. I. (1969). Reading groups and some aspects of teacher behavior. In F. Kaplan & S. B. Sarason (Eds.), *The psycho-educational clinic papers and research studies* (Vol. 4, pp. 109–118). Boston: Massachusetts Department of Mental Health.

Gordon, T. (1974). *T.E.T.: Teacher effectiveness training.* New York: McKay.

Grant, L., & Rothenberg, J. (1986). The social enhancement of ability differences: Teacher-student interactions in first- and second-grade reading groups. *Elementary School Journal, 87*, 29–49.

Haller, E. P., Child, D. A., & Walberg, H. J. (1988). Can comprehension be taught? A quantitative synthesis of "metacognitive" studies. *Educational Researcher, 17*, 5–8.

Hanhan, S. F. (1988). A qualitative and qualitatively different format for the evaluation of student teachers. *Action in Teacher Education, 10*(2), 51–55.

Harty, H., & Mahan, J. M. (1977). Student teachers' expressed orientations toward education while preparing to teach minority and mainstream ethnic groups. *Journal of Experimental Education, 46*, 34–41.

Haywood, C., & Brooks, P. (1990). Theory and curriculum development in cognitive education. In M. Schwebel, C. M. Maher, & N. S. Fagley (Eds.), *Promoting cognitive growth over the life span* (pp. 165–192). Hillsdale, NJ: Lawrence Erlbaum Associates.

Hearne, J. C., & Moos, R. H. (1978). Subject matter and classroom climate: A test of Holland's environmental propositions. *American Educational Research Journal, 15*, 111–124.

Hoy, W. K., & Woolfolk, A. E. (1990). Socialization of student teachers. *American Educational Research Journal, 27*, 279–300.

Hule, B. (1989, October). Teaching students cultural mediation. *School Safety*, pp. 20–22.

Jansma, P. (1977). Get ready for mainstreaming! *Journal of Physical Education and Recreation, 48*, 15–16.

Jussim, L. (1990). Social reality and social problems: The role of expectancies. *Journal of Social Issues, 46*, 9–34.

Kavale, K. A. (1990). Effectiveness of differential programming in serving handicapped students. In M. C. Wang, M. C. Reynolds, & H. S. Walberg (Eds.), *Special education: Research and practice* (pp. 35–55). Oxford: Pergamon.

Kitano, M. K., Stiehl, J., & Cole, J. T. (1978). Role taking: Implications for special education. *Journal of Special Education, 12*, 59–74.

Kolze, R. C. (1988). Finding first-rate teachers. *The American School Board Journal, 175*(7), 29 & 41.

Krathwohl, D. R., Bloom, B. S., & Masia, B. (1964). *Taxonomy of educational objectives: Affective domain*. New York: McKay.

Lazarus, R., & Folkman, S. (1984). *Stress, appraisal and coping*. New York: Springer.

Leigh, P. (1977). Great expectations: A consideration of the self-fulfilling prophecy in the context of educability. *Educational Review, 29*, 317–324.

Lipsky, D. K., & Gartner, A. (1989). The current situation. In D. K. Lipsky & A. Gartner (Eds.), *Beyond separate education: Quality education for all* (pp. 3–24). Baltimore: Brookes.

Madsen, C. H. Jr., Becker, W. C., Thomas, D. R., Kosen, L., & Plager, E. (1972). An analysis of the reinforcing function of "sit-down" commands. In M. H. Harris (Ed.), *Classroom uses of behavior modification* (pp. 169–182). Columbus, OH: Charles E. Merrill.

Madsen, C., & Madsen, C. (1974). *Teaching discipline: Behavioral principles toward a positive approach* (2nd ed.) Boston: Allyn & Bacon.

Maker, C. J. (1982). *Curriculum development for the gifted*. Aspen, MD: Aspen Publications.

McLaughlin, R. D., & Ross, S. M. (1989). Student cheating in high school: A case of moral reasoning vs. "fuzzy logic." *High School Journal, 72*(3), 97–104.

Merina, A. (1991, March). National teacher exam takes a new twist. *NEA Today, 9*(7), 3.

Murwin, S. & Matt, S. R. (1990). Fears prior to student teaching. *The Technology Teacher, 49*, 25–26.

Newman, C. J., & Licata, J. W. (1986–1987). Teacher leadership and the classroom climate as predictors of student brinkmanship. *The High School Journal, 70*(2), 102–110.

Ornstein, A. C. (1987). Questioning: The essence of good teaching. *NASSP Bulletin, 71*, 71–77.

Packard, K. L., Schwebel, A. I., & Ganey, J. S. (1979). Concerns of last semester baccalaureate nursing students. *Nursing Research, 28*, 302–304.

Piaget, J., & Inhelder, B. (1969). *The psychology of the child*. New York: Basic Books.

Raths, J. (1981). Evaluation of teachers. In H. E. Mitzel (Ed.) *Encyclopedia of educational research*, (5th ed., pp. 611–617). New York: The Free Press.

Rogow, S. (1978). Mainstreaming: It can work for blind children, *Education Canada, 18*, 21–48.

Rosenthal, R. (1973). The Pygmalion effect lives. *Psychology Today, 7*, 56–63.

Rosenthal, R. (1984). *Meta-analysis procedures for social research*. Beverly Hills, CA: Sage.

Rosenthal, R. (1985). From unconscious experimenter bias to teacher expectancy effects. In J. Dusek (Ed.), *Teacher expectancies* (pp. 37–65). Hillsdale, NJ: Lawrence Erlbaum Associates.

Rosenthal, R., & Jacobson, L. (1966). Teachers' expectancies: determinants of pupils' IQ gains. *Psychological Reports, 19*, 115–118.

Sarason, S. B. (1982). *The culture of the school and the problem of change* (2nd ed.). Boston: Allyn & Bacon.

Sarason, S. B. (1990). *The predictable failure of educational reform*. San Francisco: Jossey-Bass.

Sarason, S., Davidson, K., & Blatt, B. (1962). *The preparation of teachers: An unstudied problem in education*. New York: Wiley.

Schlichter, C. L. (1977). The gifted and talented: A case in point. *Focus on Exceptional Children, 9*, 1–10.

Schwebel, A. I., & Cherlin, D. L. (1972). Physical and social distancing in teacher-pupil relationships. *Journal of Educational Psychology, 63*, 543–550.

Schwebel, M., Maher, C. M., & Fagley, N. S. (1990). *Promoting cognitive growth over the life span*. Hillsdale, NJ: Lawrence Erlbaum Associates.

Seeman, H. (1988). *Preventing classroom discipline problems: A guide for educators*. Lancaster, PA: Technomic Publishing.

Shavelson, R. J., & Stern, P. (1981). Research on teachers' pedagogical thoughts, judgments, decisions, and behavior. *Review of Educational Research, 51*(4), 455–498.

Skolnick, C. L. (1986). Why I'm sorry I don't teach English. *English Journal, 75*(7), 36–37.

Starko, A. J., & Schack, G. D. (1989). Perceived need, teacher efficacy, and teaching strategies for the gifted and talented. *Gifted Child Quarterly, 33*, 118–122.

Treffinger, D. J. (1975). Teaching for self-directed learning: A priority for the gifted and talented. *The Gifted Child Quarterly, 19*, 46–59.

Wang, M. C. (1989). Adaptive instruction: An alternative for accommodating student diversity through the curriculum. In D. K. Lipsky & A. Gartner (Eds.). *Beyond separate education: Quality education for all* (pp. 99–119). Baltimore: Brookes.

Wang, M. C., & Baker, M. C. (1985–1986). Mainstreaming programs: Design features and effects, *Journal of Special Education, 19*, 503–521.

Westling, D. L., & Koorland, M. A. (1988). *The special educator's handbook*. Boston: Allyn & Bacon.

Yee, S. M-L. (1990). *Careers in the classroom: When teaching is more than a job*. New York: Teachers College Press.

Young, D., & Beier, E. (1977). The role of applicant non-verbal communication in the employment interview. *Journal of Employment Counseling, 14*, 154–165.

# Author Index

# Subject Index

open house night, 97
parent-teacher meetings, 97
reactions to student teachers, 104–105
visits during school day, 103–104
*see also* Parent-teacher conferences, 97–103
Parent-teacher conferences, 97 103
Poverty, 156–157
Principal, *see* School principal
Problem solving
CONTROL-C Method, 21–28
CONTROL-C with intimidating student, 182–183
CONTROL-C with low self-esteem students, 189–190
effective problem solving, 165–167, 196–198
impulsive problem solving, 167–170
Punishment, 90, 159, 180
*see also* Classroom management, 40–41, 158–173

## Q

Questioning, 130–132
asking probing questions, 75–76

## R

Racial issues, *see* Multicultural society
Reading, teaching of, 134
Reality therapy, 163
Resources, curriculum, 125–127
Resume, 225–229

## S

School faculty, 204–206
faculty meetings, 205–206
relationship with student teachers, 111–112
School principal, 108–111
as classroom observer, 108–109
as disciplinarian, 110
as school leader, 109–111
School staff, 112
*see also* Custodian, 112–113
Seating arrangements, 183
Self-directed learning, 150–151

Self-esteem, 189–191
Self-fulfilling prophecy, *see* Expectancy and self-fulfilling prophecy
Seminar classes, 72–73
Sexual issues, 183–186, 195
Socialization agents, 215–217
Special needs students, 145–151, 239–240
definition, 145–146
diabetics, 147
dyslexia, 101–102
evaluating, 149–150
gifted, 145, 150–151
IEP (Individualized Education Program), 148–149
learning disabled, 145, 149
mainstreaming, 146–150, 239
mentally retarded, 145
visually impaired, 147
Stress, 209–211
Student teachers
as adult leader, 161–162
concerns of, 17–21
coping with stress, 209–211
criticism of, *see* Criticism
exhaustion, 202–203
overcoming self-doubt, 206–209
relationship with school faculty, 111–112
relationship with students, 11, 83–88
self-evaluation, 138–139
socialization of, 215–217
soloing as a teacher, 29–30, 43
Student teaching
evaluation of, 80–82
first days of, 29, 36–37
preparation for, 11–16
principal's observation of, 108–109
stages of, 29–30
supervisor's observation of, 63–69
Students, 83–95, 141–157
abused, 193–194
behavioral problems, *see* Classroom management
classification of, 88–90, 238–240
cognitive development, 88
defiant, 176–179
devotion to, 218–219
devotion by, 219–220
disruptive, 191–193
gifted, *see* Special needs students
individual versus class needs, 174–176
intimidating, 179–183